SPECTATOR
OF
AMERICA

Books by Herbert Mitgang:

FICTION

The Return

BIOGRAPHY

Abraham Lincoln: A Press Portrait
(Lincoln as They Saw Him)

The Man Who Rode the Tiger: The Life
and Times of Judge Samuel Seabury

CRITICISM

Working for the Reader: A Chronicle of Culture, Literature,
War and Politics in Books, 1950's to the Present

REPORTAGE

Freedom to See: Television and the First Amendment

Edited by Herbert Mitgang:

The Letters of Carl Sandburg

Spectator of America (by Edward Dicey)

Washington, D.C., in Lincoln's Time (by Noah Brooks)

America at Random: Topics of *The Times*

Civilians Under Arms: Stars and Stripes, Civil War to Korea

Edward Dicey (1832–1911) as a young correspondent,
from a portrait by the French artist M. Laugée.

SPECTATOR OF AMERICA

BY EDWARD DICEY

Edited with an Introduction by
HERBERT MITGANG

CHICAGO

Quadrangle Books

1971

Library of Congress Catalog Card Number: 70–143574
SBN 8129–0177–0

A Note on the Text, and Acknowledgments

EARLY IN 1862, Edward Dicey went to New York—"from the Mersey to the Narrows"—as a special correspondent for *The Spectator* and *Macmillan's Magazine*. When he returned to London six months later, he assembled his articles from these periodicals, revised and rewrote them, and turned in his book to Macmillan and Company in March 1863, his personal dateline reading "Oxford and Cambridge Club."

"If anything that I have written should jar upon the feelings of my friends on either side [of] the Atlantic," he wrote, "I can only beg them to believe that I have stated simply what I conceive to be the truth, in the earnest hope that, by so doing, I might render some little service towards creating a more friendly feeling between the two great English-speaking nations of the world."

The book was published that year as *Six Months in the Federal States*—but it met a lukewarm reception because of the author's clear Northern sympathies. It was never printed in the United States. Lincoln scholars have turned to its passages for first-hand impressions of the sixteenth President. But the less well-known observations of the American people and cities and slavery have been overlooked because of the book's unavailability.

I have retitled it to underscore its meaning today. In the editing process, Dicey's language has not been changed, but historical research has revealed some factual slips and omissions, which have been corrected. Some stylistic inconsistencies have also been repaired. The book was originally published as two volumes in one and included disquisitions on territorial and state constitutions and similar non-observed material. I have pared down some rather mundane explanatory details in a number of chapters because they do not add to known and more significant research on constitutional documents. But all that Dicey saw with his own eyes, felt instinctively, and interpreted for himself and the reader is retained.

In the course of research here and abroad on Dicey and about the nature of reporting in 1863, I received help from the following kind persons: Wyndham D. Clark of London, whose great-grandmother was a Dicey and recalled seeing the author early in this century; Mme Francis Cattoir of Brussels, a niece of Mr. Clark, who provided a copy of the Edward Dicey portrait that appears as the frontispiece; C. A. Seaton, librarian of *The Spectator*; and David C. Mearns and Lloyd A. Dunlap, Lincoln scholars at the Library of Congress in Washington. For faith in this historical adventure, I acknowledge the advice of Herbert Nagourney and Alfred Rice, and, in preparing the manuscript, the help of Betty Pomerantz, a catcher of anachronisms, and Vicky Heller, a fielder of folios.

Introduction

OF ALL the European correspondents who reported on the life of the American people and on President Lincoln during the Civil War, one stood alone as a keen observer, going against the tide of prevailing narrow-mindedness and prejudice. He was Edward Dicey, a young writer for *The Spectator* and *Macmillan's Magazine*, who decided to cross the Atlantic and see the citizens and cities, the war, and Mr. Lincoln with his own eyes.

A literary man, Dicey sought out Nathaniel Hawthorne and the New England academic circle, whose notions about freedom and abolition undoubtedly gave him a wider perspective. A few years earlier, he had specialized in the classics and mathematics at Trinity College, Cambridge, traveled around Italy, and got his first taste of the Mediterranean wars for independence. He then decided to put his moral fervor to work as a journalist.

Dicey found the United States in a much different situation than had his famous French predecessor. Alexis de Tocqueville had come to America when it was in a plastic and formative condition, and what he saw was filtered through the intellectual predispositions of a man who was an heir of the Enlightenment. He had his own definite ideas about the republican form of government and the viability of various political systems. His perceptions of the American character and the future of Russia and America as the polarized powers are remarkable.

Dicey arrived in the United States when it was locked in a death struggle within its own borders. He carried with him the powers of a magnifying camera-eye: he watched and listened with his mental shutter open almost all the way. Unlike many

English travelers before him, he left his snobbery at home. His vivid descriptions of scenes at Harper's Ferry and the battlefields are visual without always being hortatory. In his evaluation of major figures in America, he is very much *l'homme moyen*, gifted with sympathetic understanding and admirable moral qualities. What he says about the condition of the Negro—and the effect of slavery upon the character of the oppressing white man—has meaning more than a century later in the United States. He had an instinct against slavery and for democracy that stands up to this day.

"Morally, I do not look on slavery, nor even the slave trade, as being a sin apart from all other sins. Whether you degrade men to the level of beasts, as the Bourbons did in Naples, . . . whether you shoot Hindoos from the cannon's mouth, in order to add the prospect of everlasting damnation to the pangs of death, as we did in India . . . whether you drill human beings into soldier-slaves . . . or whether you kidnap Negroes, sell them by auction, deny them the rights of men, and scourge them with the lash, like the planters of the South, you are, in my judgment, sinning almost equally against the moral law of God.

"Slavery, however, has one peculiar guilt, which few, if any other of the hundred modes of human cruelty and oppression, can be justly charged with. It is a gigantic, almost an isolated, attempt to reduce oppression to a system, and to establish a social order of which the misery of human beings is the fundamental principle. It is for this reason that every honest man, who hates cruelty and loves justice, is bound to lift up his voice against slavery as an accursed thing. It is thus that I think of it, let me say once and for all; and thus, as far as lies within my power, that I mean to write of it."

Again and again, as he observed the war and how it affected the home front, he returned to the immorality of the slave system. As a Civil War spectator, Dicey covered more territory than most of his foreign colleagues. The half-year he spent in the North in 1862—before the fortunes of war slowly turned in favor of the Union—was a time of testing for Mr. Lincoln and his Generals.

Dicey did not join the pack that second-guessed the President and the conduct of the war. Instead, he did what few reporters then or now are capable of doing: he played it straight. He observed the abolitionists, the role of the church, mass meetings, the call-up of the green soldiery, the reactions of the men in blue and of the citizenry to bleak battle news, the free Negro and the slave traders, the American press and Congress.

From the windows of his lodgings in Washington, Dicey looked out upon long and muddy Pennsylvania Avenue. He did not hesitate to rate the average raw material in the Union Army as "the finest." No other English correspondent dared to say in the midst of the Civil War—when there was a chance that his own country might help the Confederacy with arms and men as well as with recognition—that "in the interest of humanity, in the interest of America, and in the interest of England, the success of the North is the thing we ought to hope and wish for."

He was constantly on the move, seeming to relax only in Boston and Cambridge. His travels took him to New York and New England, to Kentucky, Tennessee, Western Virginia, Missouri, Ohio, Illinois, and the prairie country on both sides of the Mississippi. Not with rancor but matter-of-factly, he observed what many Easterners from major cities still feel west of the Hudson: "When you have taken your first half-hour's stroll about any town you happen to pass a night in, you know as much about it externally as if you had lived there a month."

His comments about the American cities he visited and their residents are enduring. Already there was great diversity in the traditions of the divided country—West and East (the route of his travels) as well as North and South. In some places he saw immigrants who wore Union blue with pride; indeed, newly minted citizens often received commands in languages other than English. "Americans drink freely and Germans drink copiously," he noted while strolling in St. Louis and hearing German spoken everywhere. "When the joint thirstiness of Americans and Germans is developed by a Southern sun, it is astonishing the quantity of liquor that can be consumed. I should think, without exaggeration, that one-tenth of all the shops in St. Louis must be establishments where, in some form or another, liquor is drunk on the premises."

Dicey saw Chicago as the handsomest of all American business cities. "A commercial panic, a change in the route of traffic, might destroy Chicago, but no human power could destroy the great corn-growing region of which, for the time, it is the capital." Cincinnati he regarded as the "Queen City of the West" because it had many book and music stores and the homes gave off an air of "education and refinement." His comments on Washington are prescient: "The whole place looks run up in a night, like the cardboard cities which Potemkin erected to gratify the eyes of his Imperial mistress on her tour through Russia; and it is impossible to remove the impression that, when Congress is over, the whole place is taken down, and packed up again till wanted. Everybody is a bird of passage in Washington."

He was impressed by New York—especially the sight of it coming up the Narrows into the landlocked bay. His word-picture of Manhattan is impressionistic: "Fairy pilot-boats, with their snow-white sails . . . vessels bearing the flag of every nation under the sun dropping down with the flood . . . the Empire City, a sort of Venice without canals . . . half-hidden by a forest of masts."

But he loved Boston and decided that—"putting aside the dreary six months' winter of ice and snow"—it would be his first choice as a dwelling place. "Even though you lose your way, it is pleasanter to an ill-regulated European mind to go wrong in Boston than to go right in St. Louis or Chicago," he says. "There is even a pleasure in being received in a hotel where the waiters wear white neckties and are pompous as well as civil. The town itself is so bright and clean, so full of life without bustle; and then the suburbs are such pleasant places." He admired the English atmosphere, the abundance of English books and newspapers, the English talk and gossip. "Indeed, it often struck me that my Boston friends knew more about England than they did about America."

Dicey's impressions of Abraham Lincoln are valuable, especially since the newspapers, including *The Times* of London and such important organs of opinion as *Punch,* regarded the six-teenth President of the United States as a country bumpkin. Dicey spent several hours with the President in the White House at a small gathering, and felt that despite all the stories he was in the presence of a great and melancholy man.

"Fancy a man six-foot [three] high, and thin out of proportion, with long bony arms and legs, which somehow seem to be always in the way, with large rugged hands, which grasp you like a vise when shaking yours, with a long scraggy neck, and a chest too narrow for the great arms hanging by its side; a face furrowed, wrinkled, and indented, as though it had been scarred by vitriol; and, sunk deep beneath bushy eyebrows, two bright, somewhat dreamy eyes, that seemed to gaze through you without looking at you." Although Lincoln in his "badly-fitting suit of black, creased, soiled and puckered up at every salient point of the figure" did not have a gentlemanly appearance, Dicey saw something more essential: "Still there is about him a complete lack of pretension, and an evident desire to be courteous to everybody, which is the essence, if not the outward form, of high breeding."

Dicey noted that Lincoln appeared to be on terms of "perfect equality" with everybody. "He spoke but little, and seemed to prefer others talking to him to talking himself. But when he did speak, his remarks were always shrewd and sensible. The President asked me several questions about the state of public feeling in England, and obviously, like almost all Americans, was unable to comprehend the causes which have alienated the sympathies of the mother country. At the same time, it struck me that the tone in which he spoke of England was, for an American, unusually fair and candid."

When some of the party began smoking, Secretary of State Seward remarked that he always wondered how any man could ever get to be President of the United States with so few vices. Mr. Seward said, "The President, I regret to say, neither drinks nor smokes." Whereupon, Lincoln answered: "That is a doubtful compliment. I recollect once being outside a stage in Illinois, and a man sitting by me offered me a cigar. I told him I had no vices. He said nothing, smoked for some time, and then grunted out,

'It's my experience in life that folks who have got no vices have plaguey few virtues.' "

Dicey himself was, in the words of *The Spectator*, "a cultured Englishman." His special correspondence was widely quoted all over Europe. Of more importance, he was reprinted in the United States as a rare example of a Northern and Lincoln sympathizer.

After returning to England, Dicey assembled his war correspondence and recollections with new perspective. Alexander Macmillan in London published his book in 1863 as *Six Months in the Federal States*. It was dedicated, by permission, to the English philosopher John Stuart Mill, who was a strong supporter of the North and constantly reprimanded his countrymen for their pro-Southern partisanship. Dicey continued to guide *The Spectator* and other publications editorially concerning the war across the Atlantic and the President. He had the satisfaction of seeing *The Times* of London and other newspapers that had criticized his writings reverse their course after the assassination.

Shortly after Lincoln's death, Dicey wrote an article for *Macmillan's* that placed the sixteenth President historically and added to his own stature: "I do not believe the late President was a man of genius. His record is grand and noble enough without our need to attribute to him qualities which he did not possess. A purer Nelson, a wiser Garibaldi, his name will, if I mistake not, be cherished by the American people much as the memory of the two heroes I have mentioned is honored in their own countries. History, I think, will say that our own days produced a yet nobler representative of American courage, and honesty, and self-sacrifice, in the person of Abraham Lincoln."

After his experiences in the United States, Dicey went looking for other wars. He acted as special correspondent in the Schleswig-Holstein War in 1864 and the Seven Weeks' War of 1866. Later he visited Russia and the Near East, writing travel books and political treatises. Although he entered Gray's Inn as a student in 1865 and was called to the bar in 1875, he did not practice law but stuck to journalism. For several years he was an editorial writer for the *Daily Telegraph* of London. Between 1870 and 1889, he served as editor of *The Observer*. He was a familiar figure at the

Athenaeum and Garrick Clubs. When he died in 1911 at his
chambers in Gray's Inn, he left neither wife nor child, both having predeceased him.

But he did leave a monument for transatlantic scholars, *Six
Months in the Federal States.* In its remarkably accurate reporting and insights about Lincoln and the Civil War, in its views
of America's cities and folkways, Edward Dicey holds up a historical mirror image worth reflecting today.

HERBERT MITGANG

Contents

xvii

SPECTATOR
OF
AMERICA

Out at Sea

It was not my purpose on going to America to write a book of
travels. I did not intend, in other words, to republish my own
diary. Everybody judges of the public by himself, and I own that,
to me, the perusal of any other person's diary is singularly uninteresting. In an unknown country, the daily record of the traveler's adventures may possess a real value. On a journey such as
mine it was not probable that a traveler would meet with any
greater personal adventures than rough quarters, bad inns, and
stormy weather. It would be a matter of little interest to the public, or, indeed, to myself, to record whether on such a night, in
such a month, I slept at Philadelphia or at Baltimore. The great
majority of mankind (and, I confess, I agree with them) are
perfectly content to travel by railroad without knowing, or caring
to know, how many revolutions the wheels make per minute, and
how many tons of coal are consumed at a given speed.

Of my voyage, therefore, I shall say but little. It was in the
depth of winter, immediately after the settlement of the *Trent*
affair, that I sailed for the New World. What with the storms at
sea and the storms in the political ocean, our complement of passengers was of the scantiest; and yet, scanty as it was, it formed a
strange epitome of the new country we were hurrying to. Most of
us were men who had seen something of the world. We had
amongst us an ex-colonial governor; the son of an English earl,
now a member of the Canadian parliament; a quondam man-
about-town, settled in the Far West, to whom the prairie and
Pall Mall were alike familiar; a Frenchman, whose home was in

3

New York, but whose heart lay in Paris; a Swiss officer of distinction; a Scotch lawyer, who had married in America; a number of New York and Boston dry-goods men; and a young Englishman, traveling for pleasure, to visit his relatives in the States. With the exception of myself, perhaps, every one of us had his fortunes more or less connected with both hemispheres.

Politics were dangerous subjects of conversation, and we avoided them as much as possible. We had strong pro-Union New Englanders amongst us, Government agents, Southern Secessionists, and an unhappy bagman, who (I believe entirely on the strength of a somewhat forbidding cast of features) was regarded as a spy. The promotion, therefore, of mutual good fellowship put a check on political discussions; and even without this, we were not intellectually equal to them.

Our passage was, I suppose, much as other passages are—of the water, watery. We had the regular experiences. We had a storm, and got blocked amongst the ice, and were enveloped in a fog off the banks of Newfoundland. We were followed by the sea gulls from the Mersey to the Narrows; sighted a ship or two; saw, or fancied we saw, an iceberg; and were visited by a sparrow in the middle of the Atlantic. These are the sole outward incidents of our voyage I can call to mind. Of the remarks made by any of us during that period of intellectual trance, there is but one, I think, worth recalling, less for its intrinsic value, than as a word of recollection to my fellow passengers, in case any of them should come across this book of mine. It was during the height of our one great storm. The waves were rolling, foaming, surging round us, as only Atlantic waves can do; the ship staggered, careened, and reeled, as wave after wave came thundering on her; the wind roared howling round us; and sea and sky seemed fused together in one watery mist of foam and spray. A small party were playing faro at the time, clinging to the table with one hand, and clutching their cards with the other, when the wave washed both players and tables away to the end of the cabin. One of them, a friend of mine, sprung up with his cards in his hands, and staggering across the cabin, groaned, amidst the howling of the tempest and the shrieks of the female passengers, "I wish Columbus had been crucified!" That such a saying should have been the brightest I can remember on our voyage will give the reader a fair impression of the mental imbecility to which seasickness and dullness had reduced us.

New York

It was on the brightest of bright winter days that I entered New York. Morally, it was about the gloomiest period of the Federal fortunes, the darkest of the night before the break of day so soon to follow. The pilot, who hailed us off Sandy Hook, brought us as the only news a rumor that [Gen. Ambrose] Burnside's expedition had been half destroyed by a storm at sea; and our American fellow passengers received the intelligence gloomily. Still, the charm of seeing land again was enough to make us forget all political troubles; and, apart from that, the approach through the Narrows into the landlocked bay of New York will remain in my mind as one of the loveliest scenes that I have ever looked upon. Out of the cold, chill, gray dawn, as I stood shivering on deck, watching for the glimpses of the New World, the sun rose in a mass of fire. The dim haze rolled slowly away, and the sky grew clear and blue, like an Italian sky when the Tramontana wind is blowing southward from across the Alps; and were it not that the hill-slopes which hemmed in the bay on either side were covered with white sparkling snow, and that my fingers tingled with a chill, numbing cold, I might have fancied myself back in Italy. But the brightness of the air and the glitter of the sunshine neutralized the depression which cold always exercises on my appreciative faculties; and, even at the risk of frostbitten toes, I lingered upon deck to gaze at the view. Past Sandy Hook Fort, where the Stars and Stripes were floating gaily; through the winding Narrows; close beneath the wooded banks of Staten Island, where villas of wood, villas of stone, villas with Doric porticoes, villas with Italian campaniles, Swiss cottages, and Grecian mansions seemed to succeed each

6

other in a never-ending panorama; we floated onward, toward the long low black line which marked the city of New York. The waters of the bay were calm and blue, like those of a Southern sea; and against the banks great masses of snow-covered ice lay huddled closely—while loose blocks, sparkling in the sunlight, came floating past us out to sea with the ebbing tide. The fairy pilot-boats, with their snow-white sails, darted across our path; vessels bearing the flag of every nation under the sun were dropping down with the flood; English, French, and American men-of-war lay anchored in the bay, where all the navies of the world might ride at pleasure; and the quaint Yankee river steamboats, which look as though, in an excess of seasickness, they had thrown their cabins inside out, and turned their engines upside down, glided around us in every direction. So we steamed slowly on till the Empire City—a sort of Venice without canals—lay before us, half-hidden by the forest of masts, which, palisade-like, girds in its quays, and we were on land at last.

It seemed hard to realize, save for the sunshine, that I had come into a foreign country. Like the traveler of Horace, I had crossed the sea, and had changed nothing but the sky. Everything around and about me looked so like the Old Country. There were neither soldiers nor *gendarmes*, not even a policeman, waiting to receive us on landing. The passports with which I, in common with my fellow passengers, had provided myself, were uncalled for; and we left the ship on our several errands without a question being asked of any one of us. Indeed, up to the hour when I quitted the States, I had never occasion to show my passport, except once, to a banker in the West, to whom it luckily served as a proof of my identity. Irish porters seized upon my luggage, as they would have done at the Tower steps in London. Street newsboys pestered me with second editions of English-printed newspapers. An old-fashioned English hackney-coach carried me to my destination, through dull, English-looking streets, with English names; and the driver cheated me at the end of my fare, with genuine London exorbitance.

It is not my purpose to describe New York—its sights, and streets, and monuments. The description has been given a score of times before, probably better than I could do it. American cities have one peculiarity, not altogether displeasing to a somewhat blasé sightseer, and that is, that they have few, if any, sights to show. New York is no exception to this general rule. There is a picture gallery; there are a few public buildings, which are supposed to possess architectural merits; and there is the Croton Aqueduct, interesting to engineers. Still, with all deference to my New York friends, I hardly think that a European traveler need go far out of his way to visit any of these curiosities. I plead guilty to not having seem them, and have as little intention of describing them as I had of visiting them.

It is the general aspect alone of the city, the impression it left upon my mind, that I wish to convey in these pages. New York is not a showplace, and, architecturally, possesses but little claim to distinction. The plan of the city is, in itself, too simple for variety, and is easy enough to understand. The Island of Manhattan, on which New York is placed, is very like the shape of a sole. Now, if you suppose that the skeleton of a sole had a network of crossbones, parallel as well as perpendicular to the backbone, you will have an exact idea of the plan of New York. The backbone is Broadway; the parallel crossbones are the avenues, numbered from east to west; and the bones at right angles to the spine are the streets, numbered consecutively from the sole's mouth to its tail. This arithmetical nomenclature of the streets, which seems so barbarous to us in Europe, is really of great practical convenience. The system is not perfect, because the streets in the old parts of the town have names of their own; but still it is sufficiently so, to enable anyone to tell, given the name of a street, whereabouts it is situated, and how to get to it. The corner end of the island, corresponding to the sole's mouth, is the commercial part, the City of New York, of which Wall Street is the Cornhill. Broadway is the great thoroughfare, where all the chief shops and stores are situated; and Fifth Avenue, with the streets running across it, is the fashionable quarter, the resort of the Upper Ten Thousand, the Belgravia of the town. Across the middle of the island stretches the Central Park, and beyond that are large, straggling suburbs, whose streets stand high up in the multiplica-

tion table, and which threaten, in a few years, if New York should
grow at its present rate, to cover the whole island of Manhattan.
Across the Hudson and the East River, which join at the city end
of the island, lie the great suburbs of Jersey City and Brooklyn—
Birkenheads, so to speak, to the New World Liverpool. So much
for the topography of New York.

The general effect of the "Empire City" is to me disappointing.
Simple magnitude is never very striking to anyone accustomed
to London; and, except in magnitude, there is not much to impress you. Broadway is, or rather ought to be, a very fine street;
and its single stores are as grand as anything can be in the way of
shop-front architecture. But a marble-faced palace, of six stories
high, has a cast-iron store, with card-paper-looking pillars, on one
side, and a two-storied red brick house on the other. There is no
symmetry or harmony about the street, so that it lacks grandeur,
without having irregularity enough to be picturesque. The rows
of stunted trees on either side give it, in parts, a French look; but
still, when I had once heard a candid American describe it
as a "one-horse boulevard," I felt he had produced a description
which could not be improved upon. Fifth Avenue is symmetrical
enough; but its semi-detached stone mansions, handsome as they
are, have not sufficient height to justify its American name of
the Street of Palaces; while its monotony is dreadful. The other
streets of the fashionable quarters are inferior editions of the
Fifth Avenue, and suggested to me, just as our own districts of
Tyburnia and Belgravia always do, two invariable reflections—
firstly, what an enormous amount of wealth there must be in a
country where such vast numbers of people can afford to live in
such houses; and, secondly, how little artistic taste there must be
amongst a people who, with such incomes, are content to live
in dwellings of such external unattractiveness. The poorer streets,
toward the banks of the island, have no architectural pretensions;
and their prototype, the famous Bowery, bears the strongest family resemblance to the Walworth Road or to Mile-end Gate. The
churches, with their towers and tall taper steeples, relieve the uniformity of the city; but, like all our modern style of ecclesiastical
architecture, they are not vast enough to be imposing. In fact, if

you could transpose New York to England, it would be externally as uninteresting a city as Manchester. But here, in this crisp clear air, there is a sort of French sparkle about the place which enlivens it strangely.

With the exception of the climate, there is far less of a foreign look about New York than I had expected. Statistics tell you that over one-half of the population of the city was born in the Old World; and it is also true that there are only three German cities in the world—Vienna, Berlin, and, I believe, Hamburg—which contain more German inhabitants than New York. All the shop-notices, and all the thousands of placards, which are stuck upon every wall, with an utterly English disregard of artistic proprieties, are in English, and addressed to English customers. Announcements in the shop-windows that, *"Ici on parle Français,"* and *"Hier spricht man Deutsch,"* are but few; while the number of persons you meet speaking any language but English is smaller, I should say, than in London or in Liverpool. There are quarters in the town which Irish, French, and Germans more especially frequent; but Ratcliffe Highway is as much Irish, Whitechapel is as much German, and Leicester Square is as much French, as any corresponding district in New York. The German population evidently retains the strongest individuality of any foreign class; and the fancy for bright inharmonious colors, so common here amongst the women of the lower classes, coupled with the custom of wearing knitted woolen caps, instead of bonnets, gives rather a German look to the people in the poorer streets. There is a German newspaper too; and two or three German theaters, which the Germans have tried unsuccessfully to obtain leave to open on the Sunday. Indeed, the dullness of New York on Sunday is so preeminently British, that it is hard to persuade oneself one is not in London or Glasgow.

The physiognomy of the population is not English; but it is very difficult to state why, or in what respect, it is not so. The difference I take to be chiefly that instead of the twenty varieties of form and feature you observe in an English crowd, one English type of face, and one only, the sallow, sharp-featured, straight-haired one, is reproduced indefinitely. An American friend of mine has a theory that the Red Indian is the type of face created by Nature for America; and that there is an irresistible tendency in each succeeding generation of Americans to approximate more and more to the natural Red Indian type. I give no opinion as to the value of the theory; but it is certainly a curious fact, how, in spite of the constant infusion of fresh foreign blood, one uniform type of face appears to be spreading itself through the American people. The colored population in New York is not numerous enough in the streets to give a foreign air to the crowd, as it forms little over one per cent of the whole. At the hotels, and in wealthy private houses, the servants are frequently black, but in the streets there are few Negroes visible. Here, as elsewhere, they form a race apart, never walking in company with white persons, except as servants.

There is a popular delusion in England that New York is a sort of gingerbread-and-gilt city; and that, contrasted with an English town, there is a want of solidity about the whole place, materially as well as morally. On the contrary, I was never in a town where externally, at any rate, show was so much sacrificed to solid comfort. The ferries, the cars, the street railroads, and the houses, are all so arranged as to give one substantial comfort, without external decoration. It is, indeed, indoors that the charm of New York is found. There is not much of luxury, in the French sense of the word—no lavish display of mirrors, and clocks, and pictures—but there is more comfort, more English luxury, about the private dwelling-houses than I ever saw in the same class of houses at home. The rooms are so light and lofty; the passages are so well warmed; the doors slide backward in their grooves so easily and yet so tightly; the chairs are so luxurious; the beds are so elastic, and the linen so clean, and, let me add, the living so excellent, that I would never wish for better quarters, or for a more hospitable welcome, than I have found in many private houses of New York. All the domestic arrangements (to use a fine word for gas, hot water, and other comforts) are wonderfully perfect. Everything, even more than in England, seems adapted for a home life. Because of the severity of the winters, there can be no outdoor amusements during a great portion of the year; but, under any circumstances, there appears to be not much of public life. There are no cafés; and the nearest approach to any place of public resort, the hotel barrooms, are not places where you can sit down, or find any amusement, as a habitué, except that of drinking.

Undoubtedly, out-of-doors, you see evidences of a public equality, or rather absence of inequality, among all classes which cannot fail to strike an inhabitant of the Old World. In the streets, the man in the hat and broadcloth coat and the man in corduroys and fustian jacket never get out of each other's way or expect the other to make way for him. In the cars and omnibuses ladies and washerwomen, gentlemen and laborers, sit huddled together without the slightest mutual sense of incongruity. In the shops and by the servants it is your own fault if you are not treated with perfect civility—but with civility as to an equal, not as to a superior. In the barrooms there is no distinction of customers; and as long as you pay your way, and behave quietly, you are welcome whatever your dress may be. No doubt the cause of this general equality is the absence of the classes brutalized by poverty whom you see in all our great cities. There is a great deal of poverty in New York, and the Five Points quarter—the Seven Dials of the city—is, especially on a bitter winter's day, as miserable a haunt of vice and misery as it was ever my lot to witness in Europe. Still, compared with the size of New York, this quarter is a very small one; and poverty there, bad as it is, is not helpless poverty. The fleeting population of the Five Points is composed of the lowest and most shiftless of the recent foreign emigrants; and in the course of a few years they, or at any rate their children, move to other quarters, and become prosperous and respectable. From these causes, and from the almost universal diffusion of education, there is no class exactly analogous to our English idea of the mob. The fact that well-nigh everybody you meet is comfortably dressed seems to disprove the existence of those dangerous classes which always attract the notice of a foreigner in England. There are few beggars about the town, and of those few, all are children. For an Anglo-Saxon population, there is very little drunkenness visible in the streets; and with regard to other forms of public vice it is not for an Englishman to speak severely.

The Broadway saloons, with their so-called "pretty waiter-girls," and the lager beer haunts in the low quarters of the town, whose windows are crowded with wretched half-dressed or undressed women, formed, indeed, about the most shameless exhibition of public vice I have ever come across, even in England or Holland; and I am glad to say that, since I left New York, the State Government, under a Republican as opposed to a Democratic legislature, has taken means to suppress these social nuisances. But in the streets at night, there are few of the scenes which habitually disgrace our own metropolis.

The great quiet and order of the city are in themselves remarkable. There is an air of unsecured security about New York I never saw equaled out of England. There are no soldiers about, as in a Continental capital; and the policemen—nearly as fine a body of men, by the way, as our London police—appear to devote their energies to preserving Broadway from being utterly jammed up by carts, and to escorting ladies across that most treacherous of thoroughfares. The people seem instinctively to keep themselves in order. How a row would be suppressed if there was one, I cannot say; I only know that, during my stay in New York, I never saw anything approaching to a disturbance in any public place or thoroughfare.

But, in truth, everything there is so different from what one would expect it to be in theory. Under a democratic republic like that of New York State, where, practically, the suffrage is universal, one would expect that in all social matters the convenience and interests of the individual would be sacrificed to those of the public. The very contrary is the fact. The principle of vested rights —the power of every individual to consult his own inclinations in defiance of his neighbor's convenience—is carried there to a perfect absurdity. Anybody may build his house after his own fancy, in total disregard of the architectural style of the houses by which it is surrounded. Anybody may stop his cart or carriage where he likes; and I have seen Wall Street in its busiest hours blocked up by a stoppage caused by some brewer's dray, which chose to stand still at the side of the narrow street. Anybody has a right to get into the cars or omnibuses so long as he can squeeze his way in; and thus the cars—in themselves the most comfortable street conveyances I have ever traveled in—are rendered at times almost insufferable by the fact that the broad space between the seats is crammed with extra passengers, standing on, or in dangerous proximity to, the toes of the seated travelers. Cheap comfortable cabs are the one great luxury in which New York is deficient, and a cab company would probably be the most profitable of speculations; but the old hackney-coach proprietors, who possess the most rickety of two-horse, tumble-down vehicles, and who charge any price they like, from a dollar upward, for any distance, have always, by their vested interests, contrived to thwart the introduction of cabs. The illustration, however, of this state of public feeling which most strikes a stranger is the state of the public streets in wintertime. It has been my fortune, or misfortune, in the course of many years of travel, to ride over a good number of bad roads of every kind of badness; but no road I have literally, as well as metaphorically, stumbled across, is to compare with Broadway during last winter's snows. When it froze hard at night, the street next day was a succession of *Montagnes Russes*, up and down which the carriages slid wildly. Over the pavement lay a coating of some three or four feet of snow, indented with holes and furrows and ridges of most alarming magnitude. Whenever there was a temporary thaw, this mass of ice and snow became a pond of slush—a very slough of despond. Without exaggeration, crossing the main streets was a work of danger. Falls of foot-passengers were things of constant occurrence, while the struggles of the floundering horses to drag the carriages out of the ruts and crevasses were really painful to witness. I believe the state of the streets was somewhat worse that year than usual; but every year there is more or less of the same sort of thing. The one cause of all this obstruction is that the contractor who has undertaken to keep the streets clean has failed to fulfill the spirit, if not the letter, of his contract. Everybody grumbles—just as we do in London when a gas company stops up the Strand for the sake of tinkering its pipes—but nobody proposes to interfere and insist on the nuisance being summarily removed. The vested rights of the individual contractor override the rights of the public.

On only one occasion did I see a mob in New York, and that was on the outbreak of a fire. It was toward midday, and, to my surprise, every clock near Wall Street, down which I was passing at the time, began striking seven solemnly and slowly, like our passing bell in a country parish. I inquired the meaning from a passerby, and learnt that it was the signal that a fire had broken out in the Seventh Ward. I turned in the direction pointed out, and soon a fire engine rattled past me, dragged by a string of boys and men through, rather than over, the uneven, broken snow-drifts. Then in a few minutes another followed, and another; and by the time I had reached the scene of the fire, not a quarter of a mile away, half a dozen engines were at work, though I had heard the first signal of the fire given but a few minutes before. A store of kerosene oil had caught fire, and the volumes of flame which shot out of the roof and windows seemed to threaten the whole street with destruction. But the engines were too hard at work to give the fire a chance; the river lay fortunately near at hand; and there was a perfect crowd of volunteers ready to work the pumps with might and main. There was nobody to keep the dense throng of spectators who crammed the neighboring streets in order, but of themselves they obeyed the instructions of the firemen, and made way readily whenever space was required for the engines or the pipes to pass. The firemen worked with a will, and seemed utterly regardless of danger. Some were dragging the water-pipes right under the walls of the burning house, which looked every minute as if they were about to fall; others were standing on the parapet of the flaming roof, hanging over the street in a way that made one dizzy to look at, and shouting out orders to the men below; others, again, were perched on ladders fixed against the house on fire, and cutting down the shutters with axes in order to let out the flames. It was a service of real danger, and one poor fellow lost his life by falling off an engine; but one and all these firemen were unpaid volunteers, who ex-pected no reward for their services. The engines are supplied by

the State, but the whole expense and labor of the service are
borne by the men themselves. There is a great esprit de corps
amongst the different companies, and admission into them is
sought for eagerly. At every engine-house a certain number of the
men always remain on duty, turn and turn about; and the moment the signal-bell is heard over the city, the members of the
company leave their homes and their business, whatever it may
be, to perform their duty as firemen. I have seen great fires in
many European countries, but I never saw a fire extinguished so
promptly or so courageously as by these volunteer firemen. Indeed, the existence in New York of such an organization as that
of the fire brigades is enough in itself to make one somewhat
skeptical as to the truth of our common impression about its
democratic lawlessness.

I had left England at the time when the fortunes of the Federal cause seemed the lowest, and when New York was popularly
believed to be on the brink of ruin and revolution. It was, I own,
a surprise to me to find how little trace there was of either. An
incurious stranger, not given to enter into conversation, or to
read the newspaper, might almost, I fancy, have lived there for
weeks at that time without discovering that the country was involved in a civil war. There were forts being thrown up rapidly
along the banks which command the Narrows; but of late years
we have learnt in England not to associate the construction of
expensive fortifications with any idea of immediate war. The
number of uniforms about the streets was small—not so large as
it used to be in London before the volunteer movement was
heard of. A score or so of tents were pitched upon the snow in
the City Park, and at the Battery, but more for show than use.
On Broadway and the Bowery there were a few recruiting offices,
in front of which hung huge placards tempting fine young men,
by the offer of a hundred dollars' bounty (to be paid not down,
but after the war), and the promise of immediate active service,
to join the Van Buren light infantry or the New York *mounted*
cavalry. It was rare to hear a military band; and in the shop windows I noticed at that time but few pictures of the war, or portraits of the war's heroes. I saw regiments passing through the

town on their way to the South, and yet only a few idlers were gathered to see them pass. In fact, the show-time of the war had passed away, and it was become a matter of sober business.

So, too, I was present at New York when the news came of Roanoke Island, and Bowling Green, and Fort Donaldson—of the first of that long uninterrupted series of victories which checked the progress of the insurrection. Our English reception of the tidings of the great battles which gave the death blow to the Indian mutiny was not more reserved or calm. There were no proclamations, no addresses to the people, no grandiloquent bulletins as there would have been under like circumstances in a Continental country. A small crowd collected round the news-paper offices—a few extra flags hung out of shop windows—a notice that Barnum's Museum would be illuminated in honor of the Union victories, by the patriotic proprietor—and a salute of cannon from the Battery; such were about the only outward symptoms of public rejoicing. There was no want of interest or feeling about the war. In society it was the one topic of thought and conversation. If you heard two people talking in the street, or in the cars, or at the church doors as you came out of service, you would be sure to find they were talking of the war. The longer I lived in the country, the more I learnt how deep the feeling of the North was; but it was like all English feeling, and came slowly to the surface.

There was as little look of public distress as of popular excite-ment. The port and quays were crowded with shipping. Broad-way was daily rendered almost impassable by the never-ending string of carts and omnibuses and carriages, which rolled up and down it for hours. Splendidly equipped sable-covered sleighs were to be seen at every turning; and, on a fine day, the pavements were thronged with ladies, the expensiveness of whose dresses, if questionable as a matter of taste, was unquestionable as a matter of fact. New stores and streets were still building, and notices of "houses to let," or of sales by auction, were very few. Though the banks had suspended specie payments, yet, by one of those mys-teries of the currency I never hope to see explained, their notes passed at full value, and were exchanged readily for coin—at least, in all such small transactions as come under a traveler's notice. There was, I have no doubt, much mercantile distress; and the shopkeepers who depended on the sale of luxuries to the wealthy classes were doing a poor trade. But work was plentiful, and the distress, as yet, had not gone down deep. There were few balls or large parties, and the opera was not regularly open, partly because public feeling was averse to much gaiety; partly, and still more, because the wealthy classes had retrenched all superfluous expenditure with a really wonderful unanimity. Residents often expressed their regret to me that I should see their city under so dull an aspect. But I know that, on a bright winter day, when the whole population seemed to be driving out in sleighs to the great skating carnivals at the Central Park, I have seldom seen a brighter or a gayer-looking city than New York.

The American Press

IT IS from the press of America, or rather from the press of one portion of America, that English opinion on American affairs is principally derived. It is the source, too, from which even English travelers in America draw their observations, largely if not chiefly. I am far from saying that opinions thus formed are necessarily erroneous. In many respects, the press is a fairer exponent of American feelings than the tone of society. However excellent a stranger's letters of introduction may be, they inevitably throw him among one class, and that the wealthy and educated class; and the newspapers are addressed to the great public, of whom he inevitably sees little more than a single section. After all, too, private acquaintanceships, however valuable, only give you individual, and often interested opinions. Now, wherever there is a free and unsubventioned press, you may be sure of one thing, that, on the whole, and in the long run, the newspapers do express the opinions and prejudices of their readers. No trade goes on for long manufacturing goods which don't suit the public taste; and the press is a trade like any other. I have always felt it to be a singularly weak line of argument when I have heard either Americans or Englishmen trying to explain away any offensive remark in the newspaper organs of their respective countries by the common remark, "It is only the press says so;" it is only the utterance of the [New York] Times, or the New York Herald. It is all very true, but the question still remains: Why is it that the readers of the Times, or the Herald, like such remarks to be made? You have proved that the elephant stands upon the tortoise, but what does the tortoise stand upon? Take it all in all, then, I admit freely that the American press, *if* you judge it correctly, is a tolerably fair—probably, *the* fairest—exponent of American opinion.

That *if*, however, is a very great one. Supposing a foreigner were to read the [London] *Times*, and half a dozen other English newspapers, daily for years, his knowledge of English life and politics would still be extremely incomplete and erroneous, unless he had actually lived enough in England to have acquired what may be called the key to the English press. Anyone who, like myself, has lived at times long out of England, must, I think, have been often struck how very soon the tone, as it were, of English papers becomes strange to you. My object in making these remarks is to point out how very liable Americans are to make mistakes in judging of England from our press, and how much more liable, for special reasons, we are to make like mistakes in taking the American press as the standard of America. The Hieroglyphics contain the history of Egypt, but, to understand the history, you must be able to read the characters.

To a great extent, London is England; and to a still greater extent is the London press the press of England. There is nothing of this kind in America. The capital is a nominal one, and there is no metropolis. Americans, with their wonted love for big phrases, are apt to talk of New York as the metropolitan city; but it is big talk only. New York is the most wealthy, the most powerful, and the most important of the many capital cities which the Union possesses. New York stands to Boston, Philadelphia, Cincinnati, St. Louis, Chicago, or New Orleans, much in the same relation as Liverpool does to Hull, Birmingham, and Southampton. She is a more important city than any of them, but in no sense whatever is she their capital. The New York papers have a wider circulation than those of any other town out of their own district, but in no part of the Union, except in New York, are they *the* newspapers of the place. If a foreigner wished to study the politics of the agricultural counties, I should recommend him to read the *Morning Herald*, or some other metropolitan organ of bucolic conservatism. I should never think of advising him to take in the *Somersetshire Sentinel*, or the

Suffolk Standard. But if you want to learn the politics of the Eastern, or Western, or Southern States, the last place you would look for them would be in a New York journal. From the facts that New York is the great port of departure for Europe, that the commercial relations of the Old and New Worlds are chiefly carried on through New York, and that the New York papers contain the latest news, its journals are, naturally enough, the only ones which reach Europe. But an Englishman who reads the New York press alone knows as much and as little about the sentiments of the other parts of the Union as an American would know about the politics of Kent and Cambridgeshire who read nothing but the *Liverpool Albion.*

The absence of a metropolis, and of a metropolitan standard of thought and refinement, tells upon the American press much as it tells upon American literature and education and refinement. According to my view, it tells unfavorably on the individual, but favorably upon the average. The New York press, which is the nearest approach to a metropolitan one, is most decidedly inferior to the English, but then the local press is superior in much the same proportion. Thus, when the low standard of the New York press is taken, not altogether without reason, as a proof of the absence of high mental culture in the United States, the relatively high standard of the local press ought fairly to be taken as evidence of the extent to which education is diffused.

Before, however, I enter on the general characteristics of the American press, I must speak of the New York press, by which alone America is unfortunately judged abroad. And first, then, on the principle of honor to whom honor is *not* due, of the *New York Herald:* I have no doubt myself that the *Herald,* in spite of many assertions I have heard made to the contrary, has far the largest circulation of any American daily paper. Away from the North, it is the only New York paper that you come across frequently; and I have seen two people reading the *Herald* for one I have observed reading any other newspaper. Each of its rivals admits it to be the second in circulation. It contains, too, always all that class of advertisements which are intended to catch the eye of the million; and advertisers are pretty sure to know what is the best channel for their advertisements. One week, when there was unusually stirring news, the *Herald* boasted that its circulation reached 113,000; and therefore I suppose its average sale would be 100,000. What its political influence may be, it is more difficult to ascertain. Every educated American you speak to on the subject rejects indignantly the idea that it has any political influence whatever; but still, I find they all read it. I saw enough of political life in America to convince me that all public men, to say the least, preferred its friendship to its hostility. I remember on one occasion, which, for obvious reasons, I do not wish to specify, I was invited to a small half-political, half-military reception, given by an officer with whom I happened to be acquainted. The party was a very select one; but, to my surprise, I met there the correspondent of the *New York Herald* with his family. The cause of my surprise, I need hardly say, was not at a newspaper correspondent being present—in truth, there is no country where any sort of literary repute is more honored than in America—but simply, that I knew the gentleman in question was not received into any kind of society at the town where he was stationed; and that I myself had been cautioned by a resident against being seen in his company. The cause of his presence I discovered afterward. He had asked for a ticket, and our entertainer being anxious to rise in public favor, was afraid of being attacked by the *Herald* in case of refusal. This incident I only mention in illustration of a well-known fact. The *Herald* is a power in the country; and though it can do little to make or mar established reputations, yet it has great opportunities of pushing a new man forward in public life, or of keeping him back; and such opportunities as it has, it uses unscrupulously. It made its first start in journalistic life by levying blackmail on public men, through threats of private exposures, and the old informer spirit still clings to it in the days of its comparative respectability. The real cause, however, of the *Herald's* permanent success, I believe to be very simple. It gives the most copious, if not the most accurate, news of any American journal. It is conducted with more energy, and probably more capital; and also, on common topics, on which its prejudices or its interests are not concerned, it is written with a rough common sense, which often reminds me of the *Times*. It has too, to use a French word, the *flaire* of journalism. Mr. [Henry J.] Raymond, the proprietor of the *New York Times*, once remarked, half laughingly and half in earnest, to a gentleman who told me the story, "It would be worth my while, sir, to give a million dollars, if the devil would come and tell me every evening, as he does [James Gordon] Bennett, what the people of New York would like to read about next morning." The story hints clearly enough at the true cause of the *Herald's* success.

The politics of the *Herald* have fluctuated constantly. There are but two principles to which it has always proved faithful; one is to support the existing administration; the other is to attack and insult the country of Mr. Bennett's birth. Wherever Mr. Bennett's character is known, the opinions of the paper carry no weight whatever; and his character, like that of all public men in America, is known and commented on in New York to a degree which an editor's private character could never be subjected to in England. Still it is impossible that any large proportion of the hundred thousand purchasers of the *Herald* can know or care much about the character of Bennett; and therefore I have no doubt the influence of the *Herald*, pandering, as it does, not without real ability, to the prejudices and vanity of the American people, is no unimportant element in the political world.

As to Mr. Bennett's social position, all parties are agreed. The *Herald* is a very valuable property; and its net profits are said to vary from £20,000 to £30,000 annually. With the one virtue, too, that a Scotchman can never get rid of, Mr. Bennett is not personally extravagant, and is reputed to be now a man of very large fortune. Still, in New York society, he is not received, or even tolerated. Not long ago, at a watering place near New York where he took up his abode, the inmates of the hotel he had honored with his company told the landlord that he must choose between Mr. Bennett's custom and theirs—and Mr. Bennett left. Probably, just as the devil is painted blacker than nature, so the editor of the *Herald* may possess some redeeming qualities; but, as yet, the New York world has not discovered them. The result of Mr. Bennett's social disrepute, whether deserved or not, is that respectable literary men do not like being connected with the *Herald;* and its writers are generally men who, for some cause or other, are not on good terms with society; and even they, as far as my observation went, are not proud of the connection.

Of the utter unscrupulousness of the *Herald,* I will only quote one example, which happens to have some slight independent interest of its own. Mr. [William Howard] Russell, [of the London *Times*] during his stay in America, was the object of the most rancorous abuse on the part of the *Herald;* partly, because he had given personal offense to the editor, by declining his invitations; still more, because he had given offense to the American public. There happened to be some private theatricals given at the British Embassy, in which Mr. Russell played the part of Bombastes Furioso. The next day, the following account appeared in the *Herald:*

"During the representation of Bombastes Furioso, one or two amusing incidents are said to have occurred. After the delivery of the lines by Bombastes (LL.D. Russell), (lies like the deuce, was, by the way, on another occasion the *Herald's* interpretation of these letters)—

> "Whate'er your Majesty shall deign to name—
> Short cut or long—to us is all the same.

"A wag on the back benches, audibly added:—

> "So from Bull Run the shortest cut *you* came.

Sensation, and a general turning round of heads to detect the interpolator. He was *non est.*

"After the tremendous apostrophe to Distaffina—

> "By all the risks my fearless heart hath run—
> Risks of all shapes, from bludgeon, sword, and gun;
> By the great bunch of laurels on my brow—

there came again, from the same quarter, this unexpected completion of the quotation:—

> "A chaplet of leeks would fit it better now.

Renewed agitation. Suspicious glances directed towards a rollick-ing-looking clerk in one of the departments. Big drops of per-spiration chased each other down the face of the perplexed Bombastes.

"When he came to the passage—

> "In some still place I'll find a gloomy cave;
> There my own hands shall dig a spacious grave;
> Then, all unseen, I'll lay me down and die,
> Since—

"All my prophecies events belie,

again added his indefatigable tormentor.

"This put the climax to Bombastes' troubles. The well-bred audience could no longer restrain their merriment. So discom-forted by it was the burly warrior, that he could scarcely muster strength enough to attach his boots—his gage of battle, to the tree. His tormentor took pity on him, and let him gurgle out in peace his last adieus to the world."

Now this story was not put in as *ben trovato*, but as a delib-erate, serious narrative of fact. From beginning to end, it was a lie, with not one single word of truth in the whole story, except that Mr. Russell acted Bombastes—and, for that matter, acted it very well too.

Day after day there is a sort of triangular duel between the editors of the *Herald*, the *Tribune*, and the *Times*, in which per-sonalities, or what in any other papers would be considered gross libels, are freely bandied to and fro. In this warfare the *Herald*, being utterly, instead of only partially, unscrupulous, comes off an easy victor. As a specimen, I can only spare the space to quote one short leader in the *Herald*, which struck me as a gem in its peculiar class of journalism. It is headed "Poor Greeley playing Jacobin," and runs thus:

"Poor old silly [Horace] Greeley cries out for a traitor, weeps salt tears for a traitor, howls like a hyena for a traitor, shouts for all the universe to bring him a traitor. What does he want of a traitor? Why, Greeley wants to be blood-thirsty—he wants to be a little Robespierre. He wants to hang a traitor with his own hands. Let him come down to our office, and we'll give him a shilling to buy a rope—since the *Tribune* is so poor—and then he may hang himself to the nearest lamp-post, and thus at once satisfy his desire to hang a traitor, and greatly gratify the loyal public."

In the advertisement department the *Herald* has one or two specialities of its own. Like almost all American papers, its columns are disfigured by "catch the eye" advertisements. Every variety of inversion and perversion of which type is capable, is adopted to attract notice. There was one advertisement constantly repeated, which used to impress me as a triumph of genius. The words were short and simple enough—*"Buy Frank Leslie's Illustrated Newspaper, with all the news of the war."* It would puzzle an ordinary English compositor how to make this extend in small type over the whole of one column, but like Columbus's method for making an egg stand on one end, the solution of the puzzle was wonderfully simple, and consisted solely in dividing the advertisement into three paragraphs. *Buy Frank Leslie's—Illustrated Newspaper—with all the news of the war*—and repeating each paragraph, line below line, some score of times in all. The Broadway saloons, where "the prettiest waiter-girls in the world afford intellectual recreation to the customers," were especial patrons of the *Herald*, and showed a peculiar fondness for this sensation typography. The *Herald*, too, was the organ of the astrologers, and of searchers after matrimony. In one copy I happened to take up at hazard, I picked out the following specimens. Under the heading "Astrology" the list was unusually small, and only contained seven advertisements, of which two samples will be enough.

"Astrologists. Great excitement—Read! read!! The beautiful Madame Henri, whose wonderful and exquisite mode of reading the future destinies of thousands are (*sic*) daily creating the wildest furor. This lovely young lady is, without exception, the most accomplished in her line of business. She will write the name you marry, show their likeness, give good luck, and her lucky numbers are sure to draw a prize. Her rooms are at 80, West Broadway, corner Leonard, name on the door."

Again. "Astonishing Madame Morrow, seventh daughter, has a gift of foresight, tells how soon and how often you will marry, and all you wish to know, even your very thoughts, or no pay. Lucky charms free. Her equal is not to be found. Her magic image is now in full force, 184, Ludlow Street, below Houston. Price 25 cents. Gentlemen not admitted."

The matrimonial column, on the other hand, was fuller than usual, and contained half a dozen offers of marriage, of which, for the sake of gallantry, I will only quote two from ladies.

"A young widow lady, with means to support herself, wishes to make the acquaintance of a gentleman with a view to matrimony. None but persons of intelligence and refinement need address Mrs. E. Harland, Station A, Spring Street."

The next lady is suspiciously silent as to means, but more positive as to age. She says that "a young lady not over twenty-five years of age would like to open a correspondence with some gentleman possessed of an affectionate disposition, and a fair share of the world's goods, with a view to matrimony. One who can appreciate a woman's good feelings may address Jennie Edwards, Station G, Broadway."

Moreover, the *Herald* has, or rather used to have when I first came to the States, a column headed "personals," of a most extraordinary character. To judge from a perusal of it, you would suppose that whenever a gay Lothario met a soft-hearted Dulcinea in the streets, it was the etiquette not to address her personally, but to publish an advertisement in next day's papers, expressive of admiration and the desire for further acquaintance. In plain words, assignations, which charity alone bids one suppose were virtuous, were daily made in the columns of the *Herald*. The way in which the "personals" were extinguished is a curious comment on the principles by which the *Herald* is guided. In one day's paper there appeared an advertisement even more flagrant than usual, purporting to be from a lady making an assignation to meet a friend at the reception room of a well-known hotel. The *Tribune* got hold of this, and in a bitter article pointed out how the advertisement, besides its intrinsic immorality, was calculated to injure the character of the hotel, and would therefore expose the publisher of the paper to an action for libel. No reply was made to this attack, and no formal notice was taken of it, but from that day forth the "personals" were discontinued or confined to bona fide inquiries for absent friends. There are two peculiarities about the *Herald* which might be copied with advantage by our English press. The first is that all advertisements are carefully classed under headings, so that you always know where to look for what you want; the second is that after every military movement, plans of the locality in which the movement occurred are published on the front page. They are very roughly, often very inaccurately drawn, but still they are sufficient to make the accounts of the movements intelligible to the reader.

With all its faults, the *Herald* is the most readable of the New York papers. The *New York Times* is, in a literary point of view, a feebler edition of the *Herald*, without its verve. It is the organ of the moderate Republican party, of whom Mr. Seward and Mr. Thurlow Weed are the leaders in the State of New York; and as this party has never yet been able to look the slavery question boldly in the face, their organ shares in their indecision, and their consequent want of vigor. It is supposed to be more or less favorable to England, and so, perhaps, it is, relative to the other papers, but, actually, I should say that the less predominated over the more. It labors, too, under the general stigma of jobbery, which hangs over the whole Seward-Weed Republican party in the state politics of New York.

The *Tribune* carries more weight by its individual opinion than any paper in the city. Whatever Mr. Greeley's faults may be, he has the reputation of personal honesty. It is better printed, more thoughtfully written, and more carefully got up than any of its contemporaries. Moreover, the simple fact that it both knows and dares to speak out its own mind on the slavery question gives its writings the force which attends strong conviction. But there is a doctrinaire tone about its articles which makes them heavy reading, and when it takes to invective, as it does frequently, it is scurrilous without being pointed.

So much for the only three American newspapers whose names

are at all known in England. As you change your district you
change your paper; and, in every district, you will find some one
or more leading papers which are in their own district what the
Herald is in the district of New York. The *Boston Post,* the
Philadelphia Enquirer, the *Cincinnati Gazette,* the *Louisville
Journal,* and the *Chicago Tribune,* have each the leading circulation in the states of Massachusetts, Pennsylvania, Ohio, Kentucky, and Illinois respectively.

In truth, the most remarkable feature about the American
press is its quantity rather than its quality. The American might
be defined as a newspaper-reading animal. I have never been into
any American town where there was not more than one daily
paper. Even in the quietest of towns, boys run about the streets
hawking newspapers. In every railway train there is a lad who
passes through the cars constantly with newspapers to sell; and
in every hotel a newspaper stand is as acknowledged a part of the
establishment as the bar. In its broad characteristics, the American newspaper, like almost every other American institution, is
fashioned on the English, not on the Continental model. It resembles our newspapers in the unwieldy size of the sheets, in the
immense quantity of news given, in the great space occupied by
advertisements, and in the fact that the leading articles are practical comments, not abstract essays. Here, however, the resemblance between the American and the London press ceases. An
American paper is a sort of cross between a county newspaper
and a penny journal. Reading is so universal an acquirement here
that a far larger, and also a far lower, class reads the newspapers
than is the case with us; and, therefore, the degree of education
found in the newspaper-reading public is probably lower than in
Great Britain. Thus (I am not speaking now of a few class journals, but of the ordinary newspaper,) you never meet, in an
American paper, with literary or scientific reviews of any research, or with any article which evinces much reading on the
part of the writer, or presupposes much on the part of the reader.
On the rare occasions when a French quotation is made, it is
generally printed wrong, and always accompanied by a translation. You seldom, if ever, come upon an article which might not

have been written right off without any reference to books or authorities. It is obvious, too, that the public of even the best American papers has not passed beyond that stage of intellectual development in which the mind takes pleasure in a column of varieties. The editor of the *Louisville Journal*, Mr. George D. Prentice, is supposed to have a special talent for manufacturing facetiæ, and as the Prenticeiana are quoted throughout the Union papers, I shall give the reader a fair impression of what American varieties consist of by quoting half a dozen of his facetiæ, which lie in the paper next at hand to me while I write. I pick out the ones about the war, as having something of more permanent interest:

"A man was arrested in London lately for stealing a picture from a dealer. When caught going out of the door, with the article under his arm, he said he was an admirer of the fine arts, and only wanted to take the picture home to examine it more closely. When Floyd is caught, the ingenious rascal will have some similar plea in abatement of his debts."

"The Atlanta (Ga) Confederacy quotes the confession of a surgeon in the Confederate army, that they 'are whipped on all sides,' and 'hell is to pay.' Walk down to the counter then, and pay your indebtedness."

"The *Charleston Mercury* thinks that the Cotton States have a right to cry aloud when all their slave property is at stake. No doubt it is a case of great cry and a good deal of wool."

"A correspondent says that Beauregard made a very good moral address to his army the other day. Probably, he thought his troops so demoralised, that they needed a little moralising."

"Beauregard certainly surprised us at Shiloh, on the first day of the fight; but we surprised him a good deal more on the second."

"We guess the *New Orleans Picayune* (penny) feels now as if it were hardly worth its name,"

And so on. But if the reader is not tired of reading Prenticeiana, I am of copying them.

An immense proportion of the American papers are sold by the street newsvendors. It is on this chance circulation that the newspapers mainly depend; and out of a given number of copies sold, a very small percentage indeed is sold to regular subscribers. The inevitable consequence of this condition of things is to encourage the sensation system of newspaper headings and paragraphs, which offends our taste so constantly. There is a carelessness about the writing which to me is indefensible. Apparently, leaders are written without the proofs being revised. Constantly one stumbles on sentences which do not construe; while clerical errors are allowed to pass, for not correcting which, the reader of any respectable English newspaper would be dismissed on the spot. Then, again, all the news is broken up into short paragraphs, with appropriate headings in large capitals, in a way which, though convenient to readers in a hurry, is almost fatal to good writing. Both paper and type, too, are usually very inferior to our own.

There are two popular impressions prevailing in England as to the American press, both of which I think erroneous. The first is that it is a very cheap press; the second, that it is a very scurrilous one. To subscribers it is undoubtedly cheap; and you can, or rather could, get any daily paper in the United States by subscription for somewhat under a penny a day, excluding delivery. But it is not so with casual purchasers. In New York alone can you buy the *Herald*, for instance, in the streets for two cents. In Washington its price was five cents; and in the West, you are charged ten cents. The price of a single copy of any local paper is always five cents, except in the very large towns, where it sinks to four or three cents. Thus as the vast majority of readers buy their papers from day to day, the price they pay varies from twopence to threepence, and upward. In fact, if you take into account the quantity of matter you get in an English paper, the English high-priced press is in reality a cheaper one than the American, and the penny press is immeasurably so. In all probability, the new taxes to be imposed on newspapers will raise their prices still higher—even if the hopes of the *Herald* are not realized, and the whole cheap press crushed for good.

Perhaps my next assertion may appear even stranger, and that is that one great merit of the American press is its comparative freedom from private personality. The virulent and discreditable invectives with which Bennett and Greeley besmear each other and themselves in the *Herald* and *Tribune* are not fair illustrations of American journalism. It is of the essence and nature of one local paper to attack another, but in all the American papers I have met with, I have never seen personal attacks from one editor to another equal either in virulence or bad taste to what I have seen in English country papers. It is true, that public characters of any kind are attacked politically with a vehemence we can hardly appreciate; but this is due to the nature of political life in America, of which I shall speak elsewhere. The American papers have not learnt yet the difference between declamation and strong writing, and, therefore, their attacks on political enemies are perfectly astonishing to us for the violence of their invective. But, still, if you examine closely, you will see, that even in declamations against public men, allusions to their private relations are but rare. On the other hand, attacks on individuals in private life are almost unknown. It is a curious fact, which I never saw noticed in any account of America, that the accounts of law cases and police reports which appear in all the American papers are infinitely more curt and meager even than those in French journals. The names of the parties to a suit, and the result of the trial, are given, but, except in cases of great public interest, rarely anything more. In England, if you are unfortunate enough to get involved in any case, either as principal or witness, which involves any disgusting details, or any ridiculous episodes, your name is hawked about the country, and you are stamped forever with having been connected with some queer trial or scandal. If you object to the hardship of an innocent man being subjected to a moral pillory, you are told that the freedom of the press demands the sacrifice. Now here, in a perfectly free country, with a free press, there is nothing of the kind. Public opinion is opposed to raking up the private affairs of individuals for the amusement of newspaper readers; and the newspapers do not publish the gossip of the police courts, simply because the public does not wish for it.

I have spoken freely about the faults of the American press;

but still, in Yankee phrase, it is a great institution. The individual developments do not rise to so high a standard as our own, but the average development is higher. In every town and village where you travel you find a press which gives news copiously, and, on the whole, fairly; which treats of practical questions with shrewd good sense and fair writing; and which discusses national topics as much, or more, than local ones. When you consider that this press is read by the whole neighborhood, and is the organ of the class which, in England, would consist of agricultural laborers and overworked mechanics, you realize more than in any other way the general education of the American people. It is something, too, that this people's press should be perfectly unobjectionable in a moral sense, and should be free from petty personalities; that, in fact, if it cannot soar, it also does not grovel.

Of course, if I chose, I could pick out hosts of eccentricities, and what we should call absurdities, in American journalism. But, after all, whether you spell traveler with two "l's" or one, whether you call a leader an editorial, and whether you talk of "posting up a bill" instead of settling an account, are all questions of taste, about which there is no use disputing. The larger and, I hold, the truer view is, to look upon the American press as a vast engine of national education, not overdelicate in its machinery, but still working out its object. As such, it is, indeed, the press of a great and a free people.

New York to Washington

IT WAS always a trouble to me in America, choosing where I should go next. It was not the embarrassment of riches but rather the opposite. One place was so marvelously like the other, that it was hard to decide why you should go to one place in preference to another. I always have had the keenest sympathy for the ass in the fable who was unable to make up his mind between the two bundles of hay that hung on either side of him. Hay is excellent food and well deserves eating; but when bundle of hay number one is the exact counterpart of bundle number two, how is an irresolute ass to decide which best deserves munching? This was my own state of mind, I confess frankly, with regard to my route in America. The country is well worth seeing—how well worth seeing I never knew till I had traveled over it; but still, one American town is just as well worth seeing as its neighbor, and not more. Columbus (Ohio) is extremely like Springfield (Indiana), and both are the very counterparts of Lafayetteville (Missouri). All are worth visiting, but why should you give the preference to Springfield over Columbus, or to Lafayetteville over both? This is a dilemma which I could never get out of, and whose solution perplexed me from the day I entered the States to the day I left them.

The first time the problem presented itself to me in all its difficulty was on leaving New York. I had intended to go from thence to Boston; but the question was propounded to me, whether it was not better to go to Washington first instead. If the solution had been left to my unassisted powers of decision, I should probably be residing at this present moment in the

Everett House, New York, making up my mind where to go next. Happily, I had two motives which decided the course of my journey. In the first place, it was cold—bitterly cold—in New York. Most European travelers visit America in the summer, and therefore their books convey no impression of the cold which prevails in winter. The winter of 1862 was an unusually mild one —so, at least, I was told by everybody; and New York, from its vicinity to the sea, is a comparatively warm city. All I can say is that, till I came to New York in the January of 1862, I never knew what cold was. The houses were beautifully warmed; but the contrast between the heat indoors and the frost out-of-doors only made the cold more painful. As to sleighing it is a mere mockery of pleasure. If you want to experience it, as an American writer said, you have only to stand for an hour in a draft, with your feet in freezing water, and your numbed fingers tinkling a string of bells. At any rate, it requires a warmer-blooded being than myself to enjoy the pleasures of an American winter. New York was too cold for me already, and I dreaded the notion of a place like Boston, where New York was counted warm by comparison.

Moreover, the advance of the Grand Army of the Potomac was expected daily. It did not take place till weeks after I arrived in Washington; but, at that period, I had been too short a time in America to make allowance for the difference between promise and performance; and when I read, day after day, that the army was on the move, I was seized with a fear that I should be too late to catch a glimpse of the war.

So, from all these causes, I traveled southward instead of northward. It is not my intention, as I have said before, to write a diary of my journeys. And of this journey in particular I have little to say, except of one adventure that befell me, illustrative in many ways of American habits. I started by the mail train for Philadelphia, where I arrived at two o'clock or thereabouts on a cold winter morning. With an Englishman's dislike for parting with my luggage, I had kept my baggage checks with me instead of consigning them to the care of the freight agent who collects them en route. Whether I was sleepy—whether I had not made up my mind which hotel I should go to—or why, I forget; but so it was. My impression is, that knowing nothing of the town, I had resolved to go to the hotel which sent up the best omnibus to the station. When I arrived, there was no omnibus, no private carriage of any kind, nothing but the street railroad car, waiting to convey passengers across Philadelphia to the Washington railroad. It is not the custom for passengers to look after their own luggage on American railroads, and it was with the greatest difficulty I got my trunks together in time to get a seat on the step of the car. I asked the conductor to recommend an inn, but found that the car did not pass any hotel on its route. The man was civil, as all American conductors are, but he could do nothing for me as he had to keep with the car; so he set me down at the corner of a street, and told me that if I followed it for four blocks, I should find a hotel. I don't know that I ever felt a more helpless individual than on that winter morning, at two o'clock, in the streets of Philadelphia. I had a most indistinct notion of which way I was to go. Whether four blocks meant four, or four hundred, or four thousand yards, I was unable to guess. There was not a soul about the streets, and I had a huge port-manteau, two large carpet-bags, a bundle of heavy wraps, and an umbrella, to transport with me. I sat upon my trunk for some time looking at my bags in the hopes that somebody might appear, but in vain. There was no hope, and so I roused myself to exertion. Necessity is the mother of invention. I carried my trunk ten yards, then left it and returned for the bags, then for the wraps and umbrella as a light easy task, and so on ad infinitum. My rate of locomotion was extremely slow; and all along I was haunted by an equal fear of meeting a thief or a policeman. The former might have robbed me with the most perfect security; the latter would have arrested me for a thief who had stolen the luggage I was dragging about. However, in the main street of Philadelphia at 2:00 A.M., I met neither thief nor policeman, nor living soul; and after an hour's labor I reached a hotel, considerably the wiser in the art of American travel by the night's experience.

But while I am speaking of traveling in the States, let me say, once for all, what I have to say of railway traveling in America. Some lines are better than others. As a rule, the Western lines are inferior to the Eastern ones; and the Southern to either. Still, in their broad features, they are very much alike. The through fares are cheap. Thus, you can go from New York to Chicago, a distance of upward of one thousand miles, for four pounds; but the way-fares are three-halfpence a mile. The arrangements about luggage are exceedingly good. As soon as you arrive at the station, you show your ticket to the luggage-master; he takes off a string he holds in his hand a number of leather straps, attached to brass plates about the size of a crown piece, on which the name of your destination and a number is inscribed. These straps he passes through the handles or cordings of your luggage, fastens them by passing the strap again through a slit in the plate, and hands you plates, which are the counterparts of the ones attached to your luggage. You keep these counterparts, and, in exchange for them when produced, receive your luggage at the end of your journey. For all main stations, however, you will find it more convenient to give them up to the luggage agent, who comes round to collect them. After that, you have no more trouble in the matter, but are sure to find it at any hotel you mention, almost as soon as you can get there yourself. But, of course, this entails an extra charge of a shilling or so a package. Practically, a foreigner gains nothing by trying to look after his luggage himself; and Americans are wonderfully careless about small expenses, so that they care little for the additional charge.

These arrangements are common to all American lines; and so, too, day after day, the company you meet with in the cars, and the incidents of your journey, are much the same. You take your seat in a long, open car, about the length of two English railroad carriages fastened together, and with all their compartments knocked down. The seats are comfortable enough, with leather or horsehair cushions, and backs of a like texture. It is wearisome, however, especially at night, to have no back high enough to lean your head upon; but, what is a real luxury in a long journey, you can move from one carriage to another at any time, and can walk up and down in the broad passage between the seats. As to the sleeping cars, I can express no opinion. I have traveled in them when the night was cool and the passengers were few, and have found them most comfortable. I have traveled, also, when the passengers were many and the night hot, and have been glad to sacrifice my money and escape from them as I would from Pandemonium. If you are not particular as to fresh air, you will find them comfortable enough. If, like myself, you would sacrifice anything to pure air, you had better save your money and pass the night in the ordinary cars, even at the risk of spraining your neck if you do happen to fall asleep.

The daytime goes by not unpleasantly. Every half-hour or so a boy passes through the car with a can of iced water, out of which you can have a drink for nothing, if you don't mind drinking out of the public glass. At other times he brings apples, oranges, and sweets for sale, together with bundles of the latest papers and magazines. It is an odd trait, by the way, of the national character, that if the sale of the newsboy's wares is flat, he will come and lay down a copy of his magazines or illustrated papers alongside of every passenger in the car, and leave it with him for half an hour or more. You may read it meanwhile, and if you return it to the boy on his coming round again he will thank you all the same. Most of the passengers, of course, return their copies, but, every now and then, someone, who had no intention of purchasing beforehand, becomes interested in a story he has taken up, and buys the book or paper. There is nothing, absolutely nothing, to hinder anyone from appropriating the work without paying for it. But in this, as in other matters, it is the custom to repose great confidence on the average honesty of the public, and that confidence is rarely found to have been misplaced. Indeed, all the arrangements for taking tickets, letting passengers in and out, and for loading and unloading luggage, are more simple and perfect than those in use on any of our European railroads, all of them being based very much on the assumption that, as a rule, the passengers don't find it worthwhile to cheat the conductors, and the conductors don't find it worthwhile to cheat the company.

At the intermediate stations you only stop for a few seconds.

The system of breaks is so excellent—one break being applied to every wheel—that the train is stopped without difficulty; and the instant, almost, the train has stopped, you hear the standard cry of "All on board!" and then again the train is in motion. Three times a day at some roadside station you are summoned by sound of gong to a meal, which is called breakfast, dinner, or supper, according to the hour, but which is the same everywhere and at all times. You eat plentifully of beefsteaks, broiled ham, poached eggs, pastry without end, and cakes; drink milk, or tea, or water —never beer or any spirituous liquors; are waited on by neat, clean-looking girls; liquor afterward at the bars, if you are so inclined; pay two shillings invariably for your repast, liquor not included; and then take your seat again, and sleep, or read, or talk, till the next feeding time arrives. So the day passes on.

Every traveler in every foreign country must have remarked how very like, at first, everybody you met was to everybody else. In America, I think, this feeling wears off less rapidly than in other lands. Especially in the Western States, the uniformity in the dress and appearance of your fellow passengers is wonderfully striking—nobody is shabbily dressed, very few are handsomely dressed, and everybody is dressed respectably. If you took a railway excursion train in England, filled it almost wholly with second-class passengers, suppressed the first and the third class, increased largely the proportion of commercial travelers, and of that class we hear so much of, and see so little of, at home—the "intelligent mechanic," eliminated utterly everybody who looked poor, according to our English ideas of poverty, and added an unusual number of lovely young girls and faded, middle-aged women, you would form an average car's company in America. I don't mean to say—far from it—that you never meet people in the trains who might ride without comment in our English first and third classes; but there are two classes of people whom you never meet, or think of meeting, at home, except in a first or third class carriage, respectively. To these classes there is nothing corresponding in the living freight of an American car. I do not know that a railway journey in America is a very lively operation; there is not much conversation, the carriages are too noisy, and there is too little privacy for confidential communications. More-over, the Americans are not, to my mind, a communicative peo-ple in traveling. Throughout the whole of my travels in the States, I never recollect making an acquaintance with a fellow passenger of the kind I have made hundreds of in Europe; and on the only occasions on which I can recall a passenger having commenced a conversation with me without my speaking first, I discovered that my interlocutors were settlers from the Old World. Everybody, however, in the railway cars, almost without exception, is quiet, well-behaved, and civil; and there is little or nothing of that offensive selfishness so often exhibited amongst English travelers in the attempt to make oneself comfortable at the expense of everybody else's discomfort. The universal polite-ness, too, shown to women is very remarkable. If a woman enters the car, and the car is full, some gentleman or other is sure to get up and make room for her. It is no matter whether she is young or old, pretty or ugly, richly or poorly dressed, she is a woman, and that suffices. If I were asked whether I consider rail-way traveling in America as comfortable as in Europe, my answer would be that that depends on circumstances. An American car is not equal to an English first-class carriage in luxury, or cleanli-ness, or society. On the other hand, it is comfortable as compared with our second-classes, and luxurious as compared with our third. Indeed, I should say about American railways as I should about most American institutions: If you are able to drive about in hansom cabs, to travel always in first-class express trains, and to give a shilling to the porter at the station, then, as far as com-fort of locomotion goes, you had better stop at home. If, on the contrary, you belong to the great public, to whom sixpences and shillings are an object, who rarely travel first-class except in an excursion train, and who have been known, under the rose, to go third-class in parliamentary trains, then you are better off, far better off, in American traveling than you are in English. The million, in fact, fares better in the New World than it does in the Old.

Of the country through which my route lay, I say little. In the first place, I traveled through most of it at night; in the second,

I shall say what I have to say of American scenery when I come to my journeyings in the West, where the characteristics peculiar to American scenery are infinitely more marked than in the East. The whole country, indeed, of Pennsylvania reminded me more than anything of England run to seed. The fields were more sprawling, the houses were more loosely built, the roads were rougher, and the towns were more straggling; but otherwise the resemblance was very close. If you can conceive our midland counties flattened out, magnified indefinitely, and diffused loosely over an area of tenfold their own, you will picture Pennsylvania to yourself.

It was upon the banks of the Susquehanna river that I came first upon the track of the war. Between Pennsylvania and Maryland, between the free North and the slave South, the great deep river, wider than the Rhine at Dusseldorf, rolls as a frontier line. The top-heavy looking steam-ferry, which, in defiance of all one's preconceived ideas of the laws of equilibrium, carries train, cars, rails, passengers, luggage and all, with scarcely a break of continuity, from one bank to another, transports one not only into a new state, but into a new country. The whole aspect of the scenery changes: the broad, thriving, cheerful expanse of carefully tilled fields, dotted over with the villa-like farm houses, gives place to long, straggling, red brick towns, half villages, half cities; to broken-down fences; to half-ploughed, hopeless-looking fields, where the Negro laborers are toiling listlessly; to dreary tracks of mud, which stand where roads ought to be; and to wide stony spaces of meager brushwood. The restless activity I witnessed everywhere north of the Susquehanna was exchanged for a sort of fussy idleness. By the house doors, and in the streets through which the train passed slowly, there stood men hanging about idly, loitering languidly, with their hands deep-buried in their trouser-pockets, watching tumble-down carts struggling spasmodically across the deep-rutted roads, and loafing visibly.

In this dull wintertime, too, Maryland looked all the drearier for the traces of the war, visible on every side. I passed along the same line again in the first burst of the early summer, when the war had moved on far away southward; and, except for the look of poverty and decay, which even the rich summer foliage could not hide, I should scarce have recognized it for the same country. Hitherto I had hardly been able to realize, from the outward look of things, that the Union was in the midst of a civil war; but here in Maryland the evidence was only too palpable. At Havre de Grace, the river station on the southern side of the Susquehanna, we passed the first camp, and the dingy grayish blue-coated Federal soldiers came running alongside the train to ask for stray papers from New York. Then, at each station as we passed further south, the train became fuller and fuller with soldiers, and the small roadside camps grew more and more frequent. In Baltimore the streets swarmed with troops, and south of this again, on to Washington, we seemed to pass through a conquered country. In the gray glimmer of the evening we could see the white tents of the camps pitched on the hill-slopes that over-hang Baltimore. Every roadside station was occupied with troops; at every bridge and crossing there were small outposts stationed; and along the line at short distances there were sentinels at watch to protect the rails. The nearest forces of the enemy lay some fifty miles away across the Potomac, and with the vast Federal army before Washington, it could not be against the Confederates that these precautions were taken. It is true that the maintenance of this single track of rails, the one means of communication between New York and Washington, was of vital importance, and, therefore, no precaution was too great to take, if necessary. On the other hand, the maintenance of the same line north of the Susquehanna was of equal importance, and yet there it was left unguarded. The inference is a very obvious one—Pennsylvania is a Free State, and loyal; Maryland is a Slave State, and therefore disloyal.

It was thus, as I entered Washington, that the bearing of the slave question upon the war was practically brought home to me. Before, then, I speak of Washington, it is time to say something of that great issue.

The Free Negro

IT IS strange to me, looking back on my sojourn in the States, to think that I could have written thus far without coming on the question of the everlasting Negro. It was the fashion amongst English critics, at the time I left England, to state that the whole Secession question had no direct bearing on, no immediate connection with, the issue of slavery. As to the letter, there was some small truth in this assertion; as to the spirit, there was none. Many of my readers, probably, have visited at some time or other a friend laboring under a mortal disease. Neither he nor you, perhaps, spoke of it; every allusion to illness of any kind was studiously avoided; you talked, and laughed, and gossiped, as though the idea of death had never crossed your minds; and yet both you and he felt all along that this idea was ever present—that it was the key to every word you uttered, the burden of every spoken phrase and unspoken thought. When the cholera was raging in Venezuela, the panic-stricken half-breed Governor had a notice placed in every room of his palace—"No one is to mention here the name of cholera;" but I suppose the Venezuelans thought and talked of little else notwithstanding. So, after a like fashion, this Negro question was the one thought which pervaded everything throughout the whole of the Secession period. Officially, no doubt, the connection between slavery and Secession was sometimes denied—more often kept studiously out of sight; but, in society of all kinds, in the press of every shade and color, from the pulpit of every sect and denomination, you heard of nothing but Secession and slavery. You might as soon have ignored the existence of Secession as ignored the existence of the

43

slavery question. I am not writing now a work on slavery—I had not the opportunity for doing so had I wished it: I am seeking rather to convey the impressions left upon me by my sojourn in the North during the Southern insurrection. If I succeed in conveying those impressions faithfully, the question of slavery must crop up in these pages at all times and all places, in season and out of season.

Before entering, therefore, on this question, it will be well to say a few words on my own feelings with regard to the "peculiar institution." Morally, I do not look on slavery, nor even on the slave trade, as being a sin apart or different from all other sins. Whether you work men to death in a tailor's slop-shop; whether you burn Arabs alive in Algeria; whether you degrade men to the level of beasts, as the Bourbons did in Naples; whether you shoot Hindoos from the cannon's mouth, in order to add the prospect of everlasting damnation to the pangs of death, as we did in India; whether you drill human beings into soldier-slaves, like that modern hero-god of Mr. Carlyle's worship; or whether you kidnap Negroes, sell them by auction, deny them the rights of men, and scourge them with the lash, like the planters of the South, you are, in my judgment, sinning about equally against the moral law of God. Slavery, however, has one peculiar guilt, which few, if any other, of the hundred modes of human cruelty and oppression can be justly charged with. It is a gigantic, almost an isolated, attempt to reduce oppression to a system, and to establish a social order of which the misery of human beings is to be the fundamental principle. It is for this reason that every honest man who hates cruelty and loves justice is bound to lift up his voice against slavery as an accursed thing. It is thus that I think of it, let me say once and for all; and thus, as far as lies within my power, that I mean to write of it.

Let me add also, as I am now, in American parlance, "entering my record," that it is a conviction that the existence or the downfall of slavery was inevitably connected with the success or failure of Secession, which created my deep sympathy with the Federal cause. I admit freely, as I shall endeavor to show ere long, that besides slavery there were many great issues depending on the struggle between North and South. I believe that, putting slavery out of the question, the cause for which the North was fighting was the cause of freedom, of national existence, and of the world's progress. Still, I hold strongly to the American confession of faith, "that a people possesses an inalienable right to choose its own form of government;" and therefore, madly mistaken as I believe the South to have been in separating from the Union, I should yet have hesitated, had it not been for the issue of slavery, as to whether the North was justified in attempting to reconquer the seceding States. If Earl Russell had modified his famous dictum by saying that the North was fighting for empire (and freedom), while the South was fighting for independence (and slavery), he would have uttered a whole truth instead of a sorry half one. Such, at any rate, is my belief; and, having confessed it, I trust the reader will understand better much that I have to say.

Having this keen interest in the whole question of slavery, the position of the Negro in the Free States was a subject which I was anxious to investigate. To an Englishman, it is a new sensation, almost the only new sensation in America, to enter for the first time a hotel where one is surrounded by Negro servants. I recollect well the first evening that I dined in the New World. It was at the Everett House in New York, one of the best hotels in the States. I was seated waiting for my soup, in that calm state of enjoyment which every well-organized human being must feel after a long sea voyage in sitting at a table which does not rock, when the folding doors leading from the kitchen to the dining hall were flung open, and a troop of Negro waiters marched in together, two abreast, paced up the rooms in step, bearing the soup tureens aloft, solemnly parted to the right and left, deposited their burdens, and then took each his appointed station, in order to lift up the lids of the tureens at one and the same moment on a given signal. This was my first experience of Negrodom. Trivial as the incident may seem, there was in it a love of stage effect, a sort of dramatic talent, which belonged to a far different race than that Anglo-Saxon one of ours. So, throughout my stay in America, I could never look upon a Negro face with-

out a strange attraction. The colored people form so marked a
contrast to everything and everybody you see around you. Living,
as one does, in a bustling, toiling, sallow, washed-out world of
men and women, it is pleasing to the mental as well as to the
physical eyesight to turn to the Negro folk, with their unwonted
complexion, varying from the darkest ebony to the faintest tinge
of saffron, with their strange passion for gaudy colors, assorted
somehow with a touch of artistic feeling, with their deep, wistful, melancholy eyes, and, above all, with their indescribable air
of physical enjoyment in the actual fact of life. If I were an
American painter, I would paint nothing but the peculiar people.
No doubt this feeling wears away. If Gypsies were an institution
in England as Negroes are in America, if we had a Gypsy camp
squatted down in every village, we should, as a nation, see very
little romantic or picturesque in the Romany race. Negroes, like
Gypsies, are all very well as isolated figures in the social land-
scape, but they are out of place as a perpetual background.
Still, with all this, I have often wondered at how very little the
Americans I met with seemed to know about the Negroes who
lived amongst them. I tried frequently to obtain information
from persons interested in the Negro question, as to the prospects and position of the free Negroes, but without much success.
The truth is, the Negroes, slave or free, are a race apart, in both
North and South. A black Ruth might say to a white Naomi,
"Thy God shall be my God;" but the promise that "Thy people
shall be my people" would be uttered in vain.

Everywhere and at all seasons the colored people form a separate community. In the public streets you hardly ever see a colored person in company with a white, except in the capacity of
servant. Boston, indeed, is the only town I visited where I ever
observed black men and women walking about frequently with
white people. I never by any chance, in the Free States, saw a
colored man dining at a public table, or mixing socially in any
manner with white men, or dressed as a man well-to-do in the
world, or occupying any position, however humble, in which he
was placed in authority over white persons. On board the river
steamboats, the commonest and homeliest of working men has a

right to dine, and does dine, at the public meals; but, for colored passengers, there is always a separate table. At the great hotels there is, as with us, a servants' table, but the colored servants are not allowed to dine in common with the white. At the inns, in the barbers' shops, on board the steamers, and in most hotels, the servants are more often than not colored people. Anybody, I think, who has traveled in America, will agree with me in saying that they are the pleasantest servants in the country, and that he would always go by preference to a house where the attendants were Negroes. But where there are black servants, you hardly ever find white ones also, except as overseers. White servants will not associate with black on terms of equality. I recollect a German servant-girl telling me that she had left a very good situation in New England, because she had been desired to take her meals with a colored servant, and she "felt that that was wrong." I hardly ever remember seeing a black employed as shopman, or placed in any post of responsibility. As a rule, the blacks you meet in the Free States are shabbily, if not squalidly dressed; and, as far as I could learn, the instances of black men having made money by trade in the North are very few in number.

I remember one day in traveling through the State of Ohio (Ohio, let me add for the benefit of English critics, is a Free State), that I was seated by one of the shrewdest and kindliest old farmers it has been my lot to meet. He had been born and bred in Ohio state, and expanded to me as a stranger, with not unnatural pride, on the beauty and prosperity of that rich garden country: "There is but one thing, sir," he ended by saying, "that we want here, and that is to get rid of the niggers." I was rather surprised at this illiberal expression of opinion; for my friend, though a staunch Union man, had been talking with unwonted good sense and moderation about the folly of adopting extreme measures of vengeance toward the South; and I questioned him about the reasons for his antipathy toward the colored people. I was answered by the old story. The free blacks did not work, and preferred doing nothing. Half the thefts and crimes in the state were committed by free Negroes. Not content with having schools of their own, they wanted to have their children admitted to the free white schools; and, for his own part, he shrewdly suspected that the schoolhouse of his town, Lebanon, which had just been mysteriously burnt down, had been set on fire by free Negroes out of spite. But the great grievance seemed to his mind to be that, in defiance of the laws of Ohio, there had been recently some few intermarriages between white men and black women. "It don't answer, sir," he concluded by saying, "it isn't right, you see, and it isn't meant to be."

These sentiments express, undoubtedly, the popular feeling of the Free States toward the free Negro. Like most popular feelings, it has a basis of truth. In every Northern city, the poorest, the most thriftless, and perhaps the most troublesome part of the population, are the free Negroes. Give a dog a bad name, and he will not only get hung, but he will generally deserve hanging. The free Negro has not a fair chance throughout the North. The legislation of the country is as unfavorable to the status of free blacks as the social sentiment of the people. It is a much-disputed point, what were the ideas of the authors of the American Constitution with regard to the Negro. The most probable solution seems to me to be that though, undoubtedly, they contemplated the possibility of the Negroes becoming freemen, they never admitted the idea of their becoming citizens of the United States. There is no distinct statement in the Constitution as to what constitutes American citizenship; but you see clearly that the Indians, though born under the American Government, were never designed to become citizens, and, in like manner, the strong presumption is that the Negroes were not either. Certainly, as a matter of fact, a free Negro citizen does not enjoy the full rights of citizenship. No colored man can hold any Government appointment, however humble, under the United States. During the last session, a bill of Mr. Sumner's was passed through the Senate, allowing the Government to employ colored men as mail-carriers; but even in a Republican House of Representatives, the bill was rejected by a large majority. About state legislation, with regard to the free Negro, there is no ambiguity whatever. In three states alone, Massachusetts, Maine, and New Hampshire, are colored men allowed to vote on an equality with white citizens. In New York, where there is manhood suffrage as far as white men are concerned, a man of color must possess a freehold estate of not less value than £50, clear of all debt, before he can exercise the right of voting. In no other state can a colored citizen vote at all; and under no state government are black men practically allowed to hold office of any kind. The free schools of every state are closed to colored children; and in the district of Washington, under the direct authority of the national government, free blacks were taxed till the other day to support the free schools for white children. In the Eastern States, intermarriage between blacks and whites is permitted by law, but in few, if any, of the other states. In several of the Western States, free Negroes are forbidden to settle within the limits of the state; while in the Border Slave States of the Union, proposals have been made recently to expel the free Negro population altogether. Under such conditions, it would be strange if the free Negroes were, as a class, an industrious or a respectable part of the Northern population. That a proscribed pariah people, forbidden to mix on terms of equality with the ruling race, should not afford by their conduct some excuse for their treatment, would be an unexampled fact in the world's history.

As far as the North is concerned, the free Negroes form too small a part of the population to be a source of real trouble. According to the census of 1850, in which the free colored population was classified separately from the white, the whole number of free colored persons in the then United States was, in round numbers, 435,000. Of these, only 198,000 were settled in the Free States. New Jersey and Pennsylvania, the great commercial and manufacturing states, had 127,000; Ohio and Indiana, the two frontier states of the North, 37,000. The New England States, the headquarters of the Abolitionists, held about 23,000; while the whole of the Northwestern States only contained 11,000 in all. As the white citizens of the Free States numbered 13,324,914, in 1850, the proportion of free men of color would have been barely one-and-a-half per cent. No doubt, these numbers had increased actually during the ten years up to 1860; but the relative proportion of colored men to white had decreased considerably. From these figures some very obvious conclusions may be drawn. From choice or necessity, a very large majority of the free Negroes remain in the Slave States, after emancipation. In the free North, it is only in the great cities that they can find occupation or a living—for there is no question that New York, Jersey City, and Philadelphia contain some nine-tenths of the colored population in the states to which they respectively belong. New England seems to be unsuited for the Negro race, probably from the length and severity of its winters. Ohio and Indiana owe the large numbers of their black population to the immediate proximity of the Slave States. And practically, either from natural causes or from adverse legislation, the Northwestern States afford no home for the free Negro. Somehow or other, the climate, or the social conditions of the free North, are not favorable to the increase of the colored race. In 1790, in the seven states of New Hampshire, Vermont, Rhode Island, Connecticut, New York, New Jersey, and Pennsylvania, in which at that period slavery existed, there were 40,370 slaves, to say nothing of free men of color, while the white population numbered 1,452,828. In 1850, the free colored population of these states, in which slavery had been gradually abolished, amounted to 139,206, while the white population had reached 6,909,826. Thus, while the whites in sixty years had more than quadrupled their numbers, the men of color have increased little more than threefold.

It is a charge very commonly brought in England against the Free States, that when they abolished slavery, they sold their slaves to the South. It is possible this may have been done in individual instances, but it is obvious that it cannot have been in any sense a state measure, from the fact that the census in every state shows an increase in the number of colored people, in the years immediately succeeding the act of emancipation. The explanation, therefore, for the comparative unproductiveness of the Negro race in the North must be sought in natural causes. Poverty, hardship, and disease have checked successfully the natural fertility of the race. Mr. Seward, in talking over this subject, told me that when he was a child in his father's house, there

were as many black as white people in the household. Circumstances had enabled him to keep a record of all the inmates of
the household whom he had known as a child; and now, after
some fifty years, while the members of the white family were
numbered almost by hundreds, he could count on the fingers of
one hand, the descendants and the living members of the black
people. This testimony was corroborated by all Americans in the
North I had the opportunity of speaking to. The majority of the
slaves in the North were household servants, and were kept as
articles of luxury, not of profit. In truth, north of Mason and
Dixon's line, the Negro is an exotic, and can be kept in existence
only by an artificial system of culture.

It is impossible to obtain any statistics as to the amount of
intermarriages which have taken place in the Free States between
blacks and whites. It is the universal belief amongst Americans
that such intermarriages are rarely fertile, and are invariably
productive of similar consequences to those which attend the repeated intermarriages of near relatives. How far this belief is
based on physiological evidence, or how far the fact, if fact it be,
may not be accounted for by the climate of the North being unfavorable to the development of the mulatto, are questions concerning which I could never satisfy myself. It is certain that if the
mixed race were a productive one in the North, the proportion
of quadroons ought to be much larger by this time than that of
mulattoes; whereas the barest traveler's observation will convince you that such is not the case. For every quadroon you meet,
you see two or three mulattoes. The actual number of mixed
marriages I gather to be very small. Amongst the higher classes,
the relative social position of blacks and whites, quite apart from
the question of color, would be a bar to intermarriage; while
amongst the poor, and amongst persons of the same average rank
of life as the free Negro, the prejudice against color is naturally
even more violent and unreasoning than amongst men of education. The connections, legal or illegitimate, which arise between
the two races, are almost, without exception, between white men
and colored women. Even in the lowest houses of ill-repute in
the Free States, no colored man is allowed to enter. Unfortu-

nately, perhaps, the white male sex is more catholic in its tastes; and of the mixed race, a very large proportion are the illegitimate offspring of white fathers and colored mothers. Of late years, however, such connections are grown less frequent, partly from an advance in public morality, partly from an increased repugnance amongst the white race to any idea of amalgamation with the black.

Now, without wishing for one moment to justify this state of feeling in the Free States, I have my doubts whether we English are, of all people in the world, the best entitled to condemn it. Wherever our Anglo-Saxon race has spread itself, it has shown a uniform intolerance of an inferior race. The treatment of the native Irish by the English settlers, of the Chinese in Australia, of the New Zealanders by the colonists, and of the Hindoos under the Company's rule, are all developments of the same national instinct. That this impatience of an inferior existence is a low *trait* in our national character, I admit freely and fully; but then I am somewhat of a skeptic as to the truth of the Yankee and Kingsley creed, and plead guilty to occasional doubts as to whether our Anglo-Saxon race, in the Old World and in the New, is altogether and in all respects the finest, and grandest, and noblest on the face of God's earth. All I state is that, however inconsistent the facts may seem, a great portion of the Northern people do unite a very genuine dislike for slavery, and a readiness to make great sacrifices for Abolition, with an extreme distaste for any kind of connection or amalgamation with the free Negro. You must take the good in this world with the bad; and I own I must doubt whether, under like circumstances, the masses in England would take a much more humane or liberal view of the Negro question than the masses do in America. The longer I lived in the States, the more I became convinced that America was, to use a mathematical metaphor, the complement of England. The national failings, as well as the national virtues of the New World, are very much those of the mother country, developed on a different and a broader scale.

In these remarks, I have assumed throughout that the Negro belongs virtually to an inferior race to that of the white man.

Many Abolition friends of mine, whose opinions I value highly, consider this assumption erroneous, and repudiate it indignantly as forming some excuse for slavery. The force of this argument was always unintelligible to me. If the Negro was as much below the white man in intellectual development as he is above the Australian savage, this is absolutely no reason why he should be bought and sold like a chattel, forced to labor and then robbed of the fruits of his own labor, scourged like a dog at the caprice of his owner, denied the right of education, or marriage, or liberty, and reduced at the very best to the level of a well-pampered beast of burden. The weaker the Negro is by nature, the less able he is to help himself, the more he needs the enjoyment of law and civil freedom, which form virtually the sole protection in this world of the feeble against the strong. Such at any rate is my belief. Even if this belief is mistaken, there is still no good in refusing to acknowledge facts. No candid observer can, I think, fail in coming to the conclusion, from his own observation and the universal testimony of impartial critics, that the Negro is not intellectually, possibly not morally, as highly developed as yet as the white man. The Uncle Tom school of Abolitionists have injured a great cause by throwing over it a veil of romantic unreality. The evils of slavery are not exposed by an attempt to prove that "the black man is as good as the white man, and better too." The Abolition party would have had far more power if they had accommodated their theory about slavery to the facts, instead of molding facts to suit their theory. No cause in the world, not even so good a one as that of emancipation, is strengthened by a suppression of the truth.

The Slave Trader Gordon

ON THE 21st February, 1862, for the first time in the annals of New York State, and I believe for the first time in the annals of the United States, a slave trader underwent the penalty of death for having been engaged in the slave trade. The case was a remarkable one in itself—remarkable still more as an illustration of the change in public feeling which had passed over the popular Northern mind since the outbreak of Secession. At the period of my first visit to New York, it was the great incident of the day. In the opinion of those best competent to judge, this execution was one of the severest blows yet struck against the whole system of slavery. It is on this account that I have recorded its general outline.

It is now more than forty years ago—if I am not mistaken, in the year 1818—that the prosecution of the African slave trade was declared an act of piracy by the Federal Government, and, as such, punishable by death. Practically, the Government contented itself with this abstract enunciation of principle, and never endeavored to turn theory into practice. It is only just to state that the slave trade had been, of late years, an unimportant item in the commerce of North America. Partly owing to the absence of a home market, partly to the vigilance of the British cruisers, and still more to the obloquy which attended any person supposed to be engaged in the traffic, the trade had been, relatively, but little prosecuted. It is just also to admit that such slave trading as there was, was carried on by Northern and not by Southern men. The North had far greater material facilities than the South for engaging in the traffic. The interests of the slave-breeding states were steadily opposed to any importation of African slaves, and also with the South, it was a point of honor to have nothing whatever to do with the slave trade. It is to the credit of human nature, if not of human consistency, that most individuals or nations addicted habitually to any sin, have some peculiar development of that sin on which they look with exaggerated aversion. Slavery was the sin the South had a mind to: for the slave trade they were not inclined, and damned it accordingly. Be this the right explanation or not, it was by Northern Yankees that the trade was mainly carried on, and New York was the headquarters of the traffic. The whole affair was kept very secret. There were in New York a certain small number of mercantile houses, surmised, rather than suspected, to be engaged in the African slave trade—perhaps a score or so in all; and every year a few vessels sailed from the port to trade with Africa, nominally for produce, but in reality for slaves. The Anti-slavery party, to their credit, kept a keen look out for all vessels engaged in the trade, and resolved that the law against slave trading should not be allowed to fall into disuse for want of protest. Whenever their agents could ascertain that a vessel was about to sail on this errand, they gave information to the State authorities, but always without effect. Under the "rowdy" Government of the Woods and Kennedys—which, till within the last few years, disgraced New York—the police were notoriously venal, and it was worth a slaver's while to bribe liberally. The more respectable authorities of the state all belonged to the extreme Democratic party, and were unwilling to do anything which might offend the pro-slavery interest, or, still more, strengthen the hands of the Abolitionists. More than all too, public opinion was not in favor of vigorous measures. There was a general though unexpressed conviction that the slave trade between Virginia and the South differed only in name, not in substance, from the slave trade between Africa and Cuba; and that the country which recognized the former as a "peculiar institution," could hardly be very severe in suppressing the latter. Indeed, the connivance of the North in the slave system of the South had so demoralized public feeling on the whole subject that the refusal to allow British cruisers to stop vessels engaged in the slave trade whilst sailing under the American flag was regarded as a national triumph. The result of this state of things was that slavers were generally allowed to escape unarrested; and even if they were brought to trial, either the juries refused to convict, or else the punishment inflicted, on the plea of insufficient evidence or of extenuating circumstances, was extremely light.

Impelled by the remonstrances of foreign powers, rather than by any pressure of public feeling at home, the United States Government, toward the end of Mr. Buchanan's Presidency, had begun to employ a little more activity in suppressing the African trade; and in the autumn of 1860 a slaver, loaded with a cargo of nine hundred slaves, and commanded by Captain [Nathan] Gordon, was seized off the coast of Africa by an American man-of-war. The slaves were landed in Monrovia, and the captain of the slaver was sent to New York—the port from which he had sailed—for trial. The case was a very bad one. The Negroes had been packed with more than usual disregard for life, and treated with more than common inhumanity. Of the nine hundred and odd shipped on the "Erie," three hundred died before the vessel reached Liberia. No excuse could be made for the captain personally: he was a New Englander from Maine, of a very respectable Presbyterian family, and a man of education. This was the fourth slave trip in which he had embarked, and in two out of the four he had made enormous profits. At the time of his seizure he hoisted British colors, and subsequently alleged that two Spaniards found on board the "Erie" were the real owners of the ship, on which he was only a passenger. But there was no doubt as to his real guilt. Still, when he was brought to trial in New York, in October, 1860, little idea was entertained that the legal penalty would be inflicted. The State Prosecutor's district attorney, Mr. Roosevelt, actually stated, in his speech for the prosecution, that "if the prisoner was found not guilty—which was highly probable—of piracy, or even if the jury found him guilty, such an outside pressure would be brought to bear upon the President as would compel him to pardon him. In either case, the prisoner would go scot free." There is little doubt that this statement, however extraordinary a one for a prosecutor to make, was substantially correct: and Gordon would have escaped had not his counsel tried to quash the case on a technical objection, that formal notice of the pleadings had not been given by the United States Government to the state authorities. The objection was not admitted as fatal, but the trial was postponed in order that the error might be rectified. Meanwhile, [James] Buchanan was succeeded by Lincoln: the Democratic officials were replaced by Republican ones. The Secession Movement broke out, and popular feeling in the North generally, and in New York especially, became anti-slavery instead of Southern and pro-slavery, as it had been hitherto. This change proved fatal to Gordon. The new district attorney took up the case, and pushed it on vigorously. At first a conviction seemed hopeless since the officer who was in command of the "Erie" when she was sent as a prize ship to New York—on whose evidence the whole case against the prisoner rested—had joined the insurgents in the South. However, for once the prosecution was in earnest. The sailors who had served under Gordon were traced out, and, by their evidence, the fact of his having been the virtual commander of the vessel while engaged in the slave trade was clearly established. There could be no reasonable doubt as to the evidence. The jury brought him in guilty of piracy, and the court sentenced him to death.

Still, little apprehension was felt, either by the condemned culprit or his partisans, that the sentence would be really executed. It was believed that the long delay in the trial, the fact that the law had never yet been put into force, and, above all, the supposed unwillingness of the Government to take any step which would place them in direct opposition to the slaveholding interest, would prove adequate grounds for the remission of the capital sentence. The prisoner was not wanting in powerful friends: the whole influence of the slave trading community was exerted vigorously, though unobtrusively, in his favor. But public sentiment proved too unanimous to get up any popular demonstration in his behalf. Not a New York paper of any weight could be found to advocate his cause; and even the *Herald* only dared to support him by passing the whole matter over in suspicious silence. The prisoner's counsel went to Washington, and employed every argument that could have weight with the Government; but, after a careful consideration of the case, the President refused to interfere with the action of the law, on the ground that the case was clear, and that it was his duty to see the laws executed. I have reason, too, to know that Mr. [William] Seward did his best to support Mr. Lincoln in this determination. Speaking to me about the case shortly afterward, the Secretary of State remarked, emphatically, that the Republican Administration would have merited the condemnation of every honest man if, whatever else it had left undone, it had not put a stop to the slave trade; and in this, as in every other instance, the resolution was acted up to. With a mercy which, at best, was a very doubtful one, a reprieve of a fortnight was granted, in order that the prisoner might prepare for death. During this fortnight the President was exposed to the most influential and painful solicitations from the friends and relatives of the prisoner for a commutation of the punishment; and a last appeal was made to him at a time when he was distracted by grief at the approaching death of his youngest and favorite child. On this occasion, however, Mr. Lincoln, in his own language, had "put his foot down," and exhibited a resolution which it would have been well if he had displayed in other matters.

When this appeal failed, the prisoner's counsel started a technical objection to the execution, on the ground that by the State law of New York, no condemned culprit could be executed till he had been imprisoned for a year after judgment was passed upon him; and that therefore Captain Gordon, though a United States prisoner, tried and sentenced by the Federal law-courts, could not be executed in the State of New York by the State authorities except in accordance with the State laws. The objection was an ingenious one, and two years before would probably have stayed the execution, but at that time the whole doctrine of state rights was out of favor: the judges before whom the application was made decided that if this appeal were correct, it would follow, as a logical consequence, that the sentences of the United

States courts could never be carried out in any state unless they were in accordance with the local legislation of that state—a consequence which manifestly would not be admitted—and that therefore the appeal must be dismissed. After this, as a last attempt, an endeavor was made to summon a mass meeting in New York to protest against the sentence being carried out. The following placard was posted during the night all over the city: "Citizens of New York, come to the rescue! Shall a judicial murder be committed in your midst, and no protesting voice raised against it? Captain Nathaniel Gordon is under sentence of execution for a crime which has been virtually a dead-letter for forty years. Shall this young man be quietly allowed to be made the victim of fanaticism?" The placard ended with a summons to the people to attend a meeting in the afternoon, at the Merchants' Exchange. The police were ordered to remove this document by the civic authorities, as tending to bring the Government into disrepute; but a sufficient number of the placards was left upon the walls, either purposely or through carelessness, to make the fact of the meeting generally known. I was present at the hour appointed, and barely a couple of hundred people were assembled. A good number were obviously idlers like myself. Several whom I knew personally were strong anti-slavery men, who had come to protest against the meeting in case it seemed likely to be influential; and the majority were rowdies, with a lot of very ill-looking Greek and Portuguese merchants. No signature was affixed to the requisition, and no one volunteered to preside at the meeting. After about an hour's delay the assemblage had dwindled down to some hundred persons, and then an unknown stranger got up, without giving his name, and stated that he had never heard of the meeting till a quarter of an hour before, but that he was opposed to staining this glad season—when Washington's birthday and the late Union victories were on the eve of celebration—by a public execution. This appeal elicited no response, and the meeting broke up.

With this fiasco the last hope was gone, and the unhappy prisoner made up his mind that the end was come. Every precaution had been taken to hinder him from committing suicide;

but, by some means or other, he procured cigars loaded with strychnine, and attempted to kill himself by smoking them; the poison, however, did not act rapidly enough, and he was unable to conceal his agony. Remedies were applied, but toward morning his strength began to fail. The execution had been fixed, by his own wish, for two o'clock, but it was feared he would not live till then; and, in obedience to their duty, the authorities of the jail had him executed in the courtyard of the Tombs Prison at noon. Very few persons were present: when I passed the prison an hour afterward, there was no sign of excitement, except the collection of a small crowd of Irish, who were waiting to see the body carried out.

The story is a painful one, and the circumstances of the execution still more so. Horrible as the man's crime was, it is impossible to feel pity for him; yet, the fact that a slave trader was hanged in New York, the headquarters of the American slave trade, and hanged amidst the approbation of the public, was a gain not only to America, but to the world at large.

Washington

It was with an odd sensation of being for the first time in a strange society, of dwelling in a slave-owning city, that I became acquainted with the metropolis of the United States.

To a stranger, Washington must be a quaint residence, even in ordinary days. Had it progressed at the rate of ordinary Northern cities, it would have been by this time one of the finest capitals of the world; as it is, it was built for a city of the future, and the future has not yet been realized. It is still, as it was once called, the city of magnificent distances. On two low hills, a couple of miles apart, stand the white marble palaces of the Houses of Congress and the Government Offices. At their feet stretches the grand Potomac, just too far off to be visible as a feature in the town; and across the low, broken, marshy valley between them runs the long, broad, irregular Pennsylvania Avenue, a secondhand Broadway out at elbows. On either side, hosts of smaller streets branch out for short distances, ending abruptly in brick fields or in the open country; and that is all. If the plan of the city had ever been carried out, the Capitol would have been the center of a vast polygon, with streets branching out from it in every direction. But owing to a characteristic quarrel between the Government and a private landowner, which could never have occurred except in an Anglo-Saxon country, the plan was abandoned; the city sprawled out on one side only of the intended polygon, and left the Capitol stranded, so to speak, at the extremity of the town. So Washington has not the one merit of American architecture—symmetry. The whole place looks run up in a night, like the cardboard cities which Potemkin erected

61

to gratify the eyes of his imperial mistress on her tour through Russia; and it is impossible to remove the impression that, when Congress is over, the whole place is taken down, and packed up again till wanted. Everything has such an unfinished "here for the day only" air about it. Everybody is a bird of passage at Washington. The diplomatic corps is transitory by its very nature. The Senators, Representatives, and ministers, reside there for two, four, possibly six sessions, as the case may be; and it can be predicted that most of those presently in office will not be returned when their terms expire. The clerks, officials, and government employes are all, too, mere lodgers. The force of necessity compels each Administration to reappoint a few of the subordinate clerks who understand the business of the office; but still, every official may be turned out in four years at the longest, and most of them know that they probably will be dismissed at the end of that period. There are no commercial or manufacturing interests to induce merchants or capitalists to settle here. The growth of Baltimore and the filling-up of the Potomac have destroyed what small prospect of commercial greatness Washington may ever have indulged in. There is nothing attractive about the place to make anyone, not brought there by business, fix on it as a place of residence. With the exception of a few landowners who have estates in the neighborhood, a score of lawyers connected with the Supreme Court, and a host of petty tradesmen and lodging-house keepers, there is nobody who looks on Washington as his home.

Hence nobody, with rare exceptions, has a house of his own there. Most of the members of Congress live in hotels or furnished lodgings. The wives and families of the married members (whose names are marked in the Congressional Directory with a row of crosses corresponding to the number of womankind they bring with them) come to Washington for a few months or weeks during the session, and for the time of their stay a furnished house is taken. In consequence, there is no style about the mode of living. The number of private carriages is very few; and people are afraid of bringing good horses to be ruined by the rut tracks (for they are not worthy of the name of roads) which serve the purposes of streets in Washington. Public amusements of any kind are scanty and poor. There is a theater about equal in size and merit to those of Margate or Scarborough in the season; at the Smithsonian Institution (the barbarity of whose designation I am afraid is due to its English benefactor) there are frequent lectures, which, when they are not political demonstrations, are about as interesting, or uninteresting, as lectures on the Glaciers and the Tertiary Formation, and similar stuff, are at home; and there are occasional concerts, dramatic readings, and pictorial exhibitions. But this, with the visit of an occasional circus, is all.

The city, in fact, is an overgrown watering place. The roads appear to have been marked out and then left uncompleted, and the pigs you see grubbing in the main thoroughfares seem in keeping with the place. The broken-down ramshackle hackney-coaches (or hacks, as they are called), with their shabby Negro drivers, are obviously brought out for the day, to last for the day only; the shops are of the stock Margate watering place stamp, where nothing is kept in stock, and where what little there is is all displayed in the shop windows. The private houses, handsome enough in themselves, are apparently stuck up anywhere the owner liked to build them, just as a traveling-van is perched on the first convenient spot that can be found for a night's lodging.

The grand hotels, too, which form a striking, if not an imposing feature in most American towns, are wanting in Washington. Even according to the American standard, there is not a decent hotel in the whole place. Willard's and the National are two huge rambling barracks where some incredible number of beds could be run up; but it is hard to say which is the shabbier and dirtier internally; and externally, neither of them have any pretensions to architectural grandeur. Of the lot, Willard's is the best, on the principle that if you are to eat your peck of dirt, you may as well eat it in as picturesque a form as possible. The aspect of this hotel during the time that the army was encamped before Manassas was indeed a wonderful one. At all times Willard's is the house of call for everybody who has business in Washington. From early morning till late at night its lobbies and passages were filled with a motley throng of all classes and all nations. With the exception of the President, there is not a statesman or general, or man of note of any kind, in Washington, whom I have not come across, at different times, in the passages of Willard's. Soldiers in every uniform, privates and officers thrown together in strange confusion; Congressmen and Senators, army contractors and Jews; artists, newspaper writers, tourists, prize-fighters, and gamblers, were mixed up with a nondescript crowd of men who seem to have no business except to hang about, and to belong to no particular nation, or class, or business. In the parlors, there was a like confusion. Half a dozen rough-looking common soldiers, with their boots encased in deep layers of Virginia mud, would be dozing with their feet hoisted on the high fenders before the fire. At the tables gentlemen, dressed in the moldy black evening suits Americans are so partial to, would sit all day writing letters. Knots of three or four, belonging apparently to every grade of society, would be standing about the room shaking hands constantly with newcomers, introducing everybody to everybody—"more Americano"—and adjourning, at intervals, in a body to the bar. Upstairs, on the floor above, splendidly-dressed ladies were strolling at all hours about the passages, chatting with friends, working, playing, and flirting with smartly bedizened officers and gay young diplomatists.

In fact, barring the presence of the ladies, an ingredient we had little of there, I was constantly reminded of Naples in the Garibaldian days, and, notably, of the Hotel Victoria. There was the same collection of all sorts of men from every country, the same Babel of languages, the same fusion of all ranks and classes, the same ceaseless conversation about the war, the same preponderance of the military element, the same series of baseless contradictory rumors, and the same feverish, restless excitement.

As to the public buildings of Washington, they add little to the splendor of the town. Of the Capitol, I shall speak presently. The Treasury, a sort of white marble Madeleine, would be magnificent if it were finished. The White House is beautiful on a moonlight night, when its snowy walls stand out in contrast to the deep blue sky, but not otherwise. As to the Post Office, Patent Office, Smithsonian Institution, and the unfinished pedestal of the Washington monument, I must refer the curious to any handbook of travel. I am ashamed to say that I never visited either the curiosities of the Patent Office or of the Smithsonian; and I am still more ashamed to add that I do not regret my shortcomings. Stock sight-seeing is an amusement that, from mental defect, I have an invincible aversion to.

Possibly this description does not do full justice to Washington. On a fine bright day, when the wooded banks that line the south side of the Potomac were in their early bloom, I have thought the city looked wondrously bright; but on nine days out of every ten the climate of Washington is simply detestable. When it rains, the streets are sloughs of liquid mud; and, by some miraculous peculiarity I could never get accounted for, even in the paved streets the stones sink into the ground and the mud oozes up between them. In a couple of hours from the time the rain ceases, the same streets are enveloped in clouds of dust. In springtime, the contrast between the burning sun and the freezing winds is greater than I ever knew it in Italy; and in summer, the heat is more dead and oppressive than in any place it has been my lot to dwell in. I had many friends in Washington, and my recollection of the weeks I spent there is a very pleasant one; but, as a place of sojourn, Washington seems to me simply detestable.

I recollect Mr. [Nathaniel] Hawthorne saying, that his impression on leaving Washington was that if Washington were really the keystone of the Union, then the Union was not worth saving; and in this opinion I cordially agreed with him.

Congress

THE ONE fact which redeems Washington from the imputation of being the ugliest capital in the world is the presence of the two grand white marble palaces of the Treasury and the Capitol, frowning at each other like old German castles. Still, in its external shape, as a matter of bricks and mortar, it was a constant wonder to me that the Houses of Congress were not grander than they are. The position, design, and material of the Capitol are all magnificent, and yet, somehow or other, it is not, to me at any rate, one of those buildings which, like St. Peter's or York Minster or the Madeleine at Paris, stand apart in a traveler's memory. The grand, half-finished front façade is turned away from the city, owing to the fact that the building was planned before the town was built. So, as a matter of fact, nobody enters, or ever will enter, by the front entrance except to see the façade; and all persons on business approach the Capitol by the back door. The completion of the edifice is suspended for the present, because funds are short and the architect is away at the war. The whole building has still an untidy, unfinished, almost tumble-down, appearance. The immense iron dome, which will vie in magnitude with that of St. Peter's, and which, like the Roman cupola, you can see from miles and miles away, rising grandly over that hilly campagna country, is still a bare framework of beams and girders, surmounted by a crane, ominously resembling its brother of Cologne Cathedral. Blocks of unhewn marble lie on every side, scattered about the pleasant grounds which lead from the Capitol to the foot of the steep hill on which it stands. The niches are still without their statues, and the grand entrance without its giant doors, while, in many parts, the staring red brick walls are still without their marble facings. Even when the building is completed, I think the effect inside will always be disappointing. Vast as the Capitol is, there is a want of great, open spaces in it; and you wander through endless passages, and richly roofed corridors, and stately staircases, without coming across one point of view which leaves a strong, definite impression on your mind. There is, too, a characteristic absence of artistic propriety about the whole arrangements. The great center circular hall is blocked up with a scaffolding, on which a number of second- or third-rate historical pictures are exposed to view, some of them for sale. Amongst them, by the way, there used to be a portrait of President Buchanan; but when the troops were quartered here at the outbreak of the war for the defense of the Capitol, a Western regiment destroyed the portrait by squirting tobacco juice over it, leaving the other pictures untouched. "And a vile indignity, too, sir, that was—" said an Abolitionist who told me the story, "—for the tobacco juice." Again, in the main passages fruit stalls are allowed to stand, where apples, and nuts, and lager beer are sold to the outside public who have not the right of entrée to the Congress refreshment-rooms, at which brandy cocktails and Bourbon whisky are administered to thirsty orators. In another hall there is a stand for the sale of guidebooks, maps of the buildings, and commemorative medals; and farther on there is a little bazaar of Indian beadwork and moccasins. In spite of these defects of taste, the arrangements of the building are wonderfully comfortable; and the rooms and passages, though less gorgeous than those of our own Houses of Parliament, are, I think, in reality, more convenient and luxurious. Show is entirely subordinate to comfort, in a way it is not with us. Like everything in America, the whole building is new, painfully so; and the one relic of antiquity is found in the old Senate Chamber, where the Supreme Court now holds its sittings. This was about the only part of the old Capitol which was not burnt down by our troops in 1814; and in the mantelpieces and cornices you still see the friezes of the consul in his car, and the lictor with his fasces, which marked the classic French taste of the early Republican era. Otherwise, the whole edifice looks as if it had been opened yesterday. There is one constant charm, however, about the Capitol, that, from its shape and its elevated position, every room faces to the light, and commands most lovely views of the Potomac and the hills that gather in round Washington on every side.

So much for the outer building. With regard to Congress itself, one's first impression is inevitably unduly favorable. To anyone who has experienced the dreary waiting in the gallery of our own House with a member's order, and the still more dreary discomfort when at last you do make your way into the close, inconvenient pen, the mere facility of access is enough to put you into good humor. I cannot conceive any intelligent being, arrived at years of discretion, subjecting himself to the annoyance of a visit to our own Houses of Parliament except as a matter of business; and I should think little of the intelligence of anybody curious in such matters who did not go constantly to the debates in Washington. Without anyone to stop you or ask you your business, you go up the long staircases, and pass through folding doors into the public gallery, where, I should think, there must be room enough for some thousand persons, and where you sit as luxuriously on stuffed benches with padded backs as if you were a favored inmate of our own Speaker's Gallery. It is true the company you find around you, like that of all places of public resort in America, is mixed in its composition. Irish workmen, with ragged coats, will be sitting next to Broadway swells, in the most elaborate of morning costume; and by the side of officers, in the brightest of uniforms, you will see common soldiers, in their gray serge coats, with the roughest of beards and the muddiest of boots. If you are fastidious, however, you can easily, supposing there is no great crowd in the house, get admission into the ladies' gallery, where you have choicer company and a better view. For my own part, however, though I was kindly given the right of entrée into the reporters' gallery, which is an admirable one for hearing, I preferred the public ones, because you could change your seats from one part of the long galleries to another, and so always get a full view of the speaker, in whatever portion of the house he might happen to be standing. The company, too, like every crowd I ever met with in the North, was perfectly civil and well behaved. Indeed, during many visits which I made to Congress, I never heard the least disturbance or breach of order on the part of the gallery. If there had been, however, I hardly know how it would have been suppressed.

With an Englishman's feeling about the relative importance of the two Houses of Parliament, his first visit will probably be to the House of Representatives. The room is rectangular in shape, with sides of an unequal length; rather low in height for architectural effect, and surrounded on every side with galleries, supported on light iron pillars. With the exception of the two small compartments set apart for the press and the diplomatic corps, the whole of this gallery is open to the public. In the body of the house the seats of the members, with desks placed before each of them, are arranged in semicircular rows round the raised platform on which the Speaker's chair is placed and in front of which the clerks of the House are seated. The defect of the arrangement, as far as the public is concerned, is that, as the speakers turn toward the Chair in speaking, it is difficult to get a front view of their faces, and it is by no means an easy thing to follow a speaker whose back is turned toward you. Moreover, the constant buzz of conversation amongst the members makes it difficult to hear a speaker who does not happen to be near the place in which you are seated.

My first impression was that there was a want of life about the whole concern, compared with our House of Commons. It recalled rather a meeting of the House of Lords on a full night, when a dull speaker is on his legs, and the peers are anxious to get away. In the old days, before Secession, as a matter of custom, the Democratic members sat on the right of the Chair, and the Opposition, whether they were Whig, Federalist, Know-nothing, or Republican, on the left. Since the Southern Democrats seceded, and the remaining fractions of the old parties had become merged, more or less, in the great party which supported the Government and the Union, this custom has fallen into abeyance; the seats have been set further apart to cover the spaces left empty by the members of the seceding States, and the Representatives sit in any part of the hall where the number assigned to them by ballot may happen to place them, without much regard to party. This absence of any line of division between the members, and the fact that no expression of applause or dissent is permitted, give a dull air to the assembly. The scene looks like a lecture room where the class is paying no attention to the lecturer. Some of the members, not many, have their legs sprawling over the desks; some are sleeping in their chairs; and the majority are writing or reading, or talking in low voices to their neighbors. The Representatives have their hats off, and are dressed, for the most part, in the seedy black suits Americans affect so much. The majority are men advanced in life; young boyish legislators are things unknown here. The House seems composed of businessmen, slightly bored at an unprofitable waste of time. Thus the ordinary demeanor of the assembly is more staid, if not more dignified, than that of our Parliament. The only distinct sound which interrupts the somewhat droning tones of the orators' voices is the constant clap-clap of the members' hands, as they summon the boy-pages to run on errands. These boys are, indeed, an institution of the place. They come and go with wonderful quickness; and when nobody wants them, with that *sans gêne* quality so peculiar to all American servants, they sit upon the steps of the Speaker's platform, or perch themselves on any member's desk that happens to be vacant.

With regard to the merit of the oratory it is difficult to judge. There is not a single speaker of great eminence in either house at present, and there was no debate, while I happened to be at Washington, of especial interest. In truth, a debate in our sense of the word, is hardly known there. There being no Ministry to turn out—or rather there being a Ministry which has no direct connection with the discussions, and which cannot be turned out—the peculiar interest which attaches to a great debate with us, where the fate of an Administration depends on the issue, is altogether wanting. Speeches are delivered to be printed and circulated amongst constituents, rather than to influence the audience to which they are addressed; and, indeed, the newspaper summaries are ordinarily so meager that any member who wishes for a full report is obliged to have his speech reprinted. Probably, in consequence of this, the custom of reading speeches, or referring constantly to memoranda, is very common, and mars the effect of the discussions. There is an amount, too, of unimpressive gesticulation which becomes painfully monotonous. I saw one member who, during a speech of an hour, kept advancing and retreating constantly up an open space of some twelve feet in length, like the polar bear at the Regent's Park gardens; another, who always sidled from one desk to another; a third, who swung his arms up and down with the regularity of a windmill; and a fourth, who kept turning like a teetotum toward every part of the house in turn. The constant accentuation, too, of unimportant words, and the frequent misplacement of the right emphasis to the wrong place, make long listening to an American debate wearisome to an Englishman. Still, the one remarkable feature is the marvelous fluency of the speakers. Everybody has the gift of speaking—the power, at least, of stringing words together without a hitch. I never heard an American member of either House stutter, or hem and haw, as nineteen-twentieths of our speakers do when in want of a word. And this is not solely because the speeches are prepared beforehand. I have constantly heard members interrupted in their speeches, and unexpected questions put to them, yet they always replied with the same perfect self-possession, and almost fatal fluency of language. Whether this arises from the fact that, "unaccustomed as I am to public speaking," is a phrase no American out of his teens could use with truth, or whether, as I think, it is due to some characteristic excitability in the race, which supplies words at command, I cannot say. The fact is certain, that though I never heard anything in the way of American parliamentary oratory which rose to the height of eloquence, I never heard so much average good speaking in any English assembly.

I was told by persons qualified to judge, that I saw the Houses of Congress under unfavorable circumstances, and that, in happier times, I should have heard much of keen discussion and sterling eloquence. It is true that the interest of the nation was fixed upon the army, not upon Congress, as in former days; and that Congress suffered, as all popular assemblies will do, from the absence of public interest in its proceedings. It is true, also, that the fusion of all parties into the one great one, which supported the Government, rendered the debates comparatively tame and colorless. Still, with all this, I doubt whether, even in the palmy times of the American Congress, in the days of [Henry] Clay and [Daniel] Webster, and [Stephen] Calhoun, an Englishman would not have experienced the same sense of unimpressiveness about Congress. I defy any rational being to take much interest in cards unless he is playing for money; and American parliamentarism always seemed to me a sort of playing for love at politics. The stake with us is the power of changing the Ministry, but where a division leads to no practical result as far as the speakers are concerned, there must inevitably be a certain tameness about the proceedings. Having made this confession, I must state, on the other hand, that judging from my own experience, I should say the American House of Representatives (as I saw it when cleared of the Southern members) was a very quiet and orderly one. The English notion that it is a public bear garden, is a mistaken one. Mutatis mutandis, making allowance for the absence of high culture which prevails in a new country, I should say that Congress relatively stands high in moderation and decorum.

The Senate is more interesting to a stranger, from the simple fact that you can hear and follow readily what is going on, which you cannot do in the Lower House. In shape and arrangement, the building is the counterpart of the Representative chamber, only smaller. With so scant a number of members at its fullest —diminished as it is now by the absence of the seceding Senators —and with the widely-parted rows of arm chairs, fronted by the small mahogany tables, the aspect of the Senate is not a lively one. It seems impossible that with such an audience any actor could work himself into a passion; and the whole look of the scene is so very staid and decorous, that it is hard to realize the stormy, passionate discussions which have taken place within these walls; harder still to imagine that bludgeons and fire arms could ever have been wielded amongst men so sober and respectable looking.

To me it was a surprise to learn how very much of the business of both Houses is conducted secretly. On all executive questions, that is, on such questions as the appointment or dismissal of public officials, the discussions are held with closed doors. Then, too, the real business of a deliberative character in both Houses is carried on in the committee rooms, where no strangers or reporters are admitted. Whenever leave has been granted to bring in a bill, it is referred, before discussion, to the standing committee appointed to investigate the class of subjects on which legislation is proposed. If the committee rejects the bill, their vote is not final; but the rejected bill is laid upon the table, and it requires a two-thirds majority to remove it from the table, or, in other words, to resume its consideration. This, of course, is rarely done, and, practically, the framework and substance of every measure is discussed in the committee rooms, not in the open House. The party in power in either House manages the selection of the committees, so that one of the party should always occupy the chairmanship, and that the majority of the members should belong to their own side. It is in the committee rooms that the real work of legislation is done; and members go into the House, as I have often heard Congressmen declare, to deliver speeches, or write their letters. With all this, with the early hours (generally from noon to five), with the fresh air and easy seats, the position of a member of Congress must be, to my mind, a more comfortable one than that of an English M.P., not to mention the £600 a year of salary,* with the mileage, stationery, and franking perquisites.

---

* The rate of exchange of the pound at the time was $5.

The Proclamation and the
Border States

I HAVE often heard it asserted, and I have seen the statement
constantly repeated in the English press, that slavery had nothing to do with the questions at issue between the North and
South. I can only say that, during my residence in Washington,
I heard little talked about except the question of slavery. At the
time I arrived there, the chief discussion was whether the President would or would not issue a proclamation advocating emancipation. At last, after much hesitation, Mr. Lincoln published
the manifesto of the 6th of March [1862], proposing gradual
emancipation throughout the Slave States. The gist of that
proclamation lay in the first paragraph. "The United States
ought to cooperate with any State which may adopt a gradual
abolishment of slavery, giving to such State pecuniary aid, to be
used by it in its discretion to compensate for the inconvenience,
public and private, produced by such change of system." This
step, unimportant as it may appear, was the first of that long
series of measures which has culminated in the final decree of
abolition. It is as such that I write of it.

I remember, at the time the proclamation appeared, speaking
to Mr. [Charles] Sumner upon the subject. He pointed out to
me the imminent danger lest the state of feeling existing between
England and America should sooner or later lead to a war between our two countries; and suggested, as the only hope he
could see of escaping the calamity, that England should join
America in crushing out what he then conceived were the last

struggles of the insurgents. To this remark my answer was one which I conceive most Englishmen would have made, that with our Government there was no possibility of such a step being taken unless the country was strongly in favor of the North, and that the only way to rouse public feeling in England in favor of the North was to convince Englishmen that the war was being carried on for the bona fide abolition of slavery. Mr. Sumner's reply was, "Is it possible that England can fail to see that this war is being carried on for this object after the publication of the President's message?"

Now there is no question that England did fail to see this. I suspect that most Englishmen, who, like myself, hate slavery, read this message at first with disappointment. "Is this all?" was my conclusion at its perusal. Here, at the crisis of a nation's fate, when, for the first time, the power is in the hands of the North; when the South, in popular opinion, was soon to be at the mercy of the victorious Union, the utmost that the Government proposed was that the status quo should be restored as regarded slavery, coupled with an abstract resolution, that if any Slave State, of its own free will and good pleasure, chose to abolish slavery, the United States Government should assist it in its good intentions by pecuniary aid. Such, I own freely, was my first impression. But subsequent conversations with American politicians led me to believe that the Emancipation Message, as it was called at the time, was capable of a far higher and more hopeful construction. Subsequent events, I need hardly say, have convinced me that, in this instance, second thoughts were the best.

In the first place, then, this step was the furthest one which the President at the time could take consistent with the Constitution. The great mistake which foreigners appeared to me to make in arguing about America is the assumption that the Government, if it likes, can do everything. Assuming that the Crown, the House of Lords, and the House of Commons, or, in other words, the Government of England, were agreed together, it is hard to say what measures they might not pass legally. And I observe that Englishmen generally assume that, practically, the

American Government could do the same. Now, the vital defect of the Union seems to me to be that it exists by means of, and in virtue of, a written Constitution, and that by this very Constitution the absolute as well as the relative powers of the different bodies in the state are so clearly defined, that, in cases not provided for by the Constitution, Government action is paralyzed.

The states which composed the Union, in the words of Justice Story, "yielded anything reluctantly, and deemed the least practical delegation of power quite sufficient for national purposes." This, to my mind, is the key to the whole American Constitution. The course of events, the progress of civilization, has gradually increased the practical power of the Central Government, but the *legal* rights of the component states remain unimpaired. Now, if there are two privileges clearly guaranteed by the Constitution to the different states, they are—the right of each state to regulate its domestic institutions, and the existence of the Fugitive Slave Law. To amend the Constitution requires a majority of three-fourths of the legislatures or conventions of the states composing the Union; and, therefore, if the Government of the United States wished to abolish slavery in the different states, they must either have declared that the consent of the insurgent states was not required, which was tantamount to confessing that the Union was at an end, or else they must have broken through the Constitution, in strength of which alone they had any legal existence. The State of New York might tomorrow reestablish slavery as an institution consistent with the law, and, by the same law, the Federal Government can no more abolish slavery in Georgia, *proprio motu*, than it can place an export duty on any single article exported from any state in the Union. No doubt the *war power* might have covered, as it has since been made to cover, any breach in the letter of the Constitution, but at this period, both in the opinion of the President and the people, the time for the exercise of this *ultima ratio* had not arrived.

In ordinary years, before the Revolution, this excuse for inaction was valid enough; and I think now that we in England were unjust to the Government of the United States in throwing it the obloquy of upholding slavery at a time when it was absolutely powerless to deal with it in the Slave States, except by overthrowing the Union, or by trampling underfoot the very Constitution in virtue of which it had its being. With the insurrection, however, a new state of things came in. If advantage was not taken of this opportunity, the blame, if blame there was, must rest with the American people, not with the United States Government. The Government throughout has followed, and not led. Had any man of genius arisen at this crisis, had there been a Cromwell, a Mirabeau, or a Jefferson, the result might have been far different. But neither Lincoln, nor Seward, nor, still less, [Gen. George] McClellan, were men to shape a nation's destinies. The one principle which the President adhered to constantly, was that he was placed in office to carry out the will of the people. It was with the people, and the people alone, that the real decision of policy rested. The national vote which brought Lincoln into power was a vote against the extension of slavery, not a vote against its maintenance. When the insurrection broke out in force, and the nation awoke to its danger at the attack on Fort Sumter, the popular cry was not to abolish slavery, but to preserve the Union. The preservation of the Union was the overwhelming national instinct. It was this instinct which attempted to suppress the insurrection, and which, if possible, will suppress it in the end. It is only by working on this instinct that any of the political parties in the States can hope to achieve their ends.

Both of the extreme parties have failed hitherto to achieve their object. The pro-slavery faction has one great argument with which it seeks to work on public opinion. The Secession movement (so they allege, and with justice) is due to a belief in the South, whether well or ill founded, that slavery was in danger from the Abolition cry in the North. Renounce this Abolition theory, convince the South that slavery is not in danger, and there is an end of Secession. In the early stages of the insurrection, this party had great weight; but their policy was unsuccessful, partly because the pride and principle of the North refused to follow their counsels heartily, still more, because the South rejected madly the last overtures of conciliation. It was during their temporary success that the resolution of Congress, proposing still further to limit its own power with regard to legislation on slavery, was proposed and carried. The success of the Abolitionist party, pure and simple, has hardly been more decisive. They have been like political John the Baptists, preaching in the wilderness, and the number of their followers has fluctuated according to the apprehension of the coming danger. Their text is as simple as it is earnest. Slavery is the one cause of Secession. Between the Free North and the Slave South there can never be union as long as slavery exists, and therefore, for the sake of the Union (not so much, remark, for the sake of the sin), slavery must be suppressed. Obviously the strength of such a cry varies inversely with the probabilities of simple military success. Whenever the fortunes of the North seemed lowest, the Abolition cry has been most powerful. At the time when this proclamation was issued, and it seemed likely that the insurrection would be suppressed without any pronunciamento as to slavery, the Abolition appeal had lost half its weight. The Union victories for the hour suspended the progress of the anti-slavery sentiment. "Six months ago," I remember a friend of McClellan's saying to me about this period, "we were all Abolitionists, now we are all for the Union."

What the numerical strength of the pro-slavery and Abolitionist parties was when Secession broke out, it is impossible to ascertain accurately. I am convinced, however, that either of them formed a very small minority compared with what might fairly be called the great Union majority. That majority had no political organization, and was probably composed pretty equally out of the Democratic and Republican parties. We should be unjust in accusing it of any sympathy with slavery; we should be doing it more than justice in asserting that it had any deliberate purpose of suppressing slavery. To account for this almost universal acquiescence in the maintenance of the status quo, the following facts should be borne in mind: The popular instinct, more acute and intelligent than we can conceive in Europe, taught the people that any outspoken decision on slavery would have alienated the loyal Slave States, and would have thus retarded, if not destroyed, the prospect of restoring the Union. Again, any vigorous action as to slavery was inconsistent with the Constitution; while the whole strength of the North, at the first outburst of the war, lay in the fact that it was upholding the Constitution. In England we have been accustomed to assert that during this insurrection —revolution as yet it is not—the Federal Constitution has been frequently violated. Whether this opinion is right or wrong in the abstract, it matters not: It is enough to say that it was not the opinion of the Americans themselves. To the written letter of the Constitution they clung with a, to me, surprising tenacity —partly, I fancy, because the national reverence for the founders of the Union is a matter of almost religious sentiment, partly because of a general conviction that strict, unswerving adherence to the Constitution is the one bar to a rule of unbridled democracy. It was for this cause that the chief opponents of any unconstitutional action on the subject of slavery were the native Americans, while the German emigrants were the staunchest supporters of Frémont and revolutionary measures. The fear of alienating the Border States, the dread of revolution, and the respect for the Constitution, were the great principles which then actuated, and still actuate, the policy of the majority. The Union before all, and above all, now and forever, one, and indivisible, was their watchword and their rallying cry.

The question at issue, moreover, was not one of principle only, but of immediate action. The capture of Fort Donelson and the evacuation of Nashville had restored the Western portion and the capital of the State of Tennessee to the Union, before either people or Government had decided upon, or even dreamed of deciding upon, any policy with regard to the manner in which the seceding States should be dealt with after subjugation. "Sufficient unto the day is the evil thereof," has been throughout the one principle of national policy, and, possibly, it may prove a wise one. There is a story reported of Blondin, that when some one asked him how he ever had the nerve to proceed, when he reflected on the long stretch of rope over which he has to pass, he answered, "I never think of anything except how to take the step before me." So it has been with the North; and thus, when the condition of Tennessee called for some immediate action, there was no policy prepared. To reestablish the power of the Union was the one thing which a nation could see its way to, and so Andrew Johnson, a Tennessee slaveholder, was appointed Provisional Governor; all questions as to the domestic institutions of the revolted state or its relations to the Union were left to decide themselves; and the status quo was reestablished.

It was hardly to be expected that a Government like that of the United States should do more than side with the decision, or rather the indecision, of the nation. This is what Mr. Lincoln did. His proposition, he stated explicitly, "sets up no claim of a right of a Federal authority to interfere with slavery within State limits." In other words, he recognized the Constitutional existence of the revolted states, and their continued possession of a right, as states, to deal with their own domestic institutions.

The step, small as, at the time, it may have seemed to us, was a great step forward. For the first time in the history of Abolitionism, a distinct, if not a feasible plan was proposed for the emancipation of the slaves. For the first time, also, in the history of the United States the expediency of Abolition was announced as a principle of Government. The *delenda est Carthago* was uttered, timidly and apologetically if you will, but still officially. On the eve of expected victory, the President called upon Congress to declare that the Abolition of slavery was in itself desirable, and that the Central Government ought to aid in its extinction. A leading Abolitionist said to me at the time, "It has taken us two months' constant pressure to induce the President to issue this message." The sensation with which it was received throughout the states showed the importance popularly attached to its issue.

To understand the feelings with which the nation entered on this, the first step in the Abolition program, it may be well to quote some expressions of the different organs of political opinion in the North upon this edict, uttered at the time of its appearance.

Let me quote, first, a paragraph from an article published at this period on the subject of the Message from the *New York Tribune*, the organ of the moderate Anti-slavery party: "No one who has not thoughtfully and carefully and earnestly considered President Lincoln's proclamation will be likely to realize how admirable and comprehensive are its suggestions, and how surely their adoption will conduce to national integrity and internal peace. Look for a moment at the question of negro expatriation, which is one of the chief difficulties of our position. There are many worthy and good men, and ten times more of the other sort, who hold, that whenever slavery is abolished the negro should be sent out of the country. We have much charity for this opinion, for we once held it, but we are now convinced that it is an error. That the negro race, wherever free, will gradually mi-grate southward, colonizing the less populous West Indies, Cen-tral America, and the adjacent portions of South America, we be-lieve. Climate, soil, natural products, ease of obtaining a rude yet ample subsistence, and the ready fraternisation of blacks with the Indian and mongrel races who now exist in those regions, and who are nowise above our Southern negroes in the social scale, not even in their own opinion, will all attract them that way. But if slavery were ended tomorrow, we are confident that even South Carolina would be in no hurry to expel from her soil the most industrious and productive half of her people; that portion amongst whom drunkards and profligates are scarce, while its office-seekers, bar-room loungers, and pot-house brawlers have yet to be developed. A State can spare its idlers far better than its workers, and it is only from dread of their influence on the slaves that a slave-holding people ever desire the expulsion of their free blacks. Were slavery dead this day, even the Carolina aristocracy would prefer, as labourers on the plantations, the negroes to whom they are accustomed, and whose manners are respectful and submissive, to any immigrants by whom they could be promptly replaced. It is quite likely that in time white labour would demonstrate its superior energy and intelligence by driving out the black. But for the present the Carolina planters would generally hire their ex-slaves more satisfactorily to themselves than they could replace them from any quarter.

"The President's proposition leaves this whole subject to the respective States. If any State chooses to exile its negroes, it will do so. The nation will not meddle with the matter in any way. When slavery dies the national peril is averted, and the national concern ceases. All beyond is remitted to local discussion and control. So with regard to paying for slaves, the nation extends pecuniary aid to the States in order to rid itself of a great danger. But we do not here raise the question of how much, nor consider how far, the compensation accorded is to be affected by rebellion. Let all such questions be decided in due time, while we improve the present in one unanimous and hearty rally around President Lincoln, for the speedy restoration of the Union, and the final overthrow and demolition of whatever can raise even a doubt of its perpetuity and internal peace."

Such being the judgment of the Abolitionists, let me now take an article from the *New York Herald* of the same date, as an exposition of the views of the pro-slavery Democrats. It should be remembered that the *Herald* has always prided itself upon being an organ of the incumbent Administration. Thus, though the one political principle to which it has been uniformly faithful is a hatred to Abolition, yet the fact of its assumed Government connection caused it to deal more tenderly with the President's edict than it would naturally have done.

The President's proposal is dismissed with the following luke-warm approbation: "The measure will most probably prove agreeable to the Conservative feeling of the North and South alike, substituting, as it does, a moderate and practical view of the question of Emancipation in place of the extreme and impracti-cable views of the Abolitionists." This faint approval was de-signed by the *Herald* to give greater force to an attack it then proceeded to make in the following words on Senator Sumner's proposal to confiscate the slaves belonging to the revolted states, which was then before the Senate.

"The progress of the debate is developing the Conservative Constitution loving sentiment in Congress. It is a struggle of law and order against anarchy and revolution. The observations of Senator McDougall, of California, are well worthy of the atten-tive consideration of the whole people; and their indorsement by Mr. Cowan is a most gratifying evidence of patriotism amidst the fierce passions of party spirit. 'Shall we,' says the latter gentleman, 'stand by the Constitution, or shall we open wide the field of revolution, and go back to the doctrines of feudal ages, and introduce feuds which centuries cannot quiet? This is what the bill proposes. The passage of such a bill will make the whole Southern people our enemies. The scheme of colonization is entirely impracticable.' . . . This covers the whole ground; and what is Mr. Cowan's opinion about emancipation? He says: 'I protest against that section of the bill for freeing the slaves, as an entire departure from the principles of the Constitution, and especially impolitic at this time: because we are in a war, we ought not to make a law which was unconstitutional before. What have the negroes done to secure freedom at this time, when the course of their masters seems especially to invite them to strike for liberty? Nothing; they simply rely on their masters with a sort of blind instinct.' This is the language of a patriot; and if all men in Congress had only so spoken and acted from the beginning, neither civil convulsion or disunion would exist to-day. There is one great result produced by this war. The eyes of millions of men at the North are open to the real character of the negro, and they have discovered, from the experience of our troops and generals, what we have so long proclaimed to them in vain, the natural inferiority of the negro to the white man, which can no more be removed than the color of his skin by any amount of legislation. It is the negro's nature to be the servant of the Caucasian race. 'He relies on his master,' says Mr. Cowan, 'with a sort of blind instinct.' It is evident, therefore, that that part of the bloody programme which contemplated servile insurrection is already exploded. The negro is happier and better off, physically and morally, socially, and religiously, under the mild, Christian servitude of his white master at the South, than he ever was in any condition since the dawn of creation, or ever will be till the coming of the millennium. To leave the negro to himself, and put him into competition with the white man, is to destroy him as effectually as our civilization has destroyed the red man of the forest. Servitude is the negro's normal condi- tion. It is calculated to preserve the race from extinction, and to render it happy and, at the same time, subservient to the happiness of the white man. That white men should wage a war of extermination against white men, to change the condition of blacks for the worse, is an absurdity too great for the common sense of any people, and much more of the intelligent and practical people of the United States. Mr. Lincoln recognises the fact, and therefore, even if the fanatics in Congress should succeed in carrying their bill, it will be met with his veto."

Besides the Abolitionists and the Democrats, there was a third party of the more moderate Republicans, whose chief representative was Mr. Seward, and who were disposed to look very jealously on any proposition to interfere with the domestic institutions of the seceding States. Just at this time a great emancipation meeting was held at New York, at which Mr. Montgomery Blair was invited to attend. This gentleman, the Postmaster General in Mr. Lincoln's Administration, is a Maryland man. By one of the political combinations so universal in American politics, he had been selected by the Republican party to fill this post on Mr. Lincoln's accession, not because he held anti-slavery views himself, but because it was believed that, out of personal connections, he would support Mr. [Salmon] Chase, who did. The result, however, proved that on all questions connected with slavery he sympathized far more strongly with Mr. Seward than with the Abolitionist portion of the Cabinet. His dereliction of strict anti-slavery principles had long been surmised; and in his letter declining to attend the above-mentioned meeting, he stated very distinctly the grounds on which he differed from his more Republican colleagues. It was in the following words that he expounded his views:

"No one who knows my political career will suspect that I am influenced by any indisposition to put an end to slavery. I have left no opportunity unimproved to strike at it, and have never been restrained from doing so by personal considerations; but I have never believed that the abolition of slavery, or any other great reform, could, or ought to be effected, except by lawful and constitutional modes. The people have never sanctioned, and never will sanction, any other; and the friends of a cause should especially avoid all questionable grounds, when, as in the present instance, nothing else can long postpone their success.

"There are two interests in slavery—the political and property interests, held by distinct parties. The rebellion originated with the political class. The property class, which generally belonged to the Whig organization, had lost no property in the regions where the rebellion broke out, and was prosperous. It was the Democratic organization, which did not represent the slaveholders as a class, that hatched the rebellion. Their defeat in the late political struggle, and in the present rebellion, extinguishes at once and for ever the political interest of slavery. . . . It is not merely a question of constitutional law or slavery with which we have to deal in securing permanent peace. The problem before us is the practical one of dealing with the relations of masses of two different races in the same community. The calamities now upon us have been brought about, not by the grievances of the class claiming property in slaves, but by the jealousy of caste, awakened by the Secessionists in the non-slaveholders. It is this jealousy of race which is chiefly to be considered. Emancipation alone would not remove it. It was by proclaiming to the labouring whites who filled the armies of rebellion that the election of Mr. Lincoln involved emancipation, equality of the negroes with themselves, and consequent amalgamation, that their jealousy was stimulated to the fighting point. Nor is this jealousy the fruit of mere ignorance and bad passion, as some suppose, or confined to the white people of the South. On the contrary, it belongs to all races, and, like all popular instincts, proceeds from the highest wisdom. It is, in fact, the instinct of self-preservation, which revolts at hybridism. Nor does this instinct militate against the natural law, that all men are created equal, if another law of nature, equally obvious, is obeyed also. We have but to restore the subject race to the same, or to a region similar to that from which it was brought by violence, to make it operative. And such a separation of races was the condition which the immortal author of the declaration himself declared to be indispensable to give it practical effect.

"I am morally certain, indeed, that to free the slaves of the

South, without removing them, would result in their massacre.

"But this antagonism of race, which has led to our present calamities, and might lead to yet greater if it continues to be ignored, will deliver us from slavery in the easiest, speediest, and best manner, if we recognise it as what it is—the real and invincible cause of trouble—and deal with it rationally. We have but to propose to let the white race have the land intended for them by their Creator, to turn the fierce spirit aroused by the Secessionists to destroy the Union to its support, and, at the same time, to break up the slave system, by which the most fertile lands of the temperate zone are monopolized and wasted. That is the result which the logic of the census shows is being worked out, and which no political management can prevent being worked out. The essence of the contest is, whether the white race shall hold these lands, or whether they shall be held by the black race in the name of a few whites.

"The blacks could never hold them in their own name, for we have seen how quickly that race has disappeared when emancipated. Experience proves what might have been inferred from their history, that they have not maintained, and cannot maintain, themselves in the temperate zone, in contact and competition with the race to which that region belongs. It is only when dependent that they can exist there. But this service-relation is mischievous, and the community so constituted does not flourish and keep pace with the spirit of the age. It has scarcely the same claim to the immense area of land it occupies which the aborigines had; for, though the Indians occupied larger spaces with fewer inhabitants, they did not waste the land as the slave-system does. No political management or sentimentalism can prevent the natural overthrow of such a system in the end any more than such means could avail to preserve the Indian possession and dominion. This rebellion, like the Indian outbreaks, is but a vain attempt to stem the tide of civilization and progress. The treachery, falsehood, and cruelty perpetrated to maintain the possession of negroes, scarcely less than that of the savages, mark the real nature of the contest. Nevertheless, I believe it might have been averted, if we had adopted Jefferson's counsels, and made provision for a separation of the races, providing suitable homes for the blacks as we have for the Indians. It is still essential, in order to abridge the conflict of arms and to fraternise the people when that is past, to follow out Jefferson's advice. No greater mistake was ever made than in supposing that the masses of the South favour slavery. They did not take up arms to defend it. The fact that they oppose emancipation in their midst is the only foundation for a contrary opinion. But the masses of the North would be equally opposed to it if the four millions of slaves were to be transported to their midst. The prohibitory laws against their coming, existing in all the States subject to such invasion, prove this. On the other hand, the intense hostility which is universally known to be felt by the non-slaveholders of the South towards all negroes expresses their real hostility to slavery, and it is the natural form of expression under the circumstances.

"It needs, therefore, but the assurance, which would be given by the mere fact of providing homes for the blacks elsewhere, that they are to be regarded as sojourners when emancipated —as, in point of fact, they are, and ever will be—to insure the co-operation of non-slaveholders in their emancipation. Nor would it require any immediate, universal, or involuntary transportation, or that any injustice whatever be done to the blacks. The more enterprising would soon emigrate, and multitudes of less energy would follow, if such success attended the pioneers, as the care with which Government should foster so important an object would, doubtless, insure; and, with such facilities, it would require but few generations to put the temperate regions of America in the exclusive occupation of the white race, and to remove the only obstacle to a permanent union of the States."

These three views will give a fair impression of the state of feeling with which the North entered upon the question of Emancipation. I believe, myself, that a very large majority of the Northern people were represented fairly by Mr. Blair. I have entered elsewhere into the question of how far that antipathy to the Negro race was reasonable or otherwise. As a matter of fact, the North, and Mr. Lincoln himself, dreaded the prospect of unconditional emancipation. The *Tribune*, which advocated emancipation on anti-slavery grounds, expressed the opinion of a small minority. The *Herald*, which supported the "peculiar institution" on pro-slavery arguments, represented a still smaller one. The general feeling of the North upon the subject was an equal desire to make an end of slavery, and to get rid of the Negro.

But throughout all these different opinions one desire reigned predominant, and that was the desire to maintain the Union. The *Herald* was ready to sacrifice slavery, Mr. Blair to give up deportation, and, I almost fear, the *Tribune* to forsake emancipation, in order to preserve the Union. It was by appealing to this national instinct that each party sought to carry out its ends; and if the Abolitionists have triumphed, or will triumph, it is solely in virtue of the fact that circumstances have given weight to their appeal. I remember at this time a leading Abolitionist saying, in the presence of myself and of several Republican Senators, "My only hope for the abolition of slavery rests upon the willful obstinacy of our opponents, not the resolution of our supporters." The event, I think, has justified his words.

Notabilities of Washington
[Abraham Lincoln]

No MAN, we all know, is a hero to his own valet; and thus, what-ever there may be of heroic amongst American public men is hard to discern from the proximity at which you view them. American majesty has no externals to be stripped off, and you see her public men always *en deshabille*. Accessibility seems the especial and universal attribute of American statesmanship. There is never any difficulty about seeing anybody, from the President downward. Of course, the overwhelming pressure of state business during the civil war rendered public men more chary of their time than they would have been otherwise. But even then, the readiness with which Washington politicians re-ceived visits from strangers, and the openness with which they discussed public questions and the characters of public men were to me perfectly astonishing. No doubt, as would be the case everywhere, a well-accredited foreigner is treated with less re-serve than a chance native visitor. But I was many times in the company of men holding high official positions in Washington, when strangers, not only to myself, but to most of the gentlemen in whose company I was, happened to be present, and yet the conversation was as unguarded as if we had been all friends on whose discretion complete reliance could be reposed. And this state of things, I think, is due, not so much to the perfect social equality prevailing in the States, as to the general good-nature so common with Americans. In consequence of the total want of *solidarité*, to use a French word, existing between public men, everybody seems to stand on his own merits, to expect no support from, and to acknowledge no responsibility toward, his own colleagues, whether in office or in Congress. If a casual stranger were to ask Earl Russell whether he was really on cordial terms with Lord Palmerston, or if Mr. Gladstone were to state in a public room that he had absolutely no opinion of Sir Charles Wood, these remarks would hardly be stranger than many I have heard made of and by public men in America. With such a state of things, gossip is an institution of the country. Before you have been a week in Washington, you may learn the private history, friendships, and antipathies of every public man in the place, if you choose to listen to the talk you hear around you.

With regard to the President himself, everybody spoke with an almost brutal frankness. Politically, at that time, Abraham Lincoln was regarded as a failure. Why he, individually, was elected, or rather, selected, nobody, to this day, seems to know. One thing is certain, amidst many uncertainties, that the North had no belief that his election would lead to the Secession movement. Had this belief been entertained, a very different man would have been chosen for the post. Whether, under such circumstances, a Republican candidate would have been chosen at all is doubtful, but there is no doubt that Lincoln would not have been the man. As it was, the North desired to make a protest, and the name of Lincoln was as good a one to protest in as any other. It was for his negative, not his positive qualities that he was chosen, and the wonder is that his positive merits have turned out as decided as they have done. A shrewd, hard-headed, self-educated man, with sense enough to perceive his own deficiencies, but without the instinctive genius which supplies the place of learning, he is influenced by men whom he sees through, but yet cannot detect. "An honest man" may be the "noblest work of God," but he is not the noblest product of humanity, and when you have called the President "honest Abe Lincoln," according to the favorite phrase of the American press, you have said a great deal, doubtless, but you have also said *all* that can be said in his favor. He works hard, and does little; and unites a painful sense of responsibility to a still more painful sense, perhaps, that his work is too great for him to grapple with.

Personally, his aspect is one which, once seen, cannot easily be forgotten. If you take the stock English caricature of the typical Yankee, you have the likeness of the President. To say that he is ugly is nothing, to add that his figure is grotesque is to convey no adequate impression. Fancy a man six-foot, and thin *out of* proportion, with long bony arms and legs, which, somehow, seem to be always in the way, with large rugged hands, which grasp you like a vise when shaking yours, with a long scraggy neck, and a chest too narrow for the great arms hanging by its side; add to this figure, a head coconut shaped and somewhat too small for such a stature, covered with rough, uncombed and uncombable lank dark hair, that stands out in every direction at once; a face furrowed, wrinkled, and indented, as though it had been scarred by vitriol; a high narrow forehead; and, sunk deep beneath bushy eyebrows, two bright, somewhat dreamy eyes, that seemed to gaze through you without looking at you; a few irregular blotches of black bristly hair in the place where beard and whiskers ought to grow; a close-set, thin-lipped, stern mouth, with two rows of large white teeth; and a nose and ears, which have been taken by mistake from a head of twice the size. Clothe this figure, then, in a long, tight, badly-fitting suit of black, creased, soiled, and puckered up at every salient point of the figure—and every point of this figure is salient—put on large, ill-fitting boots, gloves too long for the long bony fingers, and a fluffy hat, covered to the top with dusty, puffy crepe; and then add to all this an air of strength, physical as well as moral, and a strange look of dignity coupled with all this grotesqueness, and you will have the impression left upon me by Abraham Lincoln. You would never say he was a gentleman: you would still less say he was not one. There are some women about whom no one ever thinks in connection with beauty, one way or the other—and there are men to whom the epithet of "gentlemanlike" or "ungentlemanlike" appears utterly incongruous, and of such the President is one. Still there is about him a complete absence of pretension, and an evident desire to be courteous to everybody, which is the essence, if not the outward form, of high breeding. There is a softness, too, about his smile, and a sparkle of dry humor about his eye which redeem the expression of his face, and remind me more of the late Dr. [Thomas] Arnold [headmaster at Rugby], as a child's recollection recalls him to me, than any other face I can call to memory.

On the occasion when I had the honor of passing some hours in company with the President, the gathering was a very small one, and consisted of persons with all of whom, except myself, he was personally acquainted. I have no doubt, therefore, that he was as much at his ease as usual, and yet the prevailing impression left upon my mind was that he felt uncomfortable. There was a look of depression about his face, which, I am told by those who see him daily, was habitual to him, even before the then recent death of his child, whose loss he felt acutely. You cannot look upon his worn, bilious, anxious countenance, and believe it to be that of a happy man. In private life, his disposition, unless report and physiognomy both err, is a somber one; but, coupled with this, he has a rich fund of dry, Yankee humor, not inconsistent, as in the case of the nation itself, with a sort of habitual melancholy.

It was strange to me to witness the terms of perfect equality on which he appeared to be with everybody. Occasionally some of his interlocutors called him "Mr. President," but the habit was to address him simply as "Sir." There was nothing in his own manner, or in that of his guests, to have shown a stranger that the President of the United States was one of the company. He spoke but little, and seemed to prefer others talking to him to talking himself. But when he did speak, his remarks were always shrewd and sensible. The conversation, like that of all American official men I have ever met with, was unrestrained in the presence of strangers to a degree perfectly astonishing. It is a regard for English, rather than for American, rules of etiquette, which induces me to abstain from reporting the conversation that I overheard. Every American public man, indeed, appears not only to live in a glass house but in a reverberating gallery, and to be absolutely indifferent as to who sees or hears him. This much I may fairly say, that the President asked me several questions about the state of public feeling in England, and obviously, like almost all Americans, was unable to comprehend the causes which have alienated the sympathies of the mother country. At the same time, it struck me that the tone in which he spoke of England was, for an American, unusually fair and candid. There are, perhaps, one or two Lincolniana which I may fairly quote, and which will show the style of his conversation. Some of the party began smoking, and Mr. Seward, who was present, re-marked laughingly, "I have always wondered how any man could ever get to be President of the United States with so few vices. The President, you know, I regret to say, neither drinks nor smokes."

"That," answered the President, "is a doubtful compliment. I recollect once being outside a stage in Illinois, and a man sitting by me offered me a cigar. I told him I had no vices. He said nothing, smoked for some time, and then grunted out, 'It's my experience in life that folks who have got no vices have plaguey few virtues.'"

This reminds me, by the way, of the almost incredible manner in which stories are coined about Mr. Lincoln. Some time after-ward, in the West, I traveled with a gentleman who professed to be an intimate personal acquaintance of the President. After telling me a number of anecdotes to illustrate his reputed free and easy manner, he told me that he had once been present in a Western law court where Mr. Lincoln was engaged to defend a prisoner for murder. He came late, apologized to the judge for his detention, owing to his having overslept himself, and then stated that he was never comfortable until he had smoked his morning cigar, and proposed, with the judge's permission, that they should have cigars all around. The permission being granted, he proceeded, with his cigar in his mouth, to defend his client. Now, unless I had had personal reason for knowing that Mr. Lincoln was not a smoker, I should certainly have re-corded this with a variety of other similar anecdotes, as gospel truth, coming as they did on such apparently indubitable evi-dence. From all that I saw and heard myself, I have no doubt that Mr. Lincoln would say hosts of things which seem to us utterly undignified, but he is the last man to say anything which would seem undignified to himself. Unlike most Western politicians, he was noted for not being "hail fellow well met" with every barroom lounger that he came across. He is a humorist, not a buffoon.

But to return to our interview. A gentleman present happened to tell how a friend of his had been expelled from New Orleans as a Unionist, and how, on his expulsion, when he asked to see the writ by which he was expelled, the deputation, which brought him the notice to quit, told him that the Confederate Government had made up their minds to do nothing unconstitutional, and so they had issued no illegal writ, but simply meant to *make* him go of his free will. "Well," said Mr. Lincoln, "that reminds me of a hotel-keeper down at St. Louis, in the cholera time, who boasted that he had never had a death in his hotel. And no more he had, for, whenever a guest was dying in his house, he carried him out in his bed and put him in the street to die."

At another time, the conversation turned upon the discussions as to the Missouri Compromise, and elicited the following quaint remark from the President: "It used to amuse me some (*sic*) to find that the slaveholders wanted more territory because they had not room enough for their slaves, and yet they complained of not having the slave trade because they wanted more slaves for their room."

While I am talking of these Lincoln anecdotes, which used to fill the columns of the American newspapers, let me mention a few which I have reason to believe authentic. Shortly after Mr. Cameron's resignation, an old acquaintance called upon the President, and, after American fashion, asked him point-blank why, when he turned out the Secretary of War, he did not get rid of the whole Cabinet. "Well, you know," was the answer, "there was a farmer, far West, whose fields were infested with skunks, so he set a trap and caught nine; he killed the first, but that made such an infernal stench that he thought he had better let the rest go."

Again, at the first council of war, after the President assumed the supreme command-in-chief of the army, in place of McClellan, the General did not attend, and excused himself next day by saying he had forgotten the appointment. "Ah, now," re-marked Mr. Lincoln, "I recollect once being engaged in a case for rape, and the counsel for the defense asked the woman why, if, as she said, the rape was committed on a Sunday, she did not tell her husband till the following Wednesday. And when the woman answered she did not happen to recollect it, the case was dismissed at once."

The wit, indeed, of many of these anecdotes is too Aristo-phanic to be quoted here, but there is one other which will bear repeating. When the rebel armies were closely beleaguering Washington, two gentlemen insisted, late one night, on seeing the President, in order to inform him of a plot they had discov-ered on the part of some government officials for communicating with the enemy by means of signals. The President listened at-tentively to their story, which was clearly of the *gobe-mouche* order, and on inquiring what remedy his informants proposed, was told, after some hesitation, that the best plan would be to replace the traitorous officials by loyal men like themselves. "Gentlemen, gentlemen," was the President's comment, "I see it is the same old, old coon. Why could you not tell me at once that you wanted an office, and save your own time as well as mine?"

Stories such as these read dull enough in print. Unless you could give also the dry chuckle with which they are accompanied, and the gleam in the speaker's eye, as, with the action habitual to him, he rubs his hand down the side of his long leg, you must fail in conveying a true impression of their quaint humor. This sort of Socratic illustration is his usual form of conversation amongst strangers, but I believe in private life he is a man of few words, and those simple ones. Let me close my description with one re-mark he made of a more reflective character, and which, though perhaps not of great value in itself, is curious as coming from a man who has achieved distinction. Speaking of the fluency of American orators, he said, "It is very common in this country to find great facility of expression, and common, though not so common, to find great lucidity of thought. The combination of the two faculties in one person is uncommon indeed; but whenever you do find it, you have a great man."

For very obvious reasons the public press of the North was, at this period, almost unanimously, in favor of Mr. Lincoln. The Republican papers could not criticize their own nominee—the champion of their first triumph—without damaging their own party. The Democratic journals were afraid of driving the President into the arms of the Republicans, and therefore outvied their rivals in the ardor of their encomiums. From these causes, to judge from the language of the press, you might have supposed that the whole hope and confidence of the country was reposed in "Abe Lincoln." But the truth is that the talk then current of proposing him for reelection was not a genuine one, and that when the President leaves the White House, he will be no more regretted, though more respected, than Mr. Buchanan. When Wendell Phillips described him as "a first-rate second-rate man," he uttered one of those epigrammatic sarcasms which stick to their victim forever.

So much for Mr. Lincoln. At the time when I was in Washington, Mr. Seward did not stand high in popular favor. His career as Minister is curiously illustrative of the working of American politics. When Mr. Lincoln's Administration was formed, Secession was not believed in as a serious contingency, and the ministers were selected by, or rather chosen for, the President, not as the fittest men to grapple with the situation, but in order to satisfy the conflicting sections of the political party which had carried the Presidential election: New York was the headquarters of the moderate pro-slavery, or, more fairly speaking, un-anti-slavery Republicans, and Mr. Seward and Mr. Thurlow Weed were the leading politicians of the party in New York State; the latter gentleman being supposed to be the Moses, and the former the Aaron of the partnership. To satisfy this section—the most influential one of the Republicans—Mr. Seward was appointed Secretary of State; he was the one man of sterling ability and thorough energy among the ministers; and, partly by talent, still more by sheer self-assertion, became for a time almost a dictator in the Cabinet; he had, too, the merit of first recognizing that the

North was in earnest, and his passport system, his arrests, and his suspension of the habeas corpus, ill-advised, perhaps, as they may have been, were, at the time, welcome to the nation as a proof that the Government was in earnest also. If he could have kept from writing dispatches, he would have remained invincible; but, after all, explain it as you will, the *beau rôle* in the *Trent* affair was not that of the United States, and the Americans are too sharp a people to be able long to delude themselves with the flattering unction that they had won a great diplomatic victory; hence the Secretary of State suffered, perhaps unjustly, as the scapegoat for the national humiliation. For a time, General McClellan became, practically, the chief person in the state and in the Cabinet; and on his comparative decline in popularity, Mr. Stanton, the Secretary of War, directed the Presidential policy; but after every reverse, sooner or later, the Secretary of State has reestablished his position by virtue of his intellectual ability.

My first reflection, I remember, at meeting Mr. Seward, was one of wonder that so small a man should have been near creating a war between two great nations—a man, I should think little over five feet and a half in height, and of some sixty years in age, small made, with small, delicate hands and feet, and a spare, wiry body, scanty, snow-white hair, deep sunk, clear, gray eyes, a face perfectly clean shaved, and a smooth, colorless skin, of a sort of parchment texture. Such were the outward features that struck me at once. He was in his office when first I saw him, dressed in black, with his waistcoat half-unbuttoned, one leg over the side of his armchair, and a cigar stuck between his lips. Barring the cigar and the attitude, I should have taken him for a shrewd, well-to-do attorney, waiting to learn a new client's story: you are at your ease with him at once; there is a frankness and bonhomie about his manner which renders it, to my mind, a very pleasant one. In our English phrase, Mr. Seward is good company. A good cigar, a good glass of wine, and a good story, even if it is a little risqué, are pleasures which he obviously enjoys keenly. Still, a glance at that spare, hard-knit frame, and that clear, bright eye, shows you that no pleasure, however keenly appreciated, has been indulged in to excess throughout his long, laborious career; and more than that, no one who has had the pleasure of seeing him amongst his own family can doubt about the kindliness of his disposition. It is equally impossible to talk much with him without perceiving that he is a man of remarkable ability; he has read much, especially of modern literature, traveled much, and seen much of the world of men, as well as that of books. His political principles seem to me drawn from the old Whig school of the bygone *Edinburgh Review* days, and you can trace easily the influence that the teaching of Brougham, and Jeffreys, and Sidney Smith have had upon his mind. What struck me most in conversation with him was a largeness of view, very rare among American politicians. The relative position of America with respect to Europe, and the future of his country, are matters he can discuss with sense as well as patriotism. That his intellect is practical rather than philosophical, and that he is unduly impatient of abstract theories, I am inclined to suspect. In other words, he is a man of action rather than thought—a politician, not a reformer. The stories circulated over here so freely about Mr. Seward's being a man addicted to intemperance, I am convinced, are utterly unfounded. Conviviality has not gone so much out of fashion across the Atlantic as it has with us, and the Secretary of State is a man not likely to be more rigid in his observance of social rules than the society he lives amongst; but whatever Mr. Seward's indulgences may be, or may have been, they are never of such a nature as to incapacitate him for the discharge of his public duties. It is reported that not long ago some politicians of influence and of strict Puritan principles urged the President to remove the Secretary of State on the ground of incompetency, to which application the answer was made that a man who worked three times as many hours, and did three times as much in one hour as any of his colleagues, could hardly be incompetent, whatever else might be his failings.

Mr. Seward's conversation is not epigrammatic, and, though pleasant and sensible, has not much in it which will bear repeating. He talked to me on one occasion for a length of time upon the possibility of reconstructing the Union, and the purport of his remarks resembled very closely the gist of Mr. Blair's letter, which I quoted in my last chapter—so much so, indeed, as to suggest to me that, in all probability, the speaker had dictated the document. The great point on which he laid stress was that English critics failed to appreciate the difference between slavery as a social and slavery as a political institution. The two, in his opinion, were totally distinct. The effect of the present war—he was speaking then in last March—had been to destroy the political power of slavery. The Southern politicians had taken up the advocacy of "the peculiar institution," not for love of the system, but in order to establish their political predominance. When once it became clear that slavery was a decaying institution, no party, either North or South, would identify its fortunes with their own. The Democrats, or whatever new organization corresponded to the defunct Democratic party, would give up slavery, just as the English landowners have given up protection. Henceforth, every man who wished to rise in political life, would profess anti-slavery opinions, for exactly the same cause as hitherto he might have professed pro-slavery ones. The rising generation would assume Christian antipathy to slavery as part of their political creed, and the support of the system would be confined to a small and decreasing minority. This view, of course, was based upon the idea that in a fair fight the power of the Slave States would have succumbed to that of the Free States, and that, therefore, the whole prestige of slavery would be gone. When once the supremacy of the North was clearly established, the South, so he held, would reconcile itself to its fate. People in this world do not continue long fighting for a cause that is absolutely hopeless; and, if it could be proved that the cause of slavery was hopeless, its adherents would fall away from it with marvelous rapidity. In America public opinion changes with a suddenness which older states can scarcely credit; and, therefore, the fact that at this moment the South appeared to be unanimous in favor of slavery, was no reason that, in a few months' time, the majority, even of the Slave States, might not have reconciled themselves to Abolition. Of the future of the Negro, he did not speak sanguinely. Right or wrong, he obviously shared the ordinary American opinion as to the impossibility of the black and white races associating on equal terms. By the action of the same laws which had operated already in New York and New England, the Negro would die out unless protected by the artificial legislation of the slave system. His own observation throughout life had led him to the conviction that the climate and habits of the North were fatal, in the long run, to the health and prosperity of colored citizens. In his own house, he could recall, when a boy, half a dozen members of different Negro families [emancipation did not take place in New York till 1820]; but at the present moment, though he had kept in sight the Negroes of his father's household and their descendants, he did not believe that there were three or four of them left; while the white members of the same household, whose history he had also followed, now counted the number of their descendants by hundreds. In the colonization project, as it appeared to me, he had little faith; and he obviously looked to the solution of the Negro question by the gradual dying out of the black race, as soon as emancipation had really begun to work.

Probably the most striking-looking of the ministers is Mr. Chase, the Secretary of the Treasury. His head would be a treasure to any sculptor as a model of benevolence. His lofty, spacious forehead, his fresh, smooth countenance, his portly figure, and his pleasant, kindly smile, all seem to mark the stock old philanthropist of the stage, created to be the victim and providence of street beggars. One wonders how so kind-looking a man can find it in his heart to tax anybody; and I believe this much is true, that a man of less ability and sterner mold would have made a better financier than Mr. Chase has proved. Mr. Blair, though a Maryland man, is the only one of the ministers who has what we consider the characteristic Yankee type of face—the high cheek bones, sallow complexion, and long, straight hair. Of Mr. Gideon Welles, the Secretary for the Navy, who expressed such premature approval of Capt. Wilkes, there is little to be said, except that he wears a long white beard, and a stupendous white wig, which cause him to look like the heavy grandfather in a genteel comedy, and that there is such an air of ponderous deliberation about his face, that you ask yourself whether the "modern Rip-

Van-Winkle," as the *Herald* used to style him, has ever clearly realized, in so short a time as one year, that America is in a state of civil war. Mr. Stanton was laid up with illness most of the time that I was in Washington, so that I saw but very little of him. In look, he is the least distinguished of any of the ministers, and the expression of his face is by no means a pleasant one. Mr. Bates, of Missouri, the Attorney General, is a shrewd, quiet lawyer, very much like elderly legal authorities in other parts of the world.

Americans complain constantly that *we* know nothing of their public men. The complaint is hardly a fair one, as there are barely half a dozen English statesmen to whom Americans attach the slightest individuality; and the names of our minor celebrities, such as Lowe and Layard, would convey as little to American ears as those of Colfax or Conkling would do to us. Among men not in power at this period, the one, I own, that impressed me most was Caleb Cushing, known, and that not altogether favorably, to the English public as Attorney General under President Pierce's Administration, during the Frampton difficulty. From his connection with the old Democratic party, and his reputed sympathy with the Secession leaders, he was out of favor with the country and the Government, and, above all, with his own State of Massachusetts, where a bitter personal prejudice exists against him. Having had the pleasure of meeting him frequently and intimately, I found him to be a man of extreme acuteness, and immense and varied reading, and, indeed, one of the pleasantest companions whom it has been my fortune to meet with in life. While the war lasts, he has little chance of reentering public life. But I am much mistaken if a man of his power and ability does not, before long, play an important part in the politics of his country.

This record would be incomplete unless I were to say something of Mr. Sumner. He is too well known in Europe to need much description. Many of my readers are acquainted, doubtless, with that great, sturdy, English-looking figure, with the broad, massive forehead, over which the rich mass of nut-brown hair, streaked here and there with a line of gray, hangs loosely; with the deep blue eyes, and the strangely winning smile, half bright, half full of sadness. He is a man whom you would notice amongst other men, and whom, not knowing, you would turn round to look at as he passed by you. Sitting in his place in the Senate, leaning backward in his chair, with his head stooping slightly over that great, broad chest, and his hands resting upon his crossed legs, he looks, in dress, and attitude, and air, the very model of an English country gentleman. A child would ask him the time in the streets, and a woman would come to him un-bidden for protection. You can read in that worn face of his—old before its time—the traces of a life-long struggle, of disappointment and hope deferred, of ceaseless obloquy and cruel wrong. Such a life-training as this is a bad one for any man, and it has left its brand on the Senator for Massachusetts. There are wrongs which the best of men forgive without forgetting, and, since Brook's brutal assault upon him, those who know him best say they can mark a change in Charles Sumner. He is more bitter in denunciation, less tolerant in opposition, just rather than merciful. Be it so. It is not with soft words or gentle answers that men fight as Sumner has fought against cruelty and wrong.

Glimpses of Slavery

THERE ARE some things an author has a right to assume. I am perfectly justified in asserting, as a fact, that the earth moves round the sun, though, in company with nineteen-twentieths of my readers, I am utterly unacquainted with the grounds on which Galileo's discovery was established. So I do not consider it necessary to prove to my readers that slavery is a bad thing. If their knowledge of the world, and their experience of their own hearts, does not teach them what tyrants we should all be if we held irresponsible power over our fellow creatures, let them study the records and evidence of the anti-slavery reports in the days before emancipation; and if they are not convinced that slavery is an evil to master as well as slave, I hardly know what to say to them. As to the people—if there be any such in England—who bona fide believe the stories such as I have read in *Blackwood's* veracious pages, of slaves with gold watches, and monies in the savings banks, and an intelligent preference for slavery, I can no more argue with them than with lunatics of any other description.

It is not necessary—at least, I hope and trust it is not necessary—to demonstrate the evils of slavery to the vast majority of my readers. During my residence in the States, I had neither opportunity nor inclination to make researches into the cruelties of the slavery system. The sight of misery one cannot in any way relieve is a very painful one; and personally I have such a hatred of slavery, that, while in the Slave States, I always preferred to give myself the benefit of the doubt, and try to fancy, as long as it was possible for me to do so, that the Negroes I came across were free Negroes, not slaves. I see little good in quoting the individual cases of cruelty or barbarity which I heard reported privately. I had not the power to trace out the truth of any particular instance, and I doubt the use of quoting exceptional instances. Like every traveler, however, who keeps his eyes open, and who is willing to see what passes before him, I caught some glimpses of the slavery system. Let me point out a few which are matters of public notoriety, resting on unquestionable documentary evidence, not on hearsay report. There may be little, perhaps, of novelty in them, but there are some facts which should be kept before the world in season and out of season; and of such, in my mind, are the facts about slavery.

Of course we all know, or if we do not know it is not for want of telling, that the slaves are contented and happy, and have no wish for freedom. It may be so; but if so, it is hard to explain why the papers of the Slave States are filled with advertisements of runaway slaves. Every day, for instance, in the *Baltimore Sun*, which I used to see constantly in Washington, there appeared a row of advertisements, of which the following may be taken as types:

> 3d March, 1862.
> 25 dollars (5£) reward. Ran away, March 2d, from the farm of Mrs. S. B. Mayo, in Anne Arundel county, negro boy, John Stewart. He is 19 or 20 years of age; 5 feet 9 or 10 inches high; very prominent mouth and large front teeth; *light* complexion; has a stupid look when spoken to; his father lives in Annapolis. Any one who will arrest and secure him in jail can receive the above reward.
> T. H. GAITHER, *Howard Co*ᵞ.

Mr. Gaither is the owner of John Stewart, of light complexion, and had hired him to Mrs. Mayo. Doubtless, on his delivery at home, the misguided lad would have the fatted calf killed for him, in honor of the prodigal's return.

> 13th March, 1862.
> 200 dollars reward (40£). Ran away from the subscriber, living in the upper part of Calvert county, in September last, my negro man Thomas, who calls himself Thomas Jones. He is about 5 feet 6 to 9 inches high; dark chestnut colour;

stout and well built; very likely; large white teeth; with full
suit of hair (plaited when he left home); the whites of his
eyes show very much when spoken to; had on white fuiled
(*sic*) cloth peajacket, dark cloth pantaloons, and cloth cap.
I have no doubt that he is in or about Washington or Bla-
densburgh, as he left a day or two before Colonel Cowdin's
regiment left; or, if in Baltimore, he is with the Jones' or
Kayes', his free relatives. I will give the above reward, if
taken out of the State of Maryland or the district of Columbia; one hundred dollars if taken in the district of Columbia,
or any county of the State except Calvert; and fifty dollars if
taken in Calvert county. In either case, to be delivered to me
or secured in jail, so that I get him again.

> JONATHAN Y. BARBER,
> *Friendship* A. A. Co*y*.

It is melancholy to reflect, that six months' absence from the
delights of home should have failed to convince Thomas of his
mistake. What can one expect of a human being valued at 40£
sterling, and provided with cloth pantaloons, who prefers the
society of mean free men of color to involuntary servitude, and
who, reversing the example of Mr. Herbert of Clytha, has actually the audacity to appropriate the name of Jones? It is really
pleasant to consider that Jonathan Y. Barber, of Friendship, does
not yet despair of Thomas's repentance. It is not every slave who
has been demoralized by permission to use a surname, as the
next advertisement will teach us:

> 20th March, 1862.
> 180 dollars (36£) reward. Ran away from the subscriber,
> near Bladensburgh, boy Anthony, commonly called 'Toney.'
> He is 5 feet 5 inches high; very black; short hair; grum coun-
> tenance when spoken to; with a small scar over one of his
> eyes. Went away with a black jacket and United States' but-
> tons on it, casinet pants, and yellow gauntlet gloves. I will
> give 180 dollars to any one who will bring him home to me.
> FIELDER MAGRUDER.

Probably a short experience of the sorrows of freedom will
amend "Toney's" moral nature, and teach him to look pleasant
when spoken to by Fielder Magruder.
But to me the saddest of all these exhibitions of human de-

pravity was contained in an advertisement which appeared for days together. It was as short as it was sad:

> 15th March, 1862.
> Ran away from the subscriber, 13th March, negro woman, Ellen, aged about forty years, and her boy Joe, aged seven years. They are both yellow colour. Ellen has a defect in one eye; Joe is bright yellow. I will pay a liberal reward for their arrest.
>
> JOSHUA M. BOSLEY.

At last the advertisements stopped. Was the search given up as useless? Or, was the liberal reward earned and paid? God knows.

Down in the Southern States, the course of proceeding was more businesslike. In Utopia it is clear that it will be the finder of a purse, not the loser, who advertises it. If it were certain that we all followed the Christian precept of doing to others as we would that others should do to us, we should be aware that everyone who found our lost property would leave no stone unturned to restore it to us. It is pleasing to find that in the chivalrous slaveholding South there is an approach to Utopian honesty. It is the finders of stray human property there, not the losers, who advertise the fact. There is an obvious economy of labor about this arrangement. It is much cheaper for the Post Office to publish a list of unclaimed letters, than for every person who expects a letter which has been misdirected to advertise for its discovery. So it is with slaves in the South. Any slave found straying is sure to be committed to jail; so that there is no necessity for a lost slave to be advertised for. Every slaveholder is always ready to do his duty.

So, in the Slave States, the number of advertisements for runaway slaves are few, but the number of advertisements of runaways committed to jail are plentiful. In Tennessee, I observed, in one day, in one paper, thirty advertisements of commitments to jail, which ran as follows:

> Committed to jail of Davidson county, 21st April, 1862, a negro woman, who says her name is Lucinda, and belongs to William Donalson, of Davidson county. The said woman

is about 28 or 30 years old, dark copper colour. The owner is requested to come forward and prove property, and pay charges as the law directs.

JAMES M. HINTON,
Sheriff and Jailor, D.C.

Of these thirty human chattels committed to the jail of Nashville till their owners could come forward and prove property, three were women, twenty-four were men, and the rest were, according to their own statement, *free* men of color. This latter fact is worth noting. Read as follows:

Committed to jail of Davidson county, 4th April, 1862, a negro man, who says his name is Joe Bartlett: said boy claims to be a free man of colour; about 24 years old; says he lives in Henry county, Kentucky; *light* copper colour, scar on the right side of the neck; weighs about 175 or 180 lbs.; 6 feet 1 inch high.

J. M. HINTON,
Sheriff and Jailor, D.C.

Now, this advertisement is dated 20th April. If Joe Bartlett's story was true, here was a free man, a native of Kentucky, no more subject to the laws of Tennessee than I am to the laws of Russia, imprisoned for sixteen days, on account solely of a "light copper-colour." Truly a benevolent custom. If Joe Bartlett is a slave, he is restored to the tender care of a fond master; if he is free he remains in prison, in involuntary servitude, till he can prove his freedom; and when he does prove it, he has no claim for compensation, or redress for his captivity. On the contrary, he, Joe Bartlett, has to pay the costs which the State of Tennessee has incurred in imprisoning him; and, if he cannot, well then he is provided with an owner, who can pay for him, and, slave or free, he is sold back into slavery. It is a benevolent custom, startling perhaps in itself, but inevitable to the "peculiar institution." The necessity is obvious. There exists amongst slaves a peculiar malady called "drapetomania." In plain English, slaves are addicted to an inexplicable and unaccountable malady, which, without cause or reason, prompts them to run away from their masters. If slaves are to be of any value, as property, this disease must be remedied, if it cannot be cured. For the protection of the slave (and the slaveholder) any slave found at large suffering from this malady (of which absence from home without written authorization from his owner is the invariable symptom) must be confined in jail, by any good white Samaritan, who should find him in danger of falling amidst thieves. Granted this conclusion, a second follows. Another symptom of drapetomania is a tendency on the part of the sufferer to repudiate his home, to deny his lord and master, and to degrade himself by the assertion that he is a free man. There is no possibility of discovering the truth or falsehood of these statements by internal evidence. If the man of color has not papers with him, to attest his freedom, he must, in the interest of runaway slaves, be treated as a slave. Here follows a third conclusion: that the captive, if free, must pay the cost of his own captivity. If the State had to pay the expenses, State authorities would be slow to commit men of color to jail who might prove to be free men, and hence drapetomaniacs might be allowed to carry out their madness to their own destruction. In a Christian state, this idea cannot be thought of. In all legislation somebody must suffer. It is better that one innocent free man should be sold into slavery than that a hundred slaves should escape into freedom. Given the peculiar institution, the imprisonment of Joe Bartlett, and his sale into slavery for the expenses of his own imprisonment, is a logical and righteous consequence. "*Qui veut le fin,*" says the French proverb, "*veut les moyens.*" Slavery may be a good thing; but if it is good, so are the many peculiar consequences, of which Joe Bartlett's case is one, which follow inevitably from the peculiar institution. Of the runaway advertisements, there is one trait worth recording. In no Free State is there a single newspaper, however pro-slavery in its politics, which will publish hue-and-cry advertisements of escaped slaves. In no Slave State is there a paper that will refuse to publish them. By the Fugitive Slave Law, a runaway slave may be captured in free Ohio, just as well as in slave Kentucky, but no Free State newspaper can be found to promote the practical execution of the very law, which, as a matter of theory, it may defend in its columns.

I have seen lately, in certain English pro-slavery journals, a statement based upon the evidence of intelligent and high-minded Southern gentlemen, that the separation of Negro families by sale is practically unknown, and forbidden, if not by the letter of the law, by the moral sense of the community. The statement in itself is improbable. Anybody who chooses to think upon the subject must perceive that for one purchaser who wishes to buy a whole family there must be dozens who want to purchase some one member of it, and that, therefore, far higher prices can be realized by selling a slave family retail instead of wholesale. This being so, the temptation for a needy slaveowner to divide families must be enormous; and if division of families was really forbidden by the moral sense of the public, it is pretty certain that the possibility of public sensibility being outraged by the unscrupulousness of any embarrassed slaveholder would be removed by a law interdicting divided sales. In no Slave State does any such law exist. As to the evidence of candid, intelligent, and high-minded slaveowners, it must be taken for what it is worth. Where evidence is conflicting one must judge by inherent probabilities. Let me give two particles of evidence on the subject which came under my own knowledge. A friend of mine, by no means an Abolitionist, resided for some time in the Slave States. The subject of slavery was an unpleasant one, which he avoided; but on one occasion his host, a slaveowner, began to complain to him of the calumnies circulated against the South, and asserted that in the whole course of his experience he had never known an instance of a mother being separated from her children. My friend naturally enough believed the statement. On the very same day, however, it happened that some of the family began talking about a little Negro boy of theirs who had been drowned a short time before, and describing how shocked they were when the poor child's corpse was carried up to the plantation. My friend asked whether the mother's grief was very terrible to witness. "Oh," answered his informant, "the child's mother belongs to Mr. ——, who lives at the other end of the state, so that we know nothing about her." The fact seemed difficult to reconcile with his host's assertion of the morning; and so, prudently enough, he did *not* ask for an explanation of the inconsistency in the two stories. The accuracy of this story I can answer for; and it is corroborated by an incident which happened to myself. One day, after the retreat of the Confederate army from Manassas, I fell in, near Alexandria, with a party of runaway slaves, working their way northward. They asked our party about the road, and we put a few questions to them in return. One of them, the least helpless-looking of the lot, was a young worn woman carrying a child some three years old. She was going to Washington, so she told us, to look after her husband, who, she believed, was in service there, though it was two years since she had been parted from him. Of course I shall be told this case was an exceptional one; I only hope it was; but, somehow or other, all cases of cruelty are always exceptional.

If breaches of the law or of public sensibility are exceptional, it can hardly be assumed that the laws themselves are exceptional. I have before me the Maryland code of slavery, which, till last April, was in force at Washington. If you want to know what slavery is by law, note the following specimens of slave-owners' justice: "No negro, or mulatto slave, or free negro, or mulatto born of a white woman . . . . . shall be admitted and received as good and valid evidence in law, in any matter or thing whatsoever depending before any magistrate within this province, wherein any white Christian person is concerned." This Act is not a dead letter. During the present session of Congress a bill was passed by the Senate, authorizing colored persons to be employed as letter-carriers by the Government. The bill was thrown out by the House, upon the ground that, in a Slave State the evidence of a colored man could not be received, and that, therefore, if a white post-office servant was to steal letters in a Slave State, it would be impossible to prove his guilt by the evidence of colored letter-carriers.

Again, in order to suppress the assembling of slaves, it is ordained, that in case the constable shall find at any house within his district any slaves not belonging to the house, and not authorized by his master to be present, then "it shall and may be lawful for the said constable," and he is by this act required, to whip

every such Negro on the bare back, at his discretion, not exceeding thirty-nine stripes. With the view of protecting the white
man in execution of his duty, it is further ordained, that "if it
shall so happen at any time that any negro, or other slave, shall
strike any white person, it shall and may be lawful, upon proof
made thereof, either on the oath *of the party so struck*, or otherwise, before any justice of the peace, for such justice to cause one
of the negro's or other slave's ears so offending to be cropt."

The penalties against any attempt to escape are equally severe:
"Where any slave shall be guilty of rambling, riding, or going
abroad in the night, or riding horses in the day-time without
leave, or running away, it shall and may be lawful for the justices
of the county-court, and they are hereby obliged, upon the application or complaint of the master or owner of such slave, or
his, her, or their order, or on the application or complaint of any
other person, who shall be anyways damnified or injured by such
slave, immediately such slave to punish, by whipping, cropping,
or branding on the cheek with the letter "R," or otherwise, not
extending to life, or so as to render such slave *unfit for labour*."

It was found, however, that the justices did not always pay
due regard to these last provisions, and that the owners of slaves
were shy of subjecting themselves to the loss of their property,
and that, therefore, many guilty slaves escaped punishment
through their masters neglecting to commit them to justice. It
was, therefore, enacted, that in case any slave should be condemned to death, his value should be appraised by the court,
and the amount due paid over at once to the owner, at the
public expense.

These are some of the provisions of the so-called Black Code
of Maryland, still in force in that state, and, till within a few
months, in force at the Capitol. I am told that these provisions
have fallen into disuse. Why, then, are they allowed to disgrace
the statute book? And yet more, why did the Southerners in
Congress always resist with success any attempt to modify the
code on the part of the Anti-slavery party?

This legislation dates, undoubtedly, from Colonial days, when
the whole of our English law was pervaded by a spirit of brutal

ferocity. It was adopted, however, by the United States Government as the law for slaves in the District of Columbia, in 1801, and was never repealed till the abolition of slavery. The following, however, are somewhat later commentaries on its practical working, supplied by the legislation of the Washington municipality. By an act passed in 1827, for the better discipline of the colored population, free blacks or mulattoes are prohibited from giving a party at their own house without permission, from gambling or being present at gambling, and from being at large without permission after ten o'clock at night, on penalty of being fined. All slaves found offending against these provisions "may be sentenced to receive any number of stripes, not exceeding thirty-nine, on his or her bare back."

By the same act, any Negro or mulatto found in Washington who shall not be able to establish his or her title to freedom shall be committed to jail as an absconding slave.

There is a still more recent act of slavery legislation. The act against assemblages of colored people was found insufficient, and the following was passed: "All secret or private meetings, or *assemblages whatsoever,* and all meetings for *religious worship,* beyond the hour of ten o'clock at night, of free negroes, mulattoes, or slaves, shall be, and they are hereby declared to be, unlawful," under a penalty of six dollars fine for each offense, if the offender was a free man of color, or of flogging on the bare back if the offender was a slave. By this law, therefore, passed only twenty-six years ago, eight years after we passed the Catholic Emancipation Bill, any female slave who attended a prayer-meeting of any kind after ten at night was sentenced to be flogged on her bare back, with any number of stripes not exceeding thirty-nine.

I need say no more. These are a few of the glimpses of slavery, which caught my eye, unwillingly, during my residence in slavedom. Thank God, that as far as Washington is concerned, I have been writing of the past!

England and America

BEFORE I part with Washington, it may be well to say something now, once and for all, as to the feeling entertained by Americans toward England. In the metropolis of the Federal States this feeling is exhibited in its most rational and least offensive form. There is no mob at Washington, no strong commercial interest, and more of cosmopolitan sentiment about its temporary residents than is found in other parts of the North. There is no doubt, strange as it may seem to us, that the feeling against England is strongest in those parts which are most akin to the mother country. In New England, and in Boston, there is far greater animosity expressed toward this country than in New York, or in the West; why this should be the case, I will speak of presently.

Let me state, first, without comment of my own, the case of America as against England, as I have often heard it given in substance by men of education, well acquainted with Europe. The sins, then, alleged against us, are rather of omission than commission. We are blamed, not so much for what we have done as for what we have left undone. The recognition of the Confederates as belligerents is believed, whether justly or not, to have inflicted incalculable injury on the North, by raising the hopes of the insurgents in foreign intervention, and thus giving the rebellion a tenacity of life which it could not otherwise have acquired. But still, candid Americans do not profess to believe that this step was deliberately taken by our Government with a view to injure the North. The unfortunate precipitation with which our proclamation of neutrality was issued four-and-twenty hours previous to Mr. Adams' expected arrival, created, not unreasonably, a good deal of annoyance. It is a pity that an act which, whether well advised or not, could not fail to be offensive to a nation preparing to fight for its existence, should have been done in such a form as to give unnecessary offense. Our subsequent proceedings with regard to privateers are admitted by temperate critics to be the logical and inevitable consequence of our having once admitted the belligerent character of the South, while, with regard to the *Trent* affair, it is owned, though reluctantly, that England was in the right, even if she exacted her full right to the extreme letter. It is not for what we did, but for the manner in which we did it, that we are condemned. To understand this feeling, it is necessary to appreciate the estimate which the Americans form themselves of the history of the insurrection.

When Secession first began (I am giving, let me repeat, the opinions I heard constantly expressed, without now endorsing them as my own), the country was utterly unprepared for war, disbelieved even in the possibility of war. The Government was still in the hands of men who supported Secession, passively in all cases, actively in most. The North was divided among itself, and even in the Free States a numerous and powerful party looked with distrust and dread on the incoming Administration. The fall of Fort Sumter startled us, so Northerners would say, out of a dream. We had had no serious foreign war for half a century; the very idea of a civil war was as strange to us as it is to you—a soldier was almost unknown in our streets: what troops, and ships, and ammunition we had, were chiefly in the hands of the insurgents. We had few generals or statesmen, and of those we had, we could not tell who was faithful to our cause. Under these circumstances we claim it as a credit that we did not despair of the commonwealth. When the nation once awoke to the consciousness that the existence of the Union was at stake, and the Capitol itself in danger, there was neither delay nor doubt. From every portion of the North volunteers flocked to the defense of the country; from every class and state, men left their homes, forsook their businesses, and risked their lives at the call of duty.

In four months' time we, who on the fall of Fort Sumter had not 12,000 available troops, had raised, without conscription or compulsion, 500,000 men in arms, undisciplined if you will, but still prepared to fight. Unused to war, and overconfident in the force of numbers, we pushed on to action hastily; fortune did not favor us. Partly from mismanagement, partly from ill-luck, still more from want of training, we endured a succession of repulses, inflicted in a manner most disheartening to the spirit of the people; still, not for one moment did the North despair—we were confident in our strength and in our cause. Throughout the long months of trying inaction, the country consented to bide its time; and even when things seemed darkest, there was no cry for submission or compromise; no voice heard except to demand resistance to the death. In the midst of our troubles we found ourselves in a position in which, whether from our own fault or not, we had to choose between a galling act of national humiliation, extorted from us by a foreign power, and the surrender of our hopes of restoring the Union. Here, again, there was no hesitation; we were ready to submit to anything, sacrifice anything, sooner than fail in maintaining the integrity of our country. This was the unanimous voice of the nation, and we acted on it; as we have begun, so we shall continue till the end. We may be mistaken in our views—the end we are fighting for may not be worth the struggle, but, right or wrong, the resolution of the North is a matter of which, as a nation, we are justly proud. When our trouble began, we reckoned confidently on the moral support, if not the actual aid, of England. Our resolution to stop the advance of slavery was the cause and occasion of the insurrection; we were fighting in such a war as England has waged many a time, in order to maintain our empire, to preserve our honor, and to establish free government. We believed that you, of our own race, and faith, and language, would judge us fairly, if no one else did, and would wish us God speed! We imagined that old grudges had been forgotten, on your side as well as ours, but we found ourselves mistaken. Not only did your Government make haste to disavow any appearance of sympathy with our cause, by recognizing the South as belligerents with unwonted promptitude, but the people of England repudiated at once all fellowship with our cause. Every disaster of ours was magnified by your press, every success was derided, every effort refused acknowledgment; we were ridiculed in your public prints, treated as degenerate, held up by you to the contempt and laughter of the Old World, and offered counsels of submission, which you yourselves would have regarded as an insult. It was not only by the press of England that we were so treated: your states-men, and writers, and politicians openly prognosticated the downfall of our country, and rejoiced in the prospect of our dismemberment. In your society sympathy was with the South from the beginning, and even the few public men and the few organs of popular opinion that advocated our cause, did so rather on abstract principles than from any avowed sympathy with a great people fighting in a cause which is great and noble. We have been taught a bitter lesson. It is by ourselves alone, against the wishes, if not in spite of the efforts, of England, that the Union will have to be saved.

How much in this estimate there is that is false and unreasonable, I need not dwell on. Unfortunately it is only too moderate an expression of the condition of American feeling at the present day, with regard to England. It is not, however, so unnatural a one as it may seem on this side the Atlantic. In the first place, the Americans, from their isolation, immensely overestimate the relative importance of their own affairs. That American politics are only one, and not the chief, of the many influences that operate on our Government and people, is a fact they can hardly realize. The general ignorance of Englishmen about American affairs, they believe to be either affectation or else willful blindness. If you try to explain to them that English feeling has been, not unreasonably, outraged by the language of the *New York Herald*, and by the series of slights, to use the mildest term, offered us by successive Federal Governments, they answer you, with truth, that the *New York Herald* does not represent American feeling, and that the slights offered to England were, invariably, the doing of Southern statesmen, for whom the North cannot justly be held responsible. But when you proceed to urge that it is not reasonable to expect the English nation should understand these explanations instinctively, or should appreciate the difference between different journals and conflicting parties, they obviously cannot believe that Englishmen are, as a class, unacquainted with the real working or private history of American politics. They look upon the popular opinions of England with regard to America as if they were those of a community thoroughly conversant with American affairs, and caring for, or thinking of, little else. In fact, both in England and America, the extreme similarity between the two nations is, paradoxical as it may seem, the cause why they understand each other so little. With regard to a foreign nation, they would both make great allowances for different standards of thought and feeling. But two people so like each other can make little allowance for the points of unlikeness. When the Scotch laird thanked God that his French guests had left the room, "because they were no better than the brute beasts of the field, and never took a drop more than they wanted," he qualified the condemnation by the remark that, "perhaps, as Frenchmen, they knew no better." Had they belonged to an English-speaking nation, the excuse would not have been proffered so readily.

It is difficult also for Englishmen to appreciate the almost morbid anxiety which Americans feel for the judgment of England. The invariable question which every American asks you, before you have talked to him ten minutes, "How do you like the country?" is utterly unlike in tone to the manner in which a Frenchman might ask you a similar question, with a supreme conviction that it was morally impossible you should *not* like France; or to the mode with which an Englishman would ask it, with absolute indifference whether you liked England or not. The truth is—though I am afraid my Northern friends will dispute the truth of my remark—England is the real arbiter of opinion to whom educated America looks up. The affectation so common there of being like the French, is an affectation only. They speak less French, they read less French, they know less about France, than we do ourselves. More I cannot say. Their tone of thought is English, their literature is English, and their history is English also. Thus it is that even in spite of their avowed professions, the good opinion of England is a matter of so keen an interest to them. And thus it is, also, that they have felt so bitterly the coldness, to say the least, of English opinion on their behalf. "We could stand," I remember reading in the *New York Tribune*, "the railing, abuse, and systematic depreciation of the British journals. It is their affectation of candour, of impartiality, of sublime exaltation above such paltry matters as American discussions, that aggravates us. Such trifles are all remembered over here, and will, in due time, be requited." There is, I fear, too much truth in this outburst of hostility. In private life, as far as my experience goes, men resent real personal injuries far less bitterly than they do ill-natured speeches; and what is true of individuals, is true of nations also.

Moreover, this utterance of the *Tribune* confirms the fact, to which I have before alluded, that the greatest bitterness toward England is entertained by the Republican party. The abstract and somewhat sentimental hostility to slavery, which had been the fashion in England ever since the time of West Indian emancipation, and which rose to a climax in the days of the *Uncle Tom* mania, was appreciated in the North at more than its real value. The moral opinion of England had always been the great argument on which the Abolitionists based their cause, as against their own countrymen. In a war wherein slavery was at issue, they had always believed that they should have the support of England, and had expressed their belief constantly and confidently. It was a cruel disappointment to them to find that these assertions were ungrounded, and that the great patron of the anti-slavery cause, whose example they had always quoted, and whose opinion they had taught others to reverence, stood aloof from them when sentiment had to be exchanged for action; and the reaction of feeling among this party was proportionate to the extent of their previous pro-English sympathies. I recollect a lady, who was a very strong Abolitionist, telling me that just before the Secession of South Carolina, she was talking to Mrs. Jefferson Davis about the absurdity of the Secessionist scheme. On remarking that the Confederacy could have no hopes of support from England, on account of our known hostility to slavery, Mrs. Davis answered—"My dear Mrs.——, you don't know England as well as I do. She dislikes slavery very much, but she loves cotton a great deal more, and before six months are over, we shall have all England sympathizing with our cause." And my friend concluded by saying, "I never felt so much sorrow in my life as when I found that I was wrong and Mrs. Davis right." I quote this instance as illustrative of a state of feeling which is almost universal in the Abolitionist party; and I hardly think it is so monstrous as our English critics appear to assume, that men like Ward Beecher and Wendell Phillips should surpass other American orators in the vehemence of their feeling against England.

How far the existing and, I fear, increasing sentiment of hostility which the tone of England has, reasonably or not, produced, will prove a lasting one, is very hard to judge. For my own part, I believe and hope that the very susceptibility to the blame or depreciation of England, which has created such bitterness of feeling amongst Americans, will also render them, perhaps, unreasonably susceptible to any reaction of feeling on the part of the mother country; and if, at last, England begins to admit, what I feel more and more convinced is the truth, that amidst much exaggeration and absurdity, the struggle between the North and South is a grand cause grandly fought for, then there will be a return of the same kindly feeling as was exhibited, not three years ago, when the Prince of Wales visited America.

Political Speculations

THE OUTLOOK for the future of America occupies far more attention amongst foreign observers than it does at home. The crew of a vessel laboring beneath a hurricane are not likely to devote much attention to the consideration of what they are to do when they get safely into harbor; and so, in like manner, in the midst of this insurrection there is little time or care to think of anything but how it can be suppressed. After all, what is to be done, or rather what is to happen hereafter, is still a matter of abstract speculation; and the Americans, as a people, have an Anglo-Saxon distaste and incapacity for abstract speculation of any kind. The men by whom the country is ruled and represented are, as a body, shrewd, self-made men, with very little appreciation for the philosophy of government. Though the average culture of America is probably higher than that of any country in the world, yet, at the same time, any very high degree of intellectual culture is uncommon. There are no public men here of the class of Mill, Gladstone, or Lord Stanley; and if there were, their influence on the country would be very limited. It is a land of workers, not of thinkers.

Still, making all allowance for this, and for a natural reluctance to face the belief that the Union is not in itself a remedy for every evil, it seemed strange to me to observe how little thought there appeared to be in the public mind about the inevitable future. The future, too, was not only inevitable, but appeared so near at hand. The prevalent belief at this time was that the South was at its last gasp. All the plans of the Government, during the spring of 1862 (and in saying this I am not expressing merely a private opinion, but an official conviction), were based upon the idea, that by the end of June, at the very latest, the insurrection would be so far suppressed as to present no further military dangers. At this time, a stop had been put to further enlistment, contracts for army supplies were curtailed, and sufficient funds had been provided to meet the current military expenditure only for some ten weeks more. Within three months it was expected that the Federal Government would have to reorganize its rule over the revolted States; and yet neither Government, nor Congress, nor people appeared to have any definite idea or prospect of how that reorganization was to be effected. The truth is, the country was drifting toward peace just as it drifted toward war. In order to understand the history of the crisis through which America was passing, it may be well to say something here of the political speculations which were rife at the period when the "Army of the Potomac" had set forth in its full pride and strength, and when the suppression of the insurrection was believed to be imminent.

The only political question toward which public attention had been directed, so far as to form any definite ideas regarding it, was that of the Negro. The subject, indeed, was an unwelcome one, but still it forced itself upon the public mind. Almost every day, amongst the petitions presented to Congress at this period, there was a request, from somebody or other, begging the House to leave the Negro alone, and attend to business. There was something almost pitiable in the painful anxiety expressed by newspapers, and politicians, and the leaders of private society, to ignore the question of the everlasting Negro. Abolitionists were unpopular, because they kept on thrusting the wrongs of the Negro upon unwilling ears; pro-slavery men were unpopular, because they kept dinning the rights of Negro ownership on an unsympathetic public; and the men who were popular were the prophets of the "Seward stamp," who spoke pleasant things, and who recommended the people to wait upon Providence (or, in stock phrase, "not to interfere with its manifest interposition") for the ultimate solution of the Negro question. Still, the question cropped up at every moment. Runaway slaves came constantly into the Federal lines; large districts were deserted by their owners as the Northern armies advanced; and the plantations which could not be destroyed, together with the slaves who could not be removed, were left to the charge and embarrassment of the United States Government. "What shall we do with them?" was the question that everybody in the North was asking unwillingly, and to which nobody could find an answer. Meanwhile, it was growing daily clearer, that beyond the slavery question—difficult enough in itself—there lay the Negro question, almost more difficult to grapple with.

I am no great believer in Providence doing for anybody what he ought to do himself; but still I think that, without much decided action on the part of the Government, there was, in the event of Northern success, a necessary solution to the mere slavery question. Either (and this was the view of the most farsighted American politicians I met with) the insurrection would be speedily and hopelessly crushed, or else it would hold out for some time longer, with varying success. In the latter case, there would be an end to slavery at once—a rough and sharp one. The vindictiveness of the North would be roused, revolutionary measures would be required, and the first and chief of these would be compulsory emancipation. The result, I need not say, has justified these anticipations. In the former event, the decline of slavery would be less rapid, but not less certain. Hitherto, slavery had been the badge and cry of the great ruling political faction in the country. Any man who wanted power, and office, and success in public life, was obliged to put on slavery colors. With the election of President Lincoln the supremacy of this party was broken, and anti-slavery views became the political creed of the winning side, just as pro-slavery views had been formerly. As a political party, the slave-faction had lost its power, and it was the consciousness of this fact which impelled them to Secession. Still, if they had abided by Constitutional measures, this party would always have possessed strength, from the fear that, if driven to extremities, the South might secede, and, under the influence of this fear, might possibly have recovered the reins of Government. Now, supposing the insurrection to be crushed, they will have played their last card, and failed lamentably. Henceforth there will be no terror for the North in the threat of Secession. The South will not fight again a battle that has been fought and lost, and the slaveholders will be a small and declining faction in the states. Every ambitious politician, and every office-seeker who wants patronage, will profess anti-slavery views. With a free Government, such as the American, the influence of public opinion is overwhelming; and with the tide of public opinion set dead against slavery, state after state will throw off the degradation attached to the institution, and the system will fall to pieces by its own adherent weakness.

The objection to this optimist view is, that it does not take into account the extraordinary social influence of slavery. As long as slavery exists in a state, the pride of race makes the maintenance of the institution popular, even with the very classes who suffer most from its inevitable consequences. Not one white man, perhaps, in ten or twenty, even in the most populous of the Slave States, owns Negro property; but then, every non-slaveowner looks forward to the possibility of enrolling himself amidst the privileged class. Moreover, the meanest and poorest of white citizens in a Slave State belongs to the ruling caste. He is the recognized superior of the whole colored population, and the more wretched his own condition is, the more highly he values the one dignity belonging to him, as a white man, in a slave country. Undoubtedly, the popular sentiment, even in the most loyal Slave States, was bitterly averse to any measure which could place the Negro on an equality with the white man. Thus in Kentucky—the staunchest of the Border Slave States, and in which, within the last ten years, the white population has increased in a ratio of more than three to one to the slave—the State Legislature, in answer to the President's proposal of a scheme for voluntary and compensated emancipation, passed a resolution, "That any person who advocates the doctrine of the abolition or emancipation of slavery in the State of Kentucky, either directly or indirectly, or who sympathizes with the same, shall be disfranchised for life, and requested to leave the State within ten days." Happily, the majority of forty-eight to twenty-nine, by which this resolution was passed, was not sufficient to make it valid; but the fact shows the strength of the anti-Abolition sentiment. Still, in spite of this and many similar indications, I think it probable that the view quoted above (which I know to be that of leading American statesmen) is substantially correct, and that, as a system, slavery is doomed, supposing always the insurrection to be finally suppressed.

But when slavery is abolished, what is to become of the slaves? There are three solutions possible for the Negro question: Amalgamation with the white race, emigration or enforced colonization, or settlement in the states where they are stationed at present, as a free population of distinct race. The first of these solutions is, at first sight, the obvious one to a philosopher. Unfortunately, instincts of race are too powerful to admit of its adoption. It is hard for a European to quite appreciate the intensity of American feeling about color; but still, when an American asks you the usual question, whether you would like your sister to marry a Negro. I own that candor would force most Englishmen to answer in the negative. A black brother can be tolerated, but a black brother-in-law is an idea not pleasant to the Anglo-Saxon mind. And if you plead guilty to this weakness in a hypothetical case, it is not difficult to understand the aversion with which, in real life, a proud hard race, like the American, regards the notion of any infusion of black blood in their veins. That a Negro should ever sit in Congress, is to the Yankee intellect a sort of *reductio ad absurdum*—a moral anomaly, from the contemplation of which even the *New York Tribune* shrinks reluctantly. Moreover, even supposing this aversion to be removed, there seemed to be physiological objections to any amalgamation of the races. Those persons who have studied the subject most profoundly all agree that the mixed race is not a healthy one. The intellectual capacity of the mulatto is very great, but his physical power is inferior to that of the pure white or black man; and with each successive intermixture, the race becomes feebler and, as a rule, dies out with scrofulous diseases. Physiology is a science which has been so little studied in America, and the whole subject of amalgamation has been obscured by such a variety of conflicting prejudices, that it would be unsafe to attach implicit confidence to the above assertions. As a practical matter, however, it is sufficient to say that this belief as to the deterioration of the mixed race is universally entertained in the North, and thus any statesman dealing with the Negro question has to assume this doctrine as an acknowledged truth.

Colonization on a large scale presents enormous practical difficulties in execution. The expense of transporting or providing for four millions of people is a gigantic task, which it must take scores of years for America to be in a position to undertake. Moreover, the Negroes, like most nations whose intellectual faculties are but imperfectly developed, have strong local attachments, and have absolutely no desire to quit the home of their birth, cruel as that home may have proved to them. There remains, then, as the sole alternative, the settlement of the black race, in the existing Slave States, as a free population. The political difficulties, of which the advocates of slavery talk so much, do not seem to me insuperable. There is no reason why, after emancipation, the several states should extend the franchise to the colored population; and I fear there is little hope that the blacks would agitate to obtain political rights for themselves. With the exception of three or four of the Eastern States, colored citizens have not the right of voting in any of the Northern States; and except as a matter of abstract justice and logical consistency, about which the Americans trouble themselves very little, the free Negro might as well remain disfranchised for the present. The difficulty is a social one. In the Northern Hemisphere, the Negro is an exotic, and does not flourish except under an artificial system. Now, though nobody is more adverse to slavery than I am, the logic of figures compels me to admit that, from the rapid increase of population in the Slave States, the slaves must, on the whole, have been kept in physical comfort. An amount of work was abstracted from them, which no inducement but force would urge them to undergo; and in return for this, they were, as animals, treated with consideration. Remove the necessity of bondage, and, in a northern climate, where his energies are deadened, the Negro will not, as a rule, work enough to keep him in more than bare existence. I have my own doubts about the truth of our received English doctrines as to the dignity of labor, and as to work being the one essential end and aim of human existence. It seems to me possible that, even in this world, Lazarus, when the sun shone upon his rags and sores, and the crumbs thrown out to him were sufficient for the day, may have been as well off as Dives, with his hardly earned riches. Still, as a matter of fact, one cannot doubt that a people to whom work is naturally distasteful, cannot stand a chance, on the same soil and under the same conditions, with a race which works for the sake of work itself, as well as for gain. Supposing emancipation take place, the stigma to be removed from labor, and free white laborers to pour as they would into the Slave States, black labor would not, I think, stand the competition, and would gradually be driven out of the field. The probability seems to me that, in the event of Abolition, the fate of the American Negroes will not be unlike that of the Indians. A portion will move gradually further south, till they reach a climate where white labor cannot compete successfully with their own. Those left in the existing Slave States will slowly die out, by a diminution of their prolific powers, and will disappear with more or less of suffering. It seems as though, by some inscrutable law of Nature, the white man and the black cannot live and work together, on equal terms, on the same soil. Where the white man comes, the black man has disappeared hitherto, and I fear that America is not likely to prove an exception to the rule.

The difficulties of the problem are indeed fearful, and I own that the Abolitionist solution is the simplest if not the most philosophical. The Negro question—they say virtually, if not avowedly—is one with which we have nothing as yet to do. When it comes upon us, we must do our best to alleviate the working of natural laws, over which we have no control. Meanwhile, for the sake of any ulterior consideration, we have no right to maintain a system which is an outrage on the laws of God and man. The Negro question we must leave to Providence, but the slavery question is one we can deal with, and are bound to deal with, for ourselves. And this, like all simple solutions, commends itself to the plain popular instinct.

The never-ending Negro question is only the most pressing, perhaps not the most difficult, of those the country has to deal with. Throughout almost all English speculations on American affairs, there runs a constant assumption that the United States Government resembles our Old World Governments, and possesses unlimited powers of action, if only it chooses to exert them. Now the truth is that, by the very nature of its Constitution, the powers of the Government are so strictly defined that in all cases not provided for by the express letter of the law it has no authorized means of action. Thus in Europe, the refusal of the Federal Government to recognize formally the fact that the Confederates were belligerents appeared dictated by a childish reluctance to acknowledge an unwelcome truth. In reality, it was constitutionally impossible for the North to admit the belligerent character of the South. The Federal Government has power by the Constitution to suppress an insurrection in the supposed interest of the insurgent state—it has no power whatever to make war upon a state. In order to keep within the Constitution, it was essential for the Federal Government to assume the theory that the insurgent states still form part of the Union. Yet the adoption of this theory involves inconceivable difficulties in practice. If the states are still within the Union, they must be dealt with by the laws of the Constitution. Thus, to quote one simple instance, the insurgents must be tried in their own state, by a jury taken from the state; and no Southern jury would ever convict an insurgent of treason. Again, all taxes, by the Constitution, must be uniformly imposed on all the states. It would be therefore impossible, if the war was over, to tax the insurgent states, so as to make them bear the expenses of the war. These are no theoretical difficulties, but practical and pressing ones. During the height of the war, a cavalry officer with whom I was acquainted made an expedition into Virginia. He was in extreme want of horses to mount his men, and seized fifteen horses belonging to notorious rebels; but on reporting the fact, he received orders from headquarters to restore the horses at once, as there was no constitutional authority for seizing the property of insurgents; and yet at this time the Federal Government was purchasing horses right and left, at prices ranging from two hundred dollars and upward. This scrupulous regard for the theory of the Constitution may seem inconsistent with the practical character of the American mind; but, in fact, the adherence to the letter of the Constitution is a matter of practical rather than abstract interest. If the broad principle is once admitted that the welfare of the Commonwealth overrides all state interests and justifies any stretch of power, then the doctrine of state rights is virtually defunct in the North as well as in the South—in the Slave States of the Union as well as in the Slave States of the Confederacy. The Border Slave States, therefore, fight against any recognition of this doctrine, which would be fatal to the existence of slavery; and even the Free States of the North are unwilling to do anything, or permit anything to be done, which may involve the loss of their separate independence. Added to all this, the whole nation has been taught, so long and so sedulously, that the Constitution is the great bulwark of their liberties—the grandest triumph of legislative power, that they cannot yet, and dare not yet, realize the truth, that this Constitution has been tried and found wanting.

American Society

I MAY say without vanity that during my sojourn in the States I had considerable advantages in entering society. I was amply provided with letters of introduction; I came at a time when foreign travelers were rare; and also, from an impression that my sympathies were more Northern than those of the bulk of my fellow countrymen, I was received with, perhaps, undeserved kindness. Still, my great passport to society consisted in the fact that I was an Englishman. That this should have been so is a fact which throws a good deal of light on American Society.

An American once said to me: "I always envy you to whom England is a home; but, then, I think you ought to envy us for our feelings when we visit England. To you, after all, it is only a country, more or less interesting, where you make and spend your money: to us it is a sort of enchanted land, where everything that is old to you is new to us. You look upon England as a husband looks on his wife; we see her as a lover sees his mistress." The words were spoken half-jestingly, but there was still a good deal of truth in them. The average of educated Americans know as much about English literature, and more, perhaps, about English history, than the average of educated Englishmen. Their language, their history, their literature are those of England. There are few who cannot remember relatives that have come from the Old Country—who do not know of some town or village in the United Kingdom in which they have something of a personal interest. A visit to Europe and, above all, to England, is the great dream of all Americans who have not crossed the Atlantic—the holiday-time, as it were, of life to those who have performed the journey. I always found there was no subject on which Americans talked so willingly as about the recollections of their foreign travels. No doubt this sentimental feeling about England grows weaker with each succeeding generation, and, like all sentimental feelings, it gives place to the action of interests and passions. I often fancied that those Americans who entertained the feeling most strongly were the most hostile to England. Indeed, my chief fear of a war with America arises from the fact that Americans care too much, not too little, about England. The existence, however, of this national feeling is strong enough to create a very kindly sentiment toward individual Englishmen; and probably there is no country in the world where an English traveler meets with so much kindness and so much cordiality, in virtue of his nationality, as he does in America.

Certainly, I found it so in my own case. I know that other English travelers tell a different story. Fellow countrymen of mine have related anecdotes to me of rude speeches and offensive remarks made to them purposely in the States, because they were Englishmen. I suspect, in most of such instances, the narrators were to blame. If you are offended because a waiter offers to shake hands with you, or a barkeeper asks you to drink with him, or a laboring-man speaks to you without your speaking first to him—well, you had better not travel in America; but if you are willing to take people as you find them, you will get along very pleasantly. Speaking for myself, I can say that, during all my travels, I had never once an offensive or impolite remark made to me. The only occasion on which I ever met with anything like impoliteness was in the smoking-room of a fashionable hotel in New York. A number of old gentlemen sitting round the fire were talking politics and abusing England; I was smoking silently, and it struck me they were talking to me. Now, I am by no means an enthusiastic believer in our English doctrine that whatever England does is right; and, also, I made a rule to be a listener to, not a partaker in, political discussions. But still there is a limit to patience, at any rate to my patience; and at some remark about the mingled folly and knavery of English policy, I spoke out strongly and, I fear, somewhat rudely. At once I was answered by a polite expression of sincere regret that anything should have been said in my presence that could have given offense; and, thereupon, the subject was dropped at once. The incident was trivial in the extreme, and the only reason why I remember it is because it was the sole instance of anything approaching incivility I met with in the States.

To a stranger, there is something wonderfully pleasant about the first blush of American Society: the manners of your hosts appear to an Englishman so frank and cordial; people seem so glad to see you, and so anxious to make you feel at home. And I believe that the appearance is not assumed. Life, hitherto, has flowed very easily for the American people. The country is so large, that there is room for all and to spare; the battle of life is not an arduous one, compared to what it is in older countries. The morbid dread of poverty, which is the curse of English middle-class existence, is almost unknown in the New World. If the worst comes to the worst, and an American is ruined, the world lies open to him, and in a new state he can start afresh, with as fair prospects as when he set out in life. The desire to provide for one's children, and to secure them a similar position in life to that which the parent occupies himself, is almost unknown. Public opinion does not require the father of a family to do more than give his children a good education. As a rule, the daughters can always marry, and the sons can make their own way. Equal division of property amongst the children of a family is enforced by custom, though not by law. In the New England States, it has become very common for any wealthy citizen to leave a considerable sum toward some public object; and anyone who fails to comply with this custom is hardly considered to have acted correctly. The result of this state of things is that saving is very uncommon amongst the middle classes in America. Everybody, as a rule, spends the full amount of his income, and, in consequence, there is much greater luxury in Northern households than would be seen in English families of the same amount of wealth. Hospitality, therefore, is given very readily, and the wheels of life run more easily than they do with us. I was struck constantly with the extreme good nature of the Americans in their private and social relations. I attribute it, not so much to the national character—which, owing to the climate, is a somewhat irritable one—but to the comparative absence of the sordid cares and petty considerations which the fierceness of our struggle for existence, and the exorbitant value attached by us to the respectability of wealth, give rise to perpetually in a densely-peopled country like our own.

Paradoxical as the statement may seem, I think I have never known a country where money was less valued than in America. "The worship of the almighty dollar," which we are so apt to consider a characteristic of the Americans, cannot justly be charged to them in the sense in which we understand the phrase. The absence of all social distinctions, and the fact that there are no established positions to which birth, and rank, and station give an acknowledged entrance, render wealth the chief standard of distinction. In consequence, the natural ambition of every American is to acquire wealth, and thus distinguish himself in the only career which is practically open to the vast majority. Anybody who has known anything of Quakers will understand the working of the causes that I have attempted to describe. There is no body of men more liberal than the Society of Friends, and yet there is none more eager in the pursuit of money-making. So it is with the Yankee race. Money-making is the chief object of the nation; but they value the possession of the "almighty dollar" rather as a proof of success in life than as an end of existence. The mere ownership of wealth is less valued there than with us. The man who has made his own money is infinitely more respected than the man who has inherited it. Millionaires are rare in the second generation; and the bare fact of wealth gives a man fewer advantages in the North than in any Old World country.

I doubt, too, whether the accusation of extravagance, which is brought so frequently against the Northerners, is a just one. Money is spent freely, just as it is made; but, with the exception of New York, I was never in any American city where the style of living could compare for extravagance with that of the wealthy classes in the Old World. Americans in Europe are not, in this respect, fair specimens of their nation. They come over here for a holiday, and their expenditure is regulated on a holiday scale. But at home, the mode of living is in most respects remarkably simple. This is due, partly to the extreme difficulty of getting servants, and the impossibility of keeping a large household of domestics, but still more, I think, to a certain inherent simplicity of taste. Hours are much earlier than with us—equipages are few in number; and dwelling-houses, though eminently comfortable, very seldom possess any claim to splendor or magnificence. In the article of dress, and also in the dainties of the table, Americans will go to an expense that English families of the same rank in life never think of indulging in. In New York, especially, the ladies must spend what we should consider an extravagant amount on Parisian toilettes. I hardly ever remember to have been present at a dinner party in America where champagne was not distributed almost as plentifully as malt liquor would be with us; but in other respects, there is but little ostentatious expense visible to a stranger.

In a moral as opposed to a material point of view, the most striking feature about American Society is its uniformity. Everybody, as a rule, holds the same opinions about everything, and expresses his views, more or less, in the same language. These views are often correct, almost invariably intelligent and creditable to the holders. But still, even at the risk of hearing paradoxes defended, you cannot help wishing, at times, for a little more of originality. I believe that this monotony in the tone of American talk and opinion arises from the universal diffusion of education. Everybody is educated up to a certain point, and very few are educated above it. They have all learnt the same lessons under the same teachers, and, in consequence, share the same sentiments to a degree which it is difficult to an Englishman to appreciate beforehand. This monotony is infinitely more striking in the men than in the women. Ninety-nine American lads in a hundred go through exactly the same system of training. Up to eighteen or nineteen, they are carefully, if not very deeply, grounded in all the branches of a good ordinary English education. Then they go into business, and from that time their intellectual self-culture ceases. Unless they happen to travel, they have very little time for reading anything except the newspapers. The women pursue their education even after marriage, and are in consequence better read and more intellectual in their tastes than English ladies. In the long run, however, the national tone of mind is always derived from the male sex, and therefore the prevalent tone of America is not that of a highly-educated society. I do not mean to say, for one moment, that there are not hundreds and thousands of men of really first-class education in the Northern States. On the contrary, some of the most thoroughly educated men it has been my lot to meet with have been Americans. I am speaking of the mass, not of individuals. This opinion of mine, if it is correct, explains a fact which otherwise would seem discouraging: I mean the small share taken by educated men—in our sense of the word—in American politics. The truth is that if America were governed to any great extent by politicians of classical education, the country would not be fairly represented by its rulers. It is not the case that the fact of a gentleman having received a refined culture is any disqualification to him in the eyes of the constituencies. On the other hand, it is a very small recommendation. I do not deny that this is, in itself, an evil; but the true nature of the evil is not that men of education are disqualified from entering a political career in America, but that they form so small a class that they possess no political influence. Just in the same way, there is no doubt that, relative to the period, there were more highly educated men in the Union half a century ago than there are now. The early settlers in any new country bring with them a higher degree of individual culture than they can impart to their children. In the same ratio, however, that the education of the individual decreases, the average education of the mass increases, and, on the whole, the general tone of the nation gains in consequence. My friend Mr. Holmes once said to me: "We should find it very hard to match five thousand American gentlemen with five thousand English; but we could match five million ordinary Americans against the same number of your countrymen, without fear of the result."

This explanation I believe to be the correct one with regard to the intellectual development of America.

The truth is, the great mistake that we English make in judging of America is the assumption that the New World ought to be the reproduction of the Old Country. We expect our social system, our hierarchy of castes and rank, our forms of thought and feeling, to be repeated amongst a people growing up under conditions totally different from that in which we have been trained for hundreds of generations. Every departure from our own standard we consider to indicate moral degeneracy, while in reality it is only a symptom of development. No one who has lived in America can avoid coming to the conclusion that the Anglo-Saxon frame is gradually modifying itself to a form suited to the new conditions of climate and temperature under which it is called on to exist. What is true in the physical is true also in the moral world. By degrees, the imported civilization and culture of the Old World are developing themselves into new forms and aspects. What will be the ultimate social system of America it is impossible to say. Never yet in history has a nation grown up under circumstances where all men have started equal, and where want and poverty have been practically unknown. That the product of these conditions will be a remarkable one, we are beginning to see already. I recollect a common Irishwoman I once traveled alongside of in the States, saying to me, when talking about her experience of her new home, "This is a blessed country, sir; I think God made it for the poor." And I have often fancied that this saying might be the clue to the future history of America.

I have been asked frequently, whether I should like to live in America—and to this question my answer has always been that that depends entirely upon circumstances. Men of highly educated tastes, used to the social pleasures of the Old World, will not find their wants gratified as easily and as fully in a new state of society as in an old. In fact, in plain English, if your tastes and your habits are those of men whose income is counted by hundreds, you had better stop where you are. But the man who has his living to earn is better off, in almost every respect, in America than he is in England. The very circumstances that render the United States unattractive as a residence for the man of wealth and refinement are a positive boon to those who possess neither of the attributes; and I am afraid that in this world the latter class is larger and more important than the former.

These reflections on American Society would be imperfect if I said nothing as to the great charm which surrounds all family relations in the North. Compared with Europe, domestic scandals are unknown; and between parents and their grown-up children, there exists a degree of familiarity and intimacy which one seldom witnesses in this country. If family life is the foundation of all permanent good in the social system, then, in spite of its present defects and shortcomings, the outlook for the American society of the future is a very bright one.

Notes of the War

If I had ever professed to be an amateur military critic, my experience in America would have disgusted me with the task. I used to hear and read so much of profound military speculations from men who knew even less about the science of war than I did myself, that I got almost to disbelieve in the existence of such an art at all. I plead guilty to a heretical belief that even the recognized professors of the science talk about a basis of operations, a concentrated movement, a system of strategy, in order to invest themselves with an uncalled-for appearance of profundity. I remember Mr. Hawthorne once remarked to me about a certain metaphysical philosopher, that he never knew a man who had such a talent for confusing a simple question, and I confess that this talent seems to me to be largely developed amongst military critics. My own impression is, that in the American war there was very little possibility for scientific operations of any kind; and that if there was such a possibility, it certainly was not improved. However, right or wrong, I have no intention of filling my pages with descriptions of the military campaign. When I was in Italy two years ago, during the Garibaldian war, of all the facts and incidents connected with it, the one which brought the war nearest home to my mind was a scene I once witnessed in the back streets of Naples. It was at the time when the siege of Capua was going on, and a decisive battle was hourly expected. I had been hunting up and down the low purlieus of Naples, to look after a refugee who was keeping out of sight, and to whom I was anxious to deliver a letter. I was passing up the narrow squalid staircase of one of the deserted palaces, where hundreds of poor families appear to burrow in one common wretchedness. I had not succeeded in finding the object of my search, and was making my way out as rapidly as I could, when an old woman rushed out, and, in the rapid Neapolitan patois, besought me to tell her, for the love of God and of the Holy Virgin, whether it was true that there had been a battle. I tried to make her understand, in the best Neapolitan that I could muster up, that for twenty-four hours at least there was no prospect of a fight. *"Graz' a Dio!"* was her ejaculation, repeated many times; and then, turning to me, she said, in explanation, *"C'e il figlio unico nell' armata, Lei mi scusi;"** and then she crouched down again upon the ground, praying and telling her beads. And I own that whenever I think of the Italian war, I think also of the widowed mother, praying in that gloomy, squalid alley for her only son.

So, what little I have recorded of this American campaign are some few incidentals in its course which came under my own notice. These, with the reflections that at the time they forced upon me, are the sole contributions that I shall give to the military history of the war.

While at Washington, from the windows of my lodgings, I looked out upon the mile-long Pennsylvania Avenue, leading from the broad Potomac river, by the marble palace of the Presidents, up to the snow-white Capitol, and almost every hour of the day I was disturbed while writing by the sound of some military band, as regiment after regiment passed, marching southward. The Germans have brought with them into their new fatherland the instinct of instrumental music, and the bands are fine ones, above the average of those of a French or English line regiment. The tunes were mostly those well known to us across the water—"Cheer, Boys, Cheer," the "Red, White, and Blue," and "Dixie's Land," being the favorites. For the war had brought out hitherto no war-inspired melody, and the quaint, half-grotesque, half passion-stirring air of "John Brown's body lies a mould'ring in the grave," was still under McClellan's interdict.

---

* "My only son is in the army. Your Excellency will pardon me."

But yet, be the tunes what they may, the drums and fifes and trumpets rouse the same heart-beatings as in the Old World, and teach the same lessons of glory and ambition and martial pride. Can this teaching fail to work? is the question that I asked myself daily, as yet without an answer.

Surely no nation in the world has gone through such a baptism of war as the people of the United States underwent in one short year's time. With the men of the Revolution the memories of the revolutionary wars had died out. Two generations had passed away to whom war was little more than a name. The Mexican campaign was rather a military demonstration than an actual war, and the sixteen years which had elapsed since its termination form a long period in the life of a nation whose existence has not completed its first century. Twenty months ago there were not more than 12,000 soldiers in a country of 31,000,000. A soldier was as rare an object throughout America as in one of our country hamlets. I recollect a Northern lady telling me that, till within a year before, she could not recall the name of a single person whom she had ever known in the army, and that now she had sixty friends and relatives who were serving in the war; and her case was by no means an uncommon one. Once in four years, on the fourth of March, two or three thousand troops were collected in Washington to add to the pomp of the Presidential inauguration; and this was the one military pageant the country had to boast of. Almost in a day this state of things passed away. Our English critics were so fond of repeating what the North could not do—how it could not fight, nor raise money, nor conquer the South—that they omitted to mention what the North *had* done. There was no need to go farther than my windows at Washington to see the immensity of the war. It was curious to me to watch the troops as they came marching past. Whether they were regulars or volunteers, it was hard for the unprofessional critic to discern; for all were clad alike, in the same dull, gray-blue overcoats, and most of the few regular regiments were filled with such raw recruits that the difference between volunteer and regular was not a marked one. Of course it was easy enough to pick faults in the aspects of such troops. As each regiment marched, or rather waded, through the dense slush and mud which covered the roads, you could observe many inaccuracies of military attire. One man would have his trousers rolled up almost to his knees; another would wear them tucked inside his boots; and a third would appear with one leg of his trousers hanging down, and the other gathered tightly up. It was not infrequent, too, to see an officer with his epaulettes sewed on to a common plain frock-coat. Then there was a slouching gait about the men, not soldier-like to English eyes. They used to turn their heads round when on parade, with an indifference to rule which would drive an old drill sergeant out of his senses. There was an absence, also, of precision in the march. The men kept in step; but I always was at a loss to discover how they ever managed to do so. The system of march, it is true, was copied rather from the French than the English or Austrian fashion; but still it was something very different from the orderly disorder of a Zouave march. That all these, and a score of similar irregularities, are faults, no one—an American least of all—would deny. But there are two sides to the picture.

One thing is certain, that there is no physical degeneracy about a race which could produce such regiments as those which formed the army of the Potomac. Men of high stature and burly frames were rare, except in the Kentucky troops; but, on the other hand, small, stunted men were almost unknown. I have seen the armies of most European countries; and I have no hesitation in saying that, as far as the average raw material of the rank and file is concerned, the American army is the finest. The officers are, undoubtedly, the weak point of the system. They have not the military air, the self-possession which long habit of command alone can give; while the footing of equality on which they inevitably stand with the volunteer privates, deprives them of the esprit de corps belonging to a ruling class. Still they are active, energetic, and constantly with their troops. Wonderfully well equipped too, at this period of the war, were both officers and men. Their clothing was substantial and fitted easily, their arms were good, and the military arrangements were as perfect as money alone could make them. It was remarkable to me how rapidly the new recruits fell into the habits of military service. I have seen a Pennsylvanian regiment, raised chiefly from the mechanics of Philadelphia, which, six weeks after its formation, was, in my eyes, equal to the average of our best-trained volunteer corps, as far as marching and drill-exercise went. Indeed, I often asked myself what it was that made the Northern volunteer troops look, as a rule, so much more soldier-like than our own. I suppose the reason is, that across the Atlantic there was actual war, while at home there was at most only a parade. I have no doubt that, in the event of civil war or invasion, England would raise a million volunteers as rapidly as America has done —more rapidly she could not; and that, when fighting had once begun, there would only be too much of grim earnestness about our soldiering; but it is no want of patriotism to say that the American volunteers looked to me more businesslike than our own. At the scene of war itself there was no playing at soldiering. No gaudy uniforms or crack companies, no distinction of classes. From every part of the North, from the ports of New York and Boston, from the homesteads of New England, from the mines of Pennsylvania and the factories of Pittsburgh, from the shores of the Great Lakes, from the Mississippi Valley, and from the faraway Texan prairies, these men had come to fight for the Union. It is idle to talk of their being attracted by the pay alone. Large as it is, the pay of thirteen dollars a month is only two dollars more than the ordinary pay of privates in the Federal army during peace times. Thirteen shillings a week is poor pay for a laboring man in America, even with board, especially during this war, when the wages of unskilled labor amounted to from twenty to thirty shillings a week. It is false, moreover, to assert, as the opponents of the North are fond of doing, that the Federal armies were composed exclusively, or even principally, of foreigners. In the North, the proportion of foreign immigrants to native-born Americans is about thirty per cent, and the same proportions were observed in the Federal volunteer army. Judging from my own observation, I should say that the percentage of foreigners amongst the privates of the army of the Potomac was barely ten per cent. But, in the West, which is almost peopled with

Germans, foreigners are, probably, in the majority. The bulk of the native volunteers consisted of men who had given up good situations in order to enlist, and who had families to support at home; and for such men the additional pay was not an adequate inducement to incur the dangers and hardships of war. Of course, wherever there is an army, the scum of the population will always be gathered together; but the average morale and character of the couple of hundred thousand troops collected around Washington was extremely good. There was very little outward drunkenness, and less brawling about the streets than if half a dozen English militia regiments had been quartered there. The number of papers purchased daily by the common soldiers, and the quantity of letters which they sent through the military post was astonishing to a foreigner, though less strange when you considered that every man in that army, with the exception of a few recent immigrants, could both read and write. The ministers, also, of the different sects, who went out on the Sundays to preach to the troops, found no difficulty in obtaining large and attentive audiences.

The general impression left upon me by my observations of the army of the Potomac was a very favorable one. All day, and every day while I resided at Washington, the scene before my eyes was one of war. An endless military panorama seemed to be unrolling itself ceaselessly. Sometimes it was a line of artillery struggling and floundering onward through the mud—sometimes it was a company of wild Texan cavalry, rattling past, with the jingle of their belts and spurs. Sometimes it was a long train of sutlers' wagons, ambulance vans, or forage-carts, drawn by the shaggy Pennsylvania mules. Orderlies innumerable galloped up and down, patrols without end passed along the pavements, and at every window and doorstep and street corner you saw soldiers standing. You had to go far away from Washington to leave the war behind you. If you went up to any high point in the city whence you could look over the surrounding country, every hillside seemed covered with camps. The white tents caught your eye on all sides; and across the river, where the dense brushwood obscured the prospect, the great army of the Potomac stretched miles away, right up to the advanced posts of the Confederates, south of the far-famed Manassas. The numbers were so vast that it was hard to realize them. During one week fifty thousand men were embarked from Washington, and yet the town and neighborhood still swarmed with troops and camps, as it seemed, undiminished in number. And here, remember, I saw only one portion of the gigantic army. Along a line of two thousand miles or so, from the Potomac down to New Mexico, there were at that time Federal armies fighting their way southward. At Fortress Monroe too, Ship Island, Mobile, and at every accessible point along the Atlantic seaboard, expeditions numbered by tens of thousands were stationed, waiting for the signal to advance. At this time the muster-roll of the Federal army numbered 672,000 men, or, at least, that number were drawing pay daily from the Treasury, though a large allowance must be made for absentees and non-effectives.

Try to realize all this, and then picture to yourself what its effect, seen in fact, and not portrayed by feeble description, must be upon a nation unused to war. The wonder to me is that the American people were not more intoxicated with the consciousness of their new-born strength. Still the military passion—the lust of war—is a plant of rapid growth, and that, when the war is over, the nation will lay down their arms at once, and return to the arts of peace, is a thing more to be hoped for than expected. I recollect at the time reading an article in an English periodical of high repute, wherein the writer characterized as an acknowledged fact, the *essentially blackguardly nature* of the whole American war; and amidst some very clever discussion about the essence of a gentleman, paused to point a pungent paragraph by a sneer at the Federal army. Children play with lucifer-matches amongst powder-barrels, and probably the class of writers of whom this gentleman is a type, have not the faintest notion that, by words like these, they are sowing the seeds of war. Still, for the credit of their own country, I wish they would remember that power and strength and will, however misapplied, are never essentially blackguardly, and that there is something in an army of half a million men raised in six months' time worth thinking about as well as sneering at.

How bitterly Americans feel this sort of ill-natured comment from English critics, it is hard for anybody who has not lived in the country to appreciate. I recollect arguing once with a Northern gentleman, whose name as an author is known and honored in this country, about what seemed to me his unreasonable animosity toward England. After a concession on his part that possibly his feelings were morbidly exaggerated, he turned round and pointed to the portrait of a very near and dear relative of his —a brave, handsome lad—who had been killed a few months before when leading his men into action at the fatal defeat of Ball's Bluff. "How," he said to me, "would you like, yourself, to read constantly that that lad died in a miserable cause, and, as an American officer, should be called a coward?" And I own to that argument I could make no adequate reply. Let me quote, too, a paragraph from a letter I received the other day from another friend of mine, whose works have been read eagerly wherever the English tongue is spoken. "I have," he wrote, "a stake in this contest, which makes me nervous and tremulous and impatient of contradiction. I have a noble boy, a captain in one of our regiments, which has been fearfully decimated by battle and disease, and himself twice wounded within a hair's-breadth of his life." If you consider that in almost every Northern family there is thus some personal interest at stake in the war, it is not to be wondered at if the nation itself is also unduly impatient of contradiction.

But I have been wandering away from the subject of the army. At the period when I reached Washington the advance of the Potomac army was daily expected. I took an early opportunity of visiting the camp. By the kindness of General McClellan— kindness which, I would add, was extended freely to every English visitor—I had a pass furnished me on any occasion when I wished to cross the lines. I have taken few prettier or pleasanter rides in my life than those which I made at different times through the broken uplands of Virginia. One morning I can recall in particular, when I started in company with [William Howard] Russell and two other English gentlemen, to visit [Gen. Louis] Blenker's division. It was a lovely spring morning, and the trees, which are but little more forward than those of England, were just beginning to show their first buds. The whole way from Washington to Georgetown—a distance of some three miles—was an unbroken line of sutlers' wagons, carrying out provisions to the army. Anything more like the long, low English suburb of a northern manufacturing town than Georgetown, it is not possible to conceive; and if it had not been for the hosts of Negroes who swarm about this—the black—quarter of Washington, I should have fancied myself home in England. At the riverside we were stopped by the sentries, had our passes carefully inspected, and were then allowed to pass.

Close to this bridge the tide on the Potomac stops. The difference in the look of the river above and below Yorktown is very curious. Below, it is a great tidal river, as broad, though not as deep, as the Mersey at Liverpool. Above, it is a clear rapid stream, about the breadth of the Thames at Hammersmith. It was always a surprise to me that the planners of the City of Washington, who had a very definite conception in their heads of what they meant the capital to be like, seemed to have contemplated making so little use of the river. Even if the original design of Washington had ever been carried out, the Potomac could hardly have been a feature in the town. Yet in any country but America it would rank among the grandest of rivers. As it is, Washington is just too far off to enjoy the view of the river, and too near to escape its odors. The White House, which stands nearer the Potomac than any other part of the city, is rendered very unhealthy by the accumulation of refuse and garbage, which the tide washes to and fro between the piles of the long chainbridge.

With that quickness of invention which characterizes the Americans in all mechanical matters, the Federals had made a bridge across the Potomac by the device of letting the water out of a canal, which was carried over the river at Georgetown, and using the trough of the canal for a roadway. We rode at a foot's pace, in obedience to the sentry's orders, through the long narrow trench, which, with its planked sides, looked like an elongated coffin; and the moment we had emerged from it, we found ourselves not only in a new state, but in a new country. There is a marked and curious difference between the natural aspect of Virginia and Maryland. The latter is a bare open country, not unlike Sussex. The former is a wild, broken district, covered with brushwood. Our road lay through Arlington Park, the residence of the Confederate General [Robert E.] Lee. It certainly must have required a good deal of patriotism to induce any man to leave such a pleasant residence for the hardships of a camp. But then it must be remembered that when the General with his family left his mansion at the outbreak of Secession, he was confident of returning in triumph within a few weeks. When the Federals took possession of the house, and turned it into the headquarters of General [Irvin] Mcdowell's division, they found the whole place just in the state in which it would have been left if the owners had only intended to go away for a week's holiday. The ground belonging to the house must stretch over a space of some five or six square miles. Very little of the park is cultivated according to our English notion, and indeed it resembles much more nearly the hillside of the vale of Albury than Richmond Park or Blenheim. The timber, however—a circumstance which is rare in America—is remarkably fine, and the aspect of Washington owes the chief part of what little beauty it possesses to the wooded slopes of Arlington Heights, which face the city across the Potomac. Regard for this consideration, and for the historical associations with which the house is connected, and, above all, the social influence which General Lee possessed, had induced the Federal officers to use every precaution in order to protect the house and grounds from injury. The greatest difficulty was experienced in hindering the soldiers from cutting down the trees; and when at last Western regiments were stationed at Arlington Heights, it was found impossible to protect the timber. To soldiers from the backwoods settlements it seemed simply absurd to suppose that any man could object to having his ground cleared for him; and no amount of argument or expostulation could persuade them that it was not one of the rights of man to cut down any tree he came across. Hence, by this time the park had been sadly devastated. It had, too, that dreary, deserted look which a park always has when there is nobody to look after it. The ground was so covered with stumps of trees and broken fences, that it was with difficulty we could pilot our horses through the brushwood. The regiments which were formerly encamped here had now moved onward toward Manassas, and the only trace of the army was to be found in the number of blackened circles which showed where camp fires had been. Every now and then we could hear the booming of cannon toward the front, and constantly we heard, too, the less pleasant sound of the whirr of a rifle bullet, which showed us that, according to the fashion of the American army, some private or other was occupying his leisure in firing at any object he saw. Great attempts had been made to put a stop to this practice in the grounds of the park, where, from the dense character of the brushwood, it was extremely dangerous. But practically, with the extreme reluctance entertained to the infliction of any punishment on the volunteer soldiers, it was found impossible to enforce the prevention of this promiscuous shooting. After riding some miles across the park, we came out upon the main road, which led across the chain-bridge from Washington to the camp. At this period, the Government papers and the military authorities were all impressing on the public that, in the state of the Virginia roads, any immediate advance was out of the question. Now, on this and other occasions I saw the roads myself in their worst state, and in the very places where they had been most cut up by the passage of artillery. I confess frankly that the roads were shockingly bad. Like most of the American highways, they were hardly roads in our sense of the word, but mere tracks without any foundation. The soil of Virginia is a sort of sandy loam; and what with the rain and the passage of so many thousands of wheels, the surface of the high road had become a soft quicksand, or slush, into which you sunk from one to two feet. It was not pleasant riding when every hundred yards or so your horse would stumble into a hollow and half bury himself and you in this

"Slough of Despond." The only comfort was that, even if your horse fell down, the ground was so soft it was impossible for him to receive any injury. I saw artillery being dragged along these roads, and can bear witness to the fact that the task was one of great trouble and labor. Still, I doubt very much whether the condition of the roads was such as to render an advance impossible. They were not worse than many of the roads in the south of Italy, over which the Sardinian army marched in 1860. It was only for bits that these quagmires extended; and I suspect that, if any trouble had been taken to secure an efficient corps of roadmakers, the roads might have been made passable without difficulty. It is possible that in this opinion I may do injustice to McClellan, but I fancy that the impassability of the Virginia roads was as much exaggerated as the impregnability of the earthworks at Manassas.

The rear of the army of the Potomac was then stationed three or four miles to the south of the river, while the front extended nearly as far as Centreville. It had been our purpose on this occasion to ride out as far as the outposts, but with that extraordinary variability which distinguishes the American climate, the sky had clouded over almost at once, and the temperature from that of summer had become as cold as it is with us in the depth of winter. The snow began to fall in heavy flakes, and the wind blew as icy cold as if it came direct from the Arctic Ocean. In consequence, we changed our plans, and resolved to confine our visit to Blenker's division.

Of all camps I have seen, this of Blenker's seemed to me the most comfortable. Lying on a high tableland, the soil was dry; and the temperature in Virginia is rarely such for any length of time as to make living in the open air a severe trial. Every precaution, too, was taken to make the tents as warm as possible. Indeed, tents they could hardly be called. Each hut was floored with planks and fenced in with logs some three feet above the ground. The canvas tents were drawn tightly down over these log walls, so that very little air could penetrate, and each hut was provided with a stove; and except for the discomfort of having to sleep with two or three comrades in a space about eight feet square and seven high, I could not see that there was anything to complain of. The camp was arranged in a square intersected with broad passages parallel to each other. About the tents I looked into there was an air of rough comfort, and in many cases of luxury; and both drainage and ventilation appeared excellent. The result of such care was shown in the excellent health of the troops. Out of a body of some thousand men there were only thirty or so in the hospital; and most of these invalids were sufferers from drink or other maladies for which camp life is not directly responsible. Whether the result was equally favorable in training the men to undergo the hardships of a campaign I doubted at the time, and have seen cause since to doubt still more.

Blenker's division were the *enfans perdus* of the Federal army. Their commander even then enjoyed a most doubtful reputation, and the men justly or unjustly shared in the repute of the General. They had been moved as far away from Washington as possible, and not without cause. In the Potomac army commanded by McClellan the number of foreign regiments was at that period extremely small, and almost all of them were attached to Blenker's division. The camp I visited was filled with the black sheep of every nation under the sun. The word of command had to be given in four languages, and the officers were foreigners almost without exception. In a party with whom we spent the afternoon, there were officers who had served in the Papal brigade, the army of Francis II, the Garibaldian expedition, the British and Spanish legions, the wars of Baden, the Morocco campaign, and I know not where else beside. Both men and officers were a fine daredevil looking set of fellows, and might doubtless have been made excellent soldiers with strict training. The difficulty here, as to a less extent throughout the whole Federal army, was that with a volunteer organization it was impossible to use the stern discipline necessary to break the troops into order.

At the time of my visit to Blenker's camp, the army was hourly awaiting orders to march on Manassas. Within a week or so afterward, the news came that the Confederates had evacuated the mud forts and quaker guns which had kept McClellan so long at bay, and were retiring upon Richmond. Ten days had not passed before Yankee energy had reconstructed the railroad which led from Alexandria to Manassas Gap; and the offer having been made me to accompany the first trial trip after the completion of the line, I gladly availed myself of it. It was the loveliest of spring mornings when I left Washington early to join the expedition. A steamboat carried us from the foot of the chainbridge to Alexandria. The wide river was covered with fleets of transports, dropping down with the tide to convey provisions to the army which had just begun to sail for the peninsula. The wharves of Alexandria were covered with troops waiting for embarkment. The great river-steamers, which lay alongside, were crowded with troops singing and cheering lustily. The whole nation was overjoyed at the thought that at last the day of the "masterly inaction" was over, and that the long-expected hour of victory had struck. The army shared in the general enthusiasm; and there were few, I think, who contemplated even the possibility of a temporary reverse. I own, laying claim as I do to no pretensions as a military authority, that I shared in that impression. It seems to me even now incredible at times, that that grand army, which I watched for days and weeks defiling through Washington, should not have swept all before it; and I confess, that I still believe its failure was due to want of generalship. The nation, at any rate, at that time was confident, proud of its General, proud of its army, proud of its coming victory; and when the "Young Napoleon,"—with that affectation of the Napoleonic style he was so partial to—declared in the address he issued, almost on the day of which I write, that hereafter his troops "would ask no higher honor than the proud consciousness that they belonged to the army of the Potomac," he uttered a boast which found an echo in every Northern breast.

My companions on the excursion, among whom were Mr. Hawthorne and Mr. N. P. Willis, were all Northerners; and all of them, the ladies especially, showed a natural feeling of pride at the appearance of the troops about to start on that ill-fated expedition. It struck me, however, curiously at the time, how all the party talked about our excursion as if we were going to visit

a strange country. The sacred soil of Virginia seemed as imperfectly known to them as Ireland is to myself; and they looked
upon their excursion with much the same sort of interest as I
should do on a trip across St. George's Channel.

Half an hour's sail brought us to Alexandria. Like most of the
old Virginia and Maryland towns, it has a very English air about
it: the red brick houses, the broad sleepy streets, the long straggling wharves might have been imported direct from Norfolk or
Lincolnshire. The town itself was crammed with troops; but
neither then nor on the other occasions when I visited it was
there anything to be seen of the inhabitants. They had left the
place for the most part, or lived in retirement. Closely connected
as the little town is with Washington, it was bitterly "secesh;"
and the citizens of Alexandria showed their dislike of the Federal
army of occupation by every means in their power. The women,
as may be supposed, displayed their animosity most outspokenly.
Unless they were foully belied, they used to take pleasure in in-
sulting the private soldiers with epithets which will not bear repetition. The common Yankee soldiers seemed to feel these insults
from women with a susceptibility I felt it hard to account for.
English soldiers, under like circumstances, would have retorted
with language still more unmentionable, or would have adopted
the spirit of General [Benjamin] Butler's famous order without
compunction. But the Americans appeared to writhe under these
insults. The bad language of the Alexandria women was constantly complained of in the papers as a bitter personal injury.
I remember one stalwart Massachusetts soldier in the hospital,
who complained seriously, that when he was recovered, and went
back to duty, he should be subjected again to the abuse of these
Southern ladies; and said, "It was so hard to bear." It was here,
by the way, that the first blood shed in the war was spilt by the
murder of [Lieut. Col. Elmer] Ellsworth, when hoisting up the
Union flag at the first outbreak of Secession. A flagstaff, bearing
the Stars and Stripes, had been erected on the house where he
was killed; and, on that morning, it floated bravely in the sunlight, as though in honor of the approaching Union triumphs.

At the wharf, a train was waiting to convey our party. It was the first which had started, and the resumption of the traffic was the sign of returning peace and order. But the event excited no comment in that sullen, gloomy town, and only a few boys and Negroes were collected together to witness our departure. Slowly we moved on through the dead streets till we reached the camps outside the town, and then passing onward at an increased speed, we were soon in the hilly Virginia country, which a few days before had been occupied by the Confederate forces.

The country through which our road lay impressed me strangely with a sense of desolation. If the reader knows the Surrey downs, near Albury, and can fancy what they would be, if the mansions and cottages were all removed, if the woods were replaced by pine forests, if the place of roads was supplied by mud tracks, and if the whole district was intersected by steep gullies filled with clear sparkling torrent streams, he will have a pretty good notion of what Northern Virginia is like. For miles and miles together you passed through long tracts of pinewood, broken by patches of deserted fields, where the brushwood was growing up again amidst the stumps of the forest trees, which had been cleared years ago. Every now and then you came to an open space, where you caught a glimpse of the distant Blue Ridge Mountains, and then you passed again into the gloomy pinewood shade. Along the journey of twenty miles or so, you never saw a village; and the number of houses that you passed might be counted on your fingers. In the fields there was no one working; the snake fences were broken down; at the roadside stations there were no passengers; and the few people loitering about gazed sullenly at us as we passed. Of actual traces of the war there were not many. We passed a few deserted camps, and a house or two which had been burnt down by one of the two armies which had occupied the soil in turn; but that was all. Indeed, the look of desolation could have proceeded but partially from the presence of the war. I never saw the same aspect elsewhere, even in states which had suffered as much from invasion. The state of the fields and fences, and roads and farmhouses, betokened a decay of much longer standing than that of a year's time. The exhaustion of the soil, even more than the havoc of

men, was the cause of the deserted air which hung over everything. With the wasteful system of tobacco-growing and slave
labor, Virginia is rapidly sinking back into its primitive desolation.

At last we emerged from the pinewoods, and began to ascend
by a steep incline—an open tableland—at whose foot runs the
now famous stream of Bull Run. Here we had to move slowly,
and stop every few hundred yards to remove huge logs, which had
been rolled across the rails to obstruct the passage. Then, reach-
ing the top of the incline, we found ourselves in the center of
Manassas camp. It had hardly yet been visited since the departure
of the Confederates; everything which could be destroyed had
been burnt before their retreat; and the whole ground for miles
was covered with the debris of an army's stores. Smashed carriages, broken arms, empty coffins, charred planks, decaying
skeletons of horses, pots, pans, and cartridges, lay heaped together
in a weird disorder. A detachment of Federal soldiers were on
duty there, collecting any remnants of the stores which were
worth preserving; but, otherwise, there was not a soul visible.
The few soldiers' huts which were left standing were knocked
hastily together with the rudest planks, and swarmed inside with
vermin of every description. A foul smell of charred animal matter hung about the place, and flights of crows were feeding upon
the garbage strewn on every side. The whole ground was covered
with stray leaves of tracts and Bibles, which some Southern
religious society had obviously been distributing amongst the
troops. Letters, too, were to be picked up by dozens; and, indeed,
the collectors of curiosities amongst our party had their researches
richly rewarded.

As to the value of the fortifications, I could form no opinion.
To me they appeared of the rudest and poorest description of
earthworks, and I fancy were intended rather to protect the retreat of the army in case of a sudden attack than to keep off the
enemy. On the other hand, the position of Manassas in itself
was obviously a strong one. The wide plateau on which it stood
sloped down rapidly toward the North, so that an army advancing from Washington would have had to mount this slope, exposed to the full fire of the enemy's batteries. At this time, by the

way, there was an embittered discussion going on in the American press as to whether the Confederates had manned their works with wooden cannon, in order to give a false impression of strength. The Anti-slavery party asserted positively that such was the case, and that McClellan had been frightened from attacking Manassas by a scarecrow. The Democratic party asserted as stoutly that the whole story was an invention. Curious to say, the fact of the existence of the "quaker guns" was never either demonstrated or disproved. I can only say, that soldiers I saw at Manassas assured me that they had seen the wooden cannon on their first arrival. On the other hand, persons who took more trouble to investigate the truth came to the conclusion that there was no evidence of the fact; but to me the definite result seemed to be that, from some cause or other, the Federal commanders failed invariably to obtain reliable information as to the position and movements of the Southern army.

Our visit was but a short one, for the train had to return early, in order to avoid the risk of traveling through that half-hostile country after dark. On our return to the cars, we came upon a strange living evidence of the results of this strange war. Huddled together upon a truck were a group of some dozen runaway slaves. There were three men, four women, and half a dozen children. Anything more helpless or wretched than their aspect I never saw. Miserably clothed, footsore, and weary, they crouched in the hot sunlight more like animals than men. They seemed to have no idea, no plan, and no distinct purpose. They were field hands, on a farm some score of miles off, and had walked all night; so at least they told us. Now they were going North as far as Washington, which appeared to them the end of the world. They had no fear of being recaptured, partly, I think, because they had reached Northern troops, still more because their home seemed to them so far away. With the exception of one woman, who was going to look for her husband, who was hired out somewhere in the District of Columbia, they talked as if they had no friends or acquaintances in the new land they were traveling to. For the present they were content that they could sit in the sun without being forced to work. Some of our party gave them money, and broken victuals which they valued more. I overheard one of the men saying to a woman, as he munched some white bread he had picked up, "Massa never gave us food like that." Poor things, if their idea of freedom was white bread and rest, they must have been disappointed bitterly! As strangers and guests of official personages, it was impossible for us to do anything for them. We got them a lift upon the truck to Alexandria. But whenever I think of that incident, I wish that we could have done, that we had done, more. Before we reached the town they got down, and our roads parted. What became of them heaven knows.

Instead of returning by the river from Alexandria, the train carried us to the foot of the long chain-bridge which crosses the Potomac in front of Washington. For hours we found it impossible to cross, as a division of 16,000 men were marching over on their way to Alexandria, to embark for the peninsula. With colors flying, and bands playing, regiment after regiment defiled past us. In the gray evening light, the long endless files bore a phantom aspect. The men were singing, shouting, cheering; under cover of the darkness, they chanted "John Brown's Hymn," in defiance of McClellan's orders, and the heavy tramp of a thousand feet beat time to that strange weird melody. As the New England regiments passed our train, they shouted to us to tell the people at home that we had seen them in Dixie's Land, and on the way to Richmond. Ah, me! How many, I wonder, of those who flitted before us in the twilight, came home themselves to tell their own story?

Western Virginia

TOWARD THE middle of April Washington was growing empty. Willard's Hotel was rapidly losing its customers, and the managers were fast becoming oppressively civil, even to a single one-trunk-and-carpet-bag traveler like myself. Pennsylvania Avenue was no longer crowded with artillery and baggage-wagons. Officers had become few in number, passes had ceased to be required for crossing the now-deserted lines, and the weekly receptions of Senators and Representatives were being dropped one by one. All these symptoms were hints to a traveler to move elsewhere. Indeed, I should have gone some weeks before, but for three causes. The first was that, after some two or three weeks of spring as warm as most English summers, we had heavy falls of snow, covering the ground for days together; the second was that my introductions had made society in Washington so pleasant to me that it was with reluctance I parted from it; and thirdly, and lastly, I experienced a difficulty which almost all travelers must have felt of making up your mind where to go to, when there is no particular reason why you should go to one place more than to another. Naturally, my first inclination would have been to go "on to Richmond" with the grand army of the Potomac, but unfortunately there were many objections to such a proceeding. In the first place, I had such confidence in the "masterly inactivity," as the *New York Herald* used to style it, of General McClellan's tactics, that I doubted, as it proved with reason, whether I might not be kept waiting at Fortress Monroe for weeks to come. In the second, I strongly suspected that if I did follow the army, I should see very little but the smoke of the cannon in the event of a battle; and, lastly—but why should I go on, unmindful of Queen Elizabeth's answer to the magistrates of Falmouth in the matter of their not ringing the town bells, and enumerate the reasons why I *did* not go with the Potomac army, when there was one simple and decisive argument, and that was that I *could* not. I was supposed, rightly or wrongly, to be connected with the English press, and on this ground was denied access to the Richmond expedition, by orders of the Secretary of War. It is useless trying to conceal anything in America. Before I had been a couple of weeks in the country, my name, antecedents, and history, and a good deal of personal intelligence that was perfectly novel to myself, was published in the American papers. Under these circumstances, it was little use seeking to obtain permission to visit the peninsula, and I had received such uniform courtesy from all American officials I had hitherto come across that I did not like to disturb the pleasing tenor of my recollections by exposing myself to the probability of a discourteous refusal from Mr. Stanton.

So, in fact, my choice of directions in which to travel was limited. The orders of the War Department precluded my journeying East, the insurrection would not allow me to go South, and the cold forbade me from traveling North. The only path open to me lay westward in the track of the war, and it was this path I resolved to follow. My road lay through Western Virginia, whence the Confederates had just retreated, through Ohio, the great Border Free State, through Kentucky, the chief of the Union Slave States, whose loyalty, to say the most, had been a half-hearted neutrality, down to Tennessee, the stronghold and battlefield of the Confederates in the West.

I left Washington in the early morning, on the day when the President signed the measure for the emancipation of the slaves in the District of Columbia, a bright promise, as it proved, of a brighter future. By the way, the night before I left, a Washington friend of mine, the most lukewarm of Abolitionists, told me an incident worth relating: He had been driving that day in a hired carriage, whose coachman was an old Negro he had known for years. To his astonishment the driver mistook his way repeatedly. At last my friend grew angry, and asked the man what ailed him.

"Ah, massa," the Negro answered; "all this matter about the emancipation has got into my head somehow, and I feel stunned like." Well, in the words of a dear friend of mine, "God's fruit of justice ripens slow," and it is pleasant to me to think that I, too, have seen the ripening of one small fruit of justice. So as we passed on that morning through the dull barren fields of Maryland, I could not help watching the colored folk in the cars with more than usual interest. I had not been long enough in the country to lose the sense of novelty with which the black people impress a stranger. To me they are the one picturesque element in the dull monotony of outward life in America. With their dark swarthy skins varying from the deepest ebony to the rich yellow hue—with their strange love for bright colors in their dress, no matter how stained and faded, and yet, gaudy as they are, arranged with a sort of artistic instinct—with their bright laughing smiles and their deep wistful eyes, they form a race apart, a strange people in a strange land. Probably, if you lived amongst them, you would lose all sense of their picturesqueness just as we in England should see little romance about Gypsies, if there was a Romany camp squatted down in every village. As a gentleman who is known as one of the acutest of observers once said to me, "Negroes are just like a man you meet, who is an uncommonly pleasant companion for half an hour, but whom you find a monstrous bore when you are shut up all alone with him for a long rainy day." While I remained in America I was still in the early stage of investigation, and could hardly appreciate the evident distaste which even the stanchest Free-soilers have for the black race. A very strong Republican confessed to me on one occasion that he could never shake hands with a Negro without instinctive repugnance, and this feeling is, I suspect, a very universal one throughout the Free States. In Maryland, as in all slave countries, there prevails a more kindly feeling toward the individual Negro. In the car in which I traveled from Washington, black men came in and out freely, and the white passengers seemed to have no objection to their contact. Indeed, in one or two cases, I saw men get up to make room for Negro women, who, in justice I must add, were neither young nor pretty. By one of the barbarous laws of the black code of Maryland, the Washington railroad is forbidden to take free colored people as passengers unless they can obtain a bond from some responsible householder for a thousand dollars, to indemnify the company in case of their being claimed afterward as fugitive slaves. Of course, this rule was always evaded, whenever the Negro was personally known to the railroad officials, and during the war everything was in such confusion that, I fancy, it was rarely enforced. Barring this provision, colored people may pass freely in the cars of the Baltimore and Ohio line. There is not, indeed, the absolute equality in American railway traveling that we fancy in Europe. I dare say the reader may have observed how on our penny river steamboats, where there is no difference of fares, and no division of classes, yet, somehow or other, the working poor generally congregate in the bows of the vessel, rarely in the more aristocratic stern. The same thing happens across the Atlantic. On all American lines there is always one car, generally the one nearest the engine, where, without notice or order, the common soldiers, the working men, and the Negroes take their places naturally. There is nothing to hinder a rough-shod, mud-covered soldier from sitting in the hinder cars, but he rarely does so. How far a man of color might be liable to insult if he placed himself amidst the genteel society, I cannot say. It is certain he would feel uncomfortable, and avoids the experiment. The western line of the Baltimore and Ohio turns off at the famous Relay Bridge, the junction of the Washington and the Wheeling railroads, which the Confederates tried in vain to blow up at the first outburst of hostilities. The country was in appearance much the same as when I passed through it some six weeks before. The leaves had opened but little more, and the fields and villages still bore the same dreary deserted aspect. But in one respect there was a marked difference. The camps along the line were removed, there were few roadside pickets, and the army had passed on. Distances are so enormous in America that an Englishman finds it hard to realize them. My first day's journey, which was to take me from the eastern to the western frontier of the single State of Virginia, was four hundred miles in length—as far as from London to Edinburgh.

At the Relay Bridge we first began our real journey into the quondam dominions of Secession. Our train was a short one of two or three cars in all, filled chiefly with soldiers returning to their regiments stationed along the line, a good number of way passengers, going to visit their property or friends in the recovered districts, and a few travelers, like myself, journeying toward the West. There was not much of political conversation in the carriages. Every now and then, as we passed a detachment of Union soldiers, some Northern ladies in the car waved their handkerchiefs; but the bulk of the passengers made no demonstration. A Baltimore lady, who sat next to me, and who assumed—as I saw all Southern people did—that, being an Englishman, I was in heart favorable to the Confederate cause, communicated to me her indignation at the treatment of the South, and informed me, amongst other things, that if the women of Baltimore could only catch Wendell Phillips, they would not leave a bone unbroken in his body. She was so perfectly frank in her statements, that I do not doubt her assertion that she had never been in favor of Secession, and that she had never been rich enough to keep slaves herself; but the whole social creed in which she had been reared and bred was in favor of slavery; and, woman-like, she never thought of doubting the foundations of the creed she had been taught. Of all the foolish assumptions being constantly made in discussions on the slavery question, the more erroneous seems to me to be that, because there are only, say, 400,000 slaveholders in all the Slave States combined, this small figure measures the total number of persons who have any interest in, or concern about, the existence of slavery. You might just as well argue that there are not one thousand persons in Great Britain who can really feel any interest in the existence of the peerage.

Our route lay across the Allegheny Mountains, along the troughs of winding valleys, by the sides of rivers whose very names —the Patapsco and the Potomac, the Shenandoah and the

Monongahela—bear the rhythm of music with them. Jefferson said that it was worth a voyage across the Atlantic to witness such scenery as that of the Upper Potomac; and doubtless it is a scene of great beauty. Still, like all the American scenery I have seen, it is wearily monotonous. Some years ago a Yankee brought to London a panorama of the Mississippi, of I don't know how many thousand yards length. The first hundred yards or so were extremely interesting; but when you had seen the same scene unrolled slowly, yard after yard, and hour after hour, the sight became so wearisome, that I doubt if anyone ever saw the panorama to its close. So it is with American scenery, in reality as well as pictorially. One gets tired of the endless low hills of unvarying height; of the ceaseless forests in which the timber is all of the same small growth; of the scattered houses which never vary in size or aspect. After a long journey, you have much the same feeling as a pedestrian would have who walked a thousand times over one mile of road in a thousand hours. Still, if you could have compressed the journey into one-tenth of its distance, it would have been a very lovely one. From Baltimore the road winds up a narrow gorge, with wood-clad granite cliffs on either side, and a deep mountain stream rolling down the midst. Every three or four miles you pass a cotton factory, and the high smoke-begrimed chimneys, the riverside mills, and the stone-built, slate-roofed houses, give it a strange resemblance to a valley in the mountain district of Lancashire. Then you come upon the tableland, at the summit of the Allegheny ridge, wild, desolate, and dreary, and then down rapid inclines, under frequent tunnels, and over countless bridges, into the rich valley of the Ohio River. Such is the outline of the journey. Fill it up with long stretches of brush-wood forest, with stray fields surrounded with tumble-down snake-fences, with high cliffs of rock hanging over mountain torrents, with scattered wooden houses standing few and far apart, and with here and there a glimpse of a wide, rich champaign country stretching away in the far distance, and you will know as much as I can recall of the scenery of the Allegheny Pass.

The traces of the war were few. The country is too poor a one,

too little peopled, and too scantily cultivated to leave much opening for destruction. Of banditti, or bushwhackers, I need hardly
say we saw no sign. There were a few deserted camps along the
wood, and a few pickets of Union soldiers, looking very desolate
in that lone country. The two points where you come across the
track of the war are at Harper's Ferry and Cumberland. The
grand stone bridge across the Potomac, at the former spot, was
blown up by the Confederates, when they evacuated the place
in March. With true Yankee energy, a sort of makeshift wooden
bridge of most unsubstantial appearance had been run up on the
old stone buttresses, but on the day before I crossed, this temporary bridge had broken down, and our journey was brought to
an apparent standstill when we arrived at the riverside. However,
in a short time a rope was stretched across the stream, and passengers and luggage were ferried over the rapid swollen torrent to
proceed on their journey by the return train from Wheeling.
This stoppage caused a delay of some hours, and so I had time
to wander about the ruins of what once was the town of Harper's
Ferry. Here, a year before, stood the armory of the United States,
where 1,500 workmen were employed constantly. Now everything was destroyed. The walls alone were left standing, and
the town was half in ruins. There is nothing grand about the
debris of small, red brick buildings. Just after the fall of Fort
Sumter, when the Confederates were expected daily to enter
Washington, a friend of mine was passing the Treasury buildings,
with General Stone, who was afterward confined at Fort Lafay-
ette on a charge of treason. My friend said something to the
General about the beauty of the marble portico, and the answer
he received in reply was, "Yes, the Treasury will make a fine
Palmyra." So it would have done, but there is nothing Palmy-
resque about the ruins of Harper's Ferry. There is nothing but a
look of squalid misery—of wanton destruction. The ground
around the arsenal is strewed with fragments of the workmen's
cottages that stood around it, and amidst the broken masses of
brickwork the signpost of some roadside inn, left by mere chance
still standing, rose gibbet-like, with its signboard, riddled through

with rifle-shot, creaking harshly on its rusty hinges. The town itself, which bore traces of once having been busy and prosperous, was almost deserted; soldiers swarmed in every hole and corner, and sentries were placed at every turning, but otherwise the place seemed empty. There were few men visible, and even the women and children stood sullenly apart. Most of the shops were closed, and a few that remained open had little in them. There is no resurrection, I fear, possible for Harper's Ferry. Standing at the confluence of two rivers, the Shenandoah and the Potomac, between precipitous cliffs resembling the Avon at Clifton, only on a grander scale, it is one of the loveliest spots in America; but ever since the war, a fatality seems to have hung over it. Since I saw it, it has changed hands four times over from Confederates to Federals, and the battle of Antietam was fought almost within sight of it. Ever since John Brown's insurrection it has never prospered. I was shown the little outhouse where the stern old Puritan was confined after the failure of his mad attempt. It was here that, lying wounded, mangled, and at death's door, he was tortured by the questionings of Mr. James Mason. And now two years have scarcely passed, and Mr. Mason is in England, owing his liberty, if not his life, to the strength of a free country; begging in vain for help to an insurrection as fatal as that of his quondam prisoner—his slaves escaped in a body—his house occupied by Massachusetts regiments, and his property ruined—while the Northern regiments, as they marched across the Potomac into Virginia, shrouded by the dusk of the evening, used to sing in triumph that "John Brown's soul was marching on" before them.

After all, Harper's Ferry was the property of the Federal Government; and, therefore, the Confederates had perhaps a right to destroy it. But, if I had been the staunchest of Secessionists, and also for my misfortunes a shareholder in the Baltimore and Ohio line, I should have found it hard to excuse the wanton injury inflicted on private property in Cumberland. This was the chief railway depot on the line, and before the Confederates evacuated it they destroyed every piece of rolling stock along the road. For miles on either side I passed burnt-up cars, shattered engines, and coal trucks, which, being of iron, could neither be burnt nor broken, and had therefore been rolled down the embankments. Fancy Wolverton burnt down, with everything breakable in its sheds smashed and battered, and you will know the look of Cumberland junction.

As long as we remained in the manufacturing districts near Baltimore, the aspect of the houses and people was comfortable and prosperous enough; and, indeed, this region has been but little directly affected by the war. But, as soon as we left Maryland for West Virginia, the scene changed. Here, for the first time in the States, I saw the symptoms of squalid, Old World poverty. Miserable wooden shanty hovels, broken windows stuffed with rags, and dirty children playing together with the pigs on the dung heaps before the doors, gave an Irish air of decay to the few scattered villages through which the railroad passed. Our train, owing to the necessity of proceeding with extreme caution during the night, through fear of the obstructions which Secessionist sympathizers might have laid across the line, moved on at a foot's pace, and our journey occupied some thirty-six hours, instead of the twenty-four which it was advertised to take. The snow, too, still lay on the high bleak uplands, and what with the cold, the weariness of sitting for hours on low-backed seats, and the constant stoppages at the shuntings in order to allow trains moving eastward loaded with soldiers and supplies to pass by us, our progress toward the end was a dismal and a dreary one.

There is one fact for which I shall always remember Wheeling gratefully—namely, that it was the first place where I had been really hot since I had left Italy, some eight months before. Otherwise, it is a quiet sleepy little town, without much to be said about it. Like all the Southern towns I had yet seen, it was wonderfully English in appearance. The broad herringbone-flagged High Street; the small narrow-windowed red brick houses, with their black chimney pots; the shabby-looking shops, with the flies buzzing about the dirty windowpanes, the long walls and tall factory chimneys, all made the place resemble an English country town where the old country people had died out and the new manufacturing element had not prospered. Still, Wheeling is a go-ahead place, in its way, for a Southern city, and has proved loyal to the Union. It will be the capital of the new State of Western Virginia, if it ever succeeds in establishing its independence; and it is the headquarters of the emancipation party in the state, probably because its German population is considerable. General John Frémont had his headquarters here, when in command of the mountain district, and the town was, therefore, filled with foreign officers. A crowd of new arrivals had just come in, as I was making my way to bed; and there, sitting on the one hatbox which formed the whole of his luggage, composed, clean-shaven, and serene, was my old acquaintance, Major, Colonel, General, or whatever his rank now may be, Von Traubenfass. My friend is a mystery to me, as to everyone else. What man-about-the-press does not remember Traubenfass years ago, in the great military scandal case of——. Well, it is a long time ago, and there is no good raking up old sores. Where and in what strange medley has Traubenfass not been involved? He has served, of course, in the Spanish legion—in the wars of the Rio Grande—in the Schleswig-Holstein campaign. He has been in the service of half a dozen Indian princes, and has a perfect galaxy of orders from deposed potentates. When I met him last, twelve months before, he was a general unattached in the Garibaldian army, and received (and, what is more, was paid punctually) a very handsome salary for his unknown services. Then I heard of him as projector, manager, and secretary of an Italian railroad, which was to connect Sicily with the mainland. Now, he was instructor of cavalry, or inspector of horses, or military commissioner in the army of the United States. He informed me, with perfect equanimity, that he supposed the war would not last much longer, and then he should be on his legs again. But, meanwhile, he was certain that something else would turn up. What nation he belongs to, who he has been, where he comes from, or what his age is, are all questions I have often asked in vain, and doubt if he knows himself. He is perfectly quiet, temperate, and frugal, and the one weakness to which I have ever known him to plead guilty is a belief in an infallible system for winning at *rouge-et-noir*. After parting with Traubenfass, and indulging in a whisky cocktail, in augury of our next meeting in some unknown part of the globe, I retired to bed. What, I wonder, is the connection between slavery and dirt—that in all Slave States the hotels and the beds are always dirty?

Ohio

ACROSS THE mud-stained Ohio River, down which great rafts of wood, covered with huts, as in the Old Rhineland, were floating lazily, and then a long, hot day's journey through the length and breadth of the Ohio State. The early morning air was loaded with that dull, still closeness which foretells a day of sweltering heat, and the presage was fully realized. The cars were crowded with travelers; and though, for a wonder, the stoves were not lit, yet the closed windows served to maintain that stifling warmth of temperature which seems essential to an American's idea of comfort. The car in which I happened to take my seat was filled with soldiers, most of them rejoining their regiments, and a few escorting a batch of Southern prisoners. These men were bushwhackers, captured in the mountains of Western Virginia by one of Frémont's flying columns, and were being sent to Columbus for imprisonment. The party consisted of some dozen or so, all well-dressed quiet-looking men, apparently of the rank of small farmers. The younger men said nothing, and declined all conversation with their guardians; but the oldest of the band—a man, I should think, long past sixty—talked very freely, and assured anybody who would listen to him that his share in the insurrection had been entirely passive, and that the only reason he had not fought for the Union was because civil war seemed such an awful thing to him. "It's the same old story, sir, they always tell," was the remark of a private soldier, who had been one of the capturing party; and, I suspect, myself, the objection to civil war was one of late adoption. The Federal soldiers, let me add, were as quiet and well-behaved as I always found them. Many of them were reading newspapers, and none talked loudly or offensively. In fact, I should never wish for pleasanter fellow passengers; but, pleasant as they were, they still made the car uncomfortably hot, and before long, I, in company with some confirmed smokers, betook myself, in defiance of all rules, to the broad steps fixed behind the carriages. I don't know that there is any more danger in sitting on the steps than in any other part of the cars. If there were a collision or a breakdown, you, sitting there, would be tossed into the middle of the adjoining meadow, instead of into the face of your next-hand neighbor. But as a fact, the great respect for law which prevails throughout America hinders travelers from availing themselves freely of the seats upon the steps. At any rate, sitting, as I sat there, with my legs dangling over the single line of rails, I found the ride a very pleasant one.

Mile after mile, and hour after hour, the train carried us headlong through the same pleasant, rich, flat country. You seem to pass, so to speak, through the successive strata of the emigration era. Sometimes there were long tracts of forestland, where the axe was yet unknown. Then you came to the half-reclaimed lands, where, amidst an undergrowth of bushwood, the great trees stood, dead and leafless, ready for felling, killed by the fatal rim notched round their trunks. Then followed the newly reclaimed fields, with black, charred stumps still standing in their midst, and marked out by the snake-fences, with their unfastened rails, piled crosswise one upon the other; and then, from time to time, you came upon a tract of field-land, hemmed in by tight post and cross-bar fences, with every stump and trunk rooted out, and with a surface as smooth, and rich, and green as that of a Leicestershire meadow. You could mark every stage of the settler's life, from the rough shanty run up in the midst of the uncut brushwood, to the trim, neat farmhouse, with its lawn and flowerbeds, and the children playing before the door. The New World lay before you in the process of its creation. New roads were making everywhere; new villages were springing up; teams of rough, sturdy horses were ploughing up the old fallow-lands; the swamps were being cleared of their dank, reedy marsh plants, and the broad, shallow streams were being banked and damned into deep, quiet water courses. It was then that I first understood the poetry of the emigrant world—not romantic or spasmodic, but idyllic in its nature, of the Herman and Dorothea type. There was nothing grand about the monotony of the scene—not a house in a distance of a hundred miles of more than one story high; not a church spire or a hill of any kind; nothing that was old, except the forest, and that was vanishing. Still, throughout the whole district there was the same unbroken air of rough comfort, and ease, and plenty; and of want or poverty there was no trace forthcoming. Years ago I had heard the crew of an emigrant vessel singing, "Cheer, Boys, Cheer!" as the ship unmoored from its anchorage and dropped down the Mersey westward, and I had fancied that the burden of the song was as vain as most poets' promises; but now, it seemed to me, that the promise had come true, and that this rich western country was, in very truth, the "new and happy land." A long summer day's journey carried us through that pleasant state; and, as we came near Cincinnati, we passed again into a settled country. For miles before we reached the city we rattled through its suburb-villages with their broad, clean streets, and their neat wooden houses, before whose doors the women, with their long stiff hoods, sat knitting in the evening twilight. Railroads branched out on every side—no longer rough, single tracks, but smooth, broad, double lines of rail. Elegant brick-built stations succeeded the wooden sheds which did duty for stopping places in the newly settled districts, and the slopes of the low hill on either side were covered with green-shuttered stone villas, which looked as though they had been transplanted bodily from Kingston or Hampstead.

Of Cincinnati, the "Queen City of the West," there is not much that I need say. One American city is very like another. It is strange, after traveling for hundreds of miles through the half-settled country, to come in the Far West upon a great city, filled with every luxury and comfort of Old World civilization. The stalls, so it seemed to me, with their grand fronts and marble facings, were handsomer even than those of New York; and the music shops, and print-depots, and book stands, which you saw on every side, all told of wealth, and education, and refinement.

The hilly slopes, too, on which the city stands, the countless gardens, and the rows of almond trees which lined the streets, and which were then in full bloom, give the city a brighter look than you often see in the Northern capitals. There was an air about the place, and I suppose not a fallacious one, as though trade were not thriving. The Mississippi and the Ohio are the great arteries of the whole western country, and with the great rivers barred up, the trade of Cincinnati was paralyzed for the time. Many of the stores and shops were closed, in most of those open there being notices that, for the present, business could only be done for cash. The prices of the theaters and entertainments were advertised as "reduced to suit the times." There was little shipping about the wharves, and what goods there were being shipped were mostly military stores. Work was scarce, and there was much poverty, I was told, amongst the working classes, though the country is too rich for actual distress to be felt. The young men were gone to the war, and the hospitals were crowded with wounded soldiers—Confederates as well as Federal—who had just been brought up from the battlefield of Pittsburgh Landing.

But what struck me most was the German air of the place and people. It was hard, strolling through the streets, to realize that you were not in some city of the old German Vaterland. The great thoroughfares and the fashionable streets were American in every feature, and the only trace of Germany to be found *there* was in the number of German names—Hartmans, Meyers, Schmidt, and so on—written over the shop-doors. When, however, you passed into the suburbs, and the poorer parts of the city, everything, except the names of the streets, was German. A sluggish canal runs through the town, and, with one of those ponderous jokes so dear to the German mind, the quarter above the canal, where the Germans mostly dwell, is called "Ueber dem Rhein." Here, "across the Rhine," the Germans have brought their fatherland with them. Almost everybody that you meet is speaking in the harsh, guttural, German accents. The women, with their squat, stout figures, their dull blue eyes, and fair flaxen hair, sit knitting at their doors, dressed in the stuffed woolen petticoats of German fashion. The men have still the woolen jackets, the blue worsted pantaloons, and the low-crowned hats one knows so well in Bavaria and the Tyrol. There are *"Bier Gartens,"* *"Restaurations,"* and *"Tanz Saale,"* on every side. The goods in the shop windows are advertised in German, and the official notices of sheriffs' sales and ward elections are posted up on the walls, in English it is true, but with a German translation underneath. There are German operas, German concerts, and half a dozen German theaters, the very play-bills of which are printed in the old, plain, small German style, undebased by the asterisks and repetitions and sensation headings which form the pride of an American theatrical placard. Here, in the free West, the Germans have asserted their right to spend Sunday as they like; and so "across the Rhine," the dancing gardens are open, and the *Turner* feasts take place, and the first representations of the opera are given on the Sunday as in their native land. It was curious to me to note the audience at one of the small German theaters I dropped into one evening. The women had brought their babies and knitting with them; the men had their long pipes, and both men and women sat drinking the lager beer, and eating the inevitable sausages, and the "butter-brod und schinken" sandwiches. The play was full of true German commonplace moralities, and the actors, inferior as they were, acted with that conscientious laborious carefulness which supplies the place of talent on the German stage. But more curious than the resemblance of the old country was the gradual development you could notice in the audience, by which the German element was being merged in the American. The older comers had already dropped the old-fashioned German dress, and when they talked to each other it was as often in English as in German. With many, too, of the younger generation, who had probably been born in the New World, the placid expression of the German face was already changed for the sharp anxious look so universal to the native-born American. The notion is, that the heavy taxation which must follow this war for years will stop the German emigration. If so, and fresh German blood is not poured into the old settlement, the German breed will soon be swallowed into the American; and fifty years hence, the existence of the old German quarter "across the Rhine" will be a matter of tradition.

From Cincinnati I went down the Ohio River, which forms the frontier between the states of Indiana and Kentucky as far as Louisville. "*La Belle Rivière*," as the early French settlers called the Ohio, must have been a term applied rather to the river itself, than to the scenery through which it runs. If you took away the villa "chateaux" on its banks, and the picturesque old Norman towns with their Gothic churches, I don't know that the Seine would be an interesting river; and the Ohio is not unlike the Seine, without chateaux, or towns, or churches. The broad rapid stream, the low sloping hills on either side, the straggling brick-built towns scattered along the banks, form pretty well the only features that strike a traveler passing down the river. The first hour's sail is very pleasant, the second is monotonous, the third is wearily dull; and, after the third, you devote your attention much more to what is going on inside the vessel than to the external scenery. Happily, inside the steamer there is plenty of interest for a stranger. The boat itself, with its broad deck, on which the freight is stowed, its long cabin, raised on pillars above the deck, running from the bows to the stern, and its engines rising above the cabin, is a strange sight in itself to a European. The ladies, of whom we had few on board, sat at one end of the cabin, and the men gathered round the other, where they smoked, expectorated, read newspapers, liquored at the bar, and played the mysterious game of "euchre." It was your own fault if you wanted companionship. I made a chance acquaintance with a gentleman sitting beside me at dinner, and before half an hour was over, I had been introduced to, and shaken hands with, half of our fellow passengers, all of whom were strangers to both of us. The sole objection to this promiscuous introduction is that everyone you are introduced to asks you to drink as a matter of politeness. Happily, American whisky is very weak, and as you are allowed to help yourself from the bottle, you can take as little as you please. I was struck then, by the way, as I had often been before, at the great liberality in standing treat, to use a common word, of the ordinary Americans. Men to whom, from their dress and air, money must really be a matter of consequence, will spend many shillings in paying for drinks for perfect strangers; and if any friend's friend is standing by, will press him to join him as a matter of course. There is no ostentation, as far as I can see, about this custom, but a simple feeling of rough hospitality, not over refined, perhaps, but still creditable in itself. I was struck, too, as I was frequently, with the extraordinary freedom with which, in the midst of this civil war, men of all opinions expressed their sentiments in public. We had many Union soldiers on board, several Government officials, and a good sorting of Secessionists. We had various political discussions, but all in perfect good humor and frankness; and the only opinion I did not hear expressed was Abolitionist, either because there were no Abolitionists in the party, or because Abolitionist doctrines are too unpopular in these Border Slave States to be freely expressed. There was one old Kentucky farmer I was introduced to, who was just going home, after having been kept in prison at Columbus as a Secessionist. He confessed openly that he was in favor of Secession, but declared, whether truly or not, that he had taken no part for or against it, and that his imprisonment had been due to a malicious information given against him by the Union doctor of the village, whose conduct he had had to censure for immorality. "The only thing, sir," he said, "I thought *was* hard, was, that I was arrested on the very spot of ground where our regiment was encamped in 1812, when we were drawn out to fight the Britishers, begging your pardon, sir." Yet this old man was conversing in the most friendly way with another old Kentucky backwoodsman, who had sent three sons to fight in the Federal army, and was asking everybody if they could tell him whether his boys' regiment had been in the battle of Pittsburgh Landing, and who, when he was assured that the regiment had not been under fire, made the comment, "Well, I should have liked my boys to have been in at the battle." A gentlemen, by the way, who had just returned from the field of battle, assured me, that amongst all the dead bodies lying scattered over that hard-fought field, he saw but one, rebel or loyal, who had been shot in the back.

Kentucky

It was in Kentucky that Secession received its first important check. Had Kentucky passed a vote in favor of seceding, the whole of the Border Slave States would have gone with the South, and the suppression of the insurrection would have been indefinitely, if not permanently, postponed. The sentiments of Kentucky, being, as she is, an offshoot of Virginia, were all with the South, but her interests were all with the North. In this conflict of opposing forces she stood neutral. In all insurrections it is an invariable rule that whosoever is not with you is against you. So it proved here. The famous declaration of neutrality, issued by the State Government of Kentucky, proved of no service to the South, and was disregarded by both parties alike. In utter defiance of their favorite doctrine of state rights, the Confederates resolved to force Kentucky into active cooperation, and it was for this purpose, according to his own confession, that General Sidney Johnston, the ablest, perhaps, of the Confederate Generals, whose death at Pittsburgh Landing proved a heavy blow to the South, invaded Kentucky. His motive in so doing, as he stated in his report to Jefferson Davis, was political rather than military. Happily for the North, the Union feeling of Kentucky was roused at this attempt at coercion. Troops enough were raised in the state itself to check the Confederate advance until the Federal Government had time to form its armies. The result was that the Confederates were never able to establish themselves in any force farther than Bowling Green, which lies only a few miles north of the Tennessee frontier.

By a sort of moral retribution, the only state in the Union

which proposed to remain neutral, has in reality suffered most from the effects of the war. I recollect, at the time of the annexation of Savoy, reading a statement in one of the imperialist Savoyard papers, to the effect that where their rivers run, there their hearts turned also. The saying might be far more truly applied to the Western States. Their very life flows with the course of their rivers. The stoppage of the Mississippi, and the streams which flow into it, is absolute death to the trade of the West. Free access to the Gulf of Mexico is essential to its development. Thus Kentucky, though up to this time it had been saved from much actual war, experienced more loss than all the other states. In the country districts, the actual suffering was not perhaps so great. Wheat and corn and maize had fetched unusually good prices, while the demand for Government supplies created an artificial market for cattle. In the towns, however, there was nothing to neutralize the paralyzing effects of the war, and the complete stoppage of the Southern trade. Louisville, the virtual though not the nominal capital of the state (for in Kentucky, as in most other states of the Union, the actual seat of government is placed purposely in some town of small importance), has suffered terribly. Out of seventy jobbing houses which carried on business here before the war broke out, only two are left standing. The others have failed or have moved elsewhere. The pork trade with the South, which was one of the staples of Louisville commerce, has completely fallen off. The carrying trade on the Ohio River came altogether to an end, except for Government stores. The iron and metal factories had all suspended work. There has not been any absolute distress amongst the working classes. The country is so fertile that absolute want was a thing still unknown, but there was a total stoppage of the growth of Louisville, or rather an actual retrogression in its career. Within forty years Louisville had grown from a city of four thousand souls to one numbering upward of seventy thousand inhabitants; but during the first year since the outbreak of the war, the population had diminished by some ten thousand persons.

The aspect of the city bore out these statements, which were made to me by merchants resident in Louisville. In former times it must have been a place of great commercial activity, though of no great interest to the "uncommercial traveler." There is one striking peculiarity of a negative rather than a positive order, common to almost all American towns, and that is that they have no sights. When you have taken your first half-hour's stroll about any town you happen to pass the night in, you know as much about it externally as if you had lived there for a month. Every town is built on the same system, has the same series of more or less lengthy rectangular streets, the same large spacious stores, the same snug, unpicturesque rows of villas, detached or semi-detached as the case may be, the same somber churches, built in the architectural style of St. Clement Danes or St. Mary's, Bryan-stone Square, and the same nomenclature of streets—the invariable Walnut, Chestnut, Front, and Main streets—crossed by the same perpendicular streets, numbered First, Second, and so on to any number you like, according to the size of the town. I have often wondered how, supposing you could be put down unexpectedly in an ordinary American town, you could ascertain by observation that you were not in England. Of course the quantity of mules used for the carts is not English. The climate, at least between April and November, is not English. The street railroads are, or rather were, un-English, and the Negroes you see loitering about the streets with the colored silk handkerchiefs, which, in all Slave States, they wear bound about their heads, are happily not English also. Still, the main difference is, that everything about you would look so new and so unfinished; and this is a difference which it is easier to understand than to describe. I should think that even the compiler of a local handbook would find it difficult to say much about Louisville. When I was there, there was a sleepy, drowsy look about the place which could not have been usual to it. On every side you saw long rows of shut-up stores, and large factories whose gates were closed, and from whose chimneys no smoke issued. The riverside was crowded with numbers of steamers, laid up for want of freights. There were no trucks about the streets, and no appearance of goods being carried between the different stations. The common people to whom I spoke all told me the same story, that prices of living were uncommonly high, that work was unusually slack, and that instead of making money, as in former years, the most they could hope for was to be able to pay their way.

Still, with all this, the country around Louisville is so rich that it seems impossible to a stranger to associate the idea of distress with it. During my stay there, which I prolonged for some days, partly because there is one of the best hotels in all the Union at Louisville, I went out a good deal into the surrounding country. The institution of slavery has not been able to mar the appearance of physical prosperity, and that is saying a good deal. I doubt whether even a Bourbon regime could destroy it in less than a century. Even more than the State of Ohio, Kentucky is the garden country of the States. When you get out into the little country towns, you seem to have got into an England where the sun shines, and where there is no poverty. The German element has no great strength there, and the old English element of Virginia is still in the ascendant. In Frankfort, or in Lexington, or in any of the country towns of what is called the Blue Grass region of Kentucky, you require the sight of the railroad running along the streets to show you that you are not in an English county town. The main street, with its quiet little shops, its depots of agricultural implements, its small town houses standing a little way back from the road, and fronted by the plots of lawn, and its whole sleepy, lazy air, is the exact counterpart of an English High Street. The inns, too, are not called "houses," or even hotels, but inns, with old-fashioned English signs of the Phœnix and the Lion swinging over their doors; and the stages which meet the trains at the different stations are like resuscitated four-horse coaches, only that the drivers are Negroes. All around the towns there are small country houses standing in their own grounds, which might have been transported bodily from the Old Country. In the early Maytime, when I was there, the weather was like that of an English summer, and the pasture lands were as green, and the crops as rich, and the fields as carefully tilled and hedged in, as they would have been in Warwickshire. There was hardly a trace of that shiftless slovenliness I observed in every other Slave State, and the slaves themselves were better dressed, and brighter looking. In the houses, too, whose doors and windows were thrown open to let in the cool air, you saw the Negro children playing about carelessly in a way that seemed to bespeak a considerable degree of kindness on the part of their masters. From all inquiries I could make, I gathered that the feelings of Kentucky with regard to Secession were of a very mixed character. Up to the beginning of the spring, the southern portion of the state was more or less subject to the Confederate government. The first of the Union victories was that of Mill Springs, in Kentucky, where General [Felix] Zollicoffer was killed. But, with this exception, there had been then little actual fighting in the state, and, with the evacuation of Bowling Green, the authority of the Union was restored without resistance. In the Federal armies there were thirty-two Kentucky regiments, which would represent a force of some twenty-five thousand men, and there were supposed to be about six thousand Kentuckians in the Confederate service. At the battle of Shiloh, two Federal Kentucky regiments charged a Confederate one from their own state, and the belief is, judging from their own heavy loss, that they destroyed full half of it. In Kentucky, perhaps, more than anywhere else, the civil war produced that division of families and friends which forms the most fearful incident in the struggle. I suppose there is scarcely a Kentuckian who has not friends or relations fighting on each side. As far as I could collect, whenever there was a direct political issue laid before the state, the Unionists carried all before them.

There was, however, a very large, and what is more, a very noisy Secession element in Kentucky. Residents in Louisville, Unionists as well as Secessionists, assured me that the number of sympathizers with the South was very great, and that any reverse of the Federal forces would be the signal for an anti-Union demonstration. The Confederate prisoners whom I visited seemed in good condition and in high spirits; and the jailers complained to me that there was much more charity shown by private families in Louisville toward the rebels than toward the wounded Federal soldiers. If the charitable donations of the friends of Secession included soap, I can only say that their protégés made a thankless return for the kindness displayed. It was a startling fact, also, that the Government had to prohibit the public burial of Confederate soldiers in Kentucky, on account of the Secession demonstrations to which they gave place. Shortly before I was there, at the funeral of a Confederate officer, at Louisville, over three thousand persons assembled to escort the corpse. It is true that the officer in question was well known and respected in the town, and that his wife was the daughter of the most popular of the Episcopalian clergymen in the city; but still these facts would not account for a tenth part of the crowd. Again, soon after the battle of Shiloh, a wounded Confederate soldier of Louisiana, a private, who died of his wounds on the voyage up the Ohio, was left at the little town of Owensburgh for burial. He was not personally known at the place, but this was the account of his funeral, as given by a local paper: "A meeting was called by the Southern citizens of the town, and preparations made for a suitable burial. Long before the appointed time, our streets were crowded with people, from all sections of the county, who had come to witness the solemn ceremony. At two o'clock the remains were conveyed to the Methodist church, where an impressive and eloquent funeral oration was delivered by the Rev. Dr. Nicolson. The number of spectators at the church was variously estimated at from one thousand to fifteen hundred. After the exercises at the church were concluded, the procession repaired to the cemetery, where they deposited the remains of the brave but unfortunate soldier, who died while nobly battling in defense of his country and his country's cause. It may be some consolation to the friends of the deceased to know that, though buried amongst strangers, in a strange land, he was interred in a manner becoming his cause, and that thousands of sympathizing tears were shed over his grave for the loved ones at home, and many a fervent prayer offered up to God for his safe deliverance to that haven of rest where strife, dissensions, and *abolitionism* never enter, and where peace and harmony reign for ever."

I have quoted this article, not only as a proof of Secession feeling, but as evidence of the extreme liberty of speech allowed by the Federal Government in Kentucky. Even in Ireland, the *Nation* could hardly be more outspoken without danger of suppression. At the public barrooms in Louisville, I myself was present at conversations in which open sympathy for the South and bitter animosity toward the Lincoln Government was expressed as freely as it could have been in Mr. Mason's drawing room in London. In the towns it was found necessary to exclude all women suspected of Secession proclivities from the military hospitals, because they insulted the wounded Federal soldiers. In fact, the feeling of Kentucky toward Secession is entirely different from what it is in the North. Events have proved that the majority—the great majority—of Kentuckians were opposed to Secession, and were ready to suppress it at the cost of war. They looked upon it as unwise, destructive to their own interests, and unjustified by law, but they did not, as Northern men did, look upon it as unprovoked. They sympathized keenly with the sentiment of Secession, though they disapproved its active manifestation. In plainer words, Kentucky is a slaveholding state, and therefore against her judgment, and in spite of her interest, could not help sympathizing with slaveholders. The bitterness against the Abolitionists and the Administration was extreme. As early as last spring, in Kentucky, the Washington Administration was regarded as completely in the hands of the Abolitionist party. The emancipation of the slaves in the District of Columbia had given great offense, and was stated openly by Union men to be a certain step toward prolonging the war. In talking to an old Kentucky statesman—the staunchest of Union men, and a member, some years ago, of the Federal Government—about a rumored intention of the Border States members to withdraw from Congress, I learnt, to my surprise, that he completely approved of the idea, if, by rendering either House unable to form a quorum, it could bring the anti-slavery legislation to a deadlock. This gentleman, I should add, was not a slaveholder, and had never, as a matter of personal feeling, held slaves; but as a Kentuckian, his sympathies were all with the Slave States.

Indeed, the old Democratic politicians, of whom my friend had been a leading member, reckoned confidently that as soon as the insurrection was suppressed, the insurgent states would resume their seats in Congress; that, throughout the North, there would be a great reaction against the Republican party after the war, and that in consequence there would be a return of something like the old pro-slavery Democratic rule. I believe myself this calculation would probably have turned out correct, and might still prove correct, at least for a certain period, if the insurgent states possessed wisdom enough to see their own interests, and accept frankly the restoration of the Union. On the other hand, the course of events in Kentucky and Tennessee, after the Union authority was restored, held out no probability that such would be the case. At this time I heard a leading Republican Senator say to Mr. Sumner, "What will save us will be not our own merits, but the mistakes of our enemies"; and I take this to be the truth. Already, in the Free State papers you could see indications of impatience at the want of loyalty shown toward the Union in the Border Slave States; and even in other than Abolition organs an opinion began to be timidly suggested that the power of the slaveholding interest was the one obstacle in the way of reunion. In truth, Kentucky, like all the so-called loyal Slave States, was about equally afraid of the triumph of its friends and of its opponents. The result was that the state was still halting between the North and South. Its sentiments drew it toward the latter, and its interest toward the former.

Let me add, in passing, that Kentucky is the first state in the Union where I saw lottery offices in every street, and where the old notices in the shop windows, that I remember so well in Italy, caught my eye, requesting passersby to tempt fortune, and to win five thousand dollars at the risk of one.

Tennessee

THE ROAD from Louisville to Nashville lay right on the track of the war, through Kentucky and Western Tennessee. The railroad had only been reopened ten days or so before I passed over it. The Confederate forces had been till quite recently in possession of Nashville, and the first great battle of the Western campaign had been expected to take place along the railroad, at Bowling Green station, and would doubtless have taken place there, had not the Confederates evacuated the position on the advance of the Union troops. Still, the traces of the recent war, and of the march and retreat of great armies, were not so numerous as I expected. Where houses are so few and far between as they are in these new states, and where so much of the country is still uncultivated, it is difficult, even for wanton destruction, to produce much outward appearance of desolation; and, besides, from the nature of this civil war, both armies in these Border States have proceeded on the assumption that they were in a friendly country, and have, therefore, as a rule, spared private property. Yet there were evidences enough of the war, after all. Along a line of some hundred and eighty odd miles, there was not a bridge that had not been burnt or broken down. Rickety wooden structures, which made a stranger tremble at the idea of passing over them, had been run up in their stead, and small detachments of Union soldiers were posted by these makeshift bridges to preserve them from destruction. The rails had often been torn up, for many hundred yards together, and the cars run over a newly-laid-down trackway, side by side with the old line of rails. There were broken engines, too, and burnt cars lying alongside the line;

and, wherever there were the traces of a Confederate encamp-
ment, there the blackened ruins of the roadside houses told you
of the reckless destruction worked by the retreating army in the
despair of defeat. The great Confederate fort of Bowling Green
struck me, on a rapid view, as of no great military strength. But,
long after the war is over, the earthworks of the camp on the
Green River, and the shattered buttresses of the grand stone
arches, will remain as tokens of the great insurrection.

But, in truth, this Tennessee country is so bright and pleasant
a one, that it would take years of war to make it look other than
prosperous, especially above all other seasons, in the early and
short-lived bloom of a Southern spring. My impression of Tennessee, like most of one's impressions about the localities of the
Southern States, was taken from the old melody of the darkie
who fell in love with the "lovely Rosa Lee, courting down in
Tennessee." For once the impression was a correct one; and, of
all pleasant places to go courting in, it would be "down in Tennessee," in that sweet April time. As far as country goes, I should
be hard put to choose, if I had to fix my dwelling-place in Ohio
or in Tennessee. In the latter state the climate is softer, and more
Southern; but there is less life, less energy, perhaps, about the
Slave State—less sign of rapid progress. The fields are worked by
gangs of Negroes. Every now and then, too, you see the wretched
wood hovels, telling of actual poverty—things which you do not
see in Ohio; and, also, I grieve to say, when you look closely into
the Tennessee paradise, the garden of Eden is somewhat of a
dirty one.

Of all American cities which I have seen, Nashville, or "Nase-
ville," as they call it, in the soft Southern lisp, is the most picturesque. Perched upon a high steep ridge hanging over the
Cumberland river, the "Rocky City" is perforce divorced from
that dismal rectangular system so fatal to the beauty of American towns. The streets run up and down all sorts of slopes, and
at all kinds of angles. The rows of houses stand terrace-like one
above the other; and, highest of all, the State Capitol towers
grandly above the city. The main thoroughfares are broad and
bright, shaded over pleasantly by the rows of lime and chestnut

trees, which grow on either side. All around the city, on every inequality of the broken ground, there are placed well-built stone villas, and the whole place had a sort of New World Bath air about it, which struck me curiously.

In happier days, Nashville must have been a very pleasant dwelling-place; but when I saw it, the whole aspect of the city was, even for a stranger, a dreary and dismal one. An American —a staunch Union man himself—described its state as being like that of Italian cities he had seen, shortly after the Austrians re-occupied them in '49. But, I own, to me this description seemed, externally, rather overdrawn. I should say myself that Nashville looked more like a city still stunned by the blow of some great public calamity. Outwardly, it had not suffered much from its various military occupations. The Louisville trains stopped on the Northern side of the river, at Edgefield, for the great railway-bridge which spanned the Cumberland was blown up by the Confederates on leaving. With a reckless wantonness, the beautiful suspension bridge was cut to pieces at the same period, so that all communication between Nashville and the North had to be carried on by boats and ferries. Otherwise, the city had received little material injury; but I think this absence of external ruin rather increased the effect of the general depression visible throughout the town. When Mr. Seward went over to Winchester, on its first occupation by General Banks' division, Mr. Sumner, who had often disputed with him as to the existence of a strong Union sentiment in the South, asked him what he thought of the look of things at the Virginian town. "Well," he answered, "all the men were gone to the war, and all the women were she-devils." The same description would not, I suspect, have applied badly to Nashville. The town had a deserted air. If you took away the Union soldiers, there would have been very few people about the streets at all. There were numbers of Negroes, apparently idling about the town, but the white population seemed scanty for the size of the place. Young men you met very seldom about—and, indeed, the proportion of women to men was unusually large. What is stranger still, the children seemed to have been sent away. At any rate, contrary to the custom of other

American towns, they were not visible in the streets. The Union regiments quartered here were from the neighboring states, and, one would suppose, would have had many acquaintances in the town, but there was, avowedly, little intercourse between the military and the inhabitants, while the soldiers complained bitterly of the manner in which the Nashville women expressed their dislike on every possible occasion. Half the shops were closed, and in the few of any size still open the owners sat moodily among empty shelves. Trade, however, was gradually reviving. In every shop there were notices put up of "No Southern money taken"; and the shopkeepers seemed willing enough to sell what goods they had at exorbitant prices to the Federal soldiers. On the walls there still hung the tattered half-torn-down official notices of the Confederate government, and on a building right in front of the hotel where I lodged you could still read an inscription over the door, "Head Quarters of the Confederate States' Army," while displayed openly in the windows of the stationers, I saw copies of patriotic Confederate dance music, headed "The Confederate Prize Banner Quadrille," "The Lady Polk Polka," and the "Morgan Schottische." Of any pro-Union exhibition of feeling on the part of private individuals I could see little trace. Over the public buildings the Stars and Stripes floated gaily; but on no single dwelling-house could I see a Union flag. In the shop windows there were no prints of Federal victories, no display of the patriotic books and pamphlets so universal throughout the North. In the way of business, indeed, nothing seemed stirring, unless it was the undertaking trade, which, from the number of coffins I saw about, ought to have been thriving. Of the women I met, a majority were in deep mourning, not so much, I fear, as an exhibition of political sentiment, as in memory of husbands, and sons, and brothers, who had fallen on the slaughter field of Pittsburgh Landing. Martial law was not enforced, but after dark the streets were almost deserted; sentries were posted at frequent intervals, and ever and anon the death-like stillness of the town was broken by the jangle of swords and spurs, as the mounted patrols rode slowly past. The theater had been reopened, more, I should fancy, from political motives than from any prospect of pecuniary profit.

The house was almost exclusively filled with Federal soldiers, and on the two occasions when I went there I saw only one lady amongst the audience, and she was a Frenchwoman. The wealthier inhabitants were daily leaving the town, on account of the general depression which prevailed there. Politics seemed to be a tabooed subject in private conversation. In several houses that I went into, I found that the heads of the family were under arrest, and there were constant rumors, though I believe mostly exaggerated ones, of collisions between the inhabitants and the soldiery. All barrooms were closed by military orders, a circumstance which must in itself have been a bitter grievance to a liquor-loving, bar-frequenting people, and neither for love nor money could a stranger obtain a drink more intoxicating than lager beer within the bounds of Nashville.

The press of Nashville represented, curiously enough, the disorganized condition of society. The editors of the old local papers, who were all bitter Secessionists, had left the town at the approach of the Federal forces, and their papers were either suspended or suppressed. The existing press of Nashville consisted of two small single sheet papers, the *Nashville Union* and the *Nashville Dispatch*. The former, of course, was the official organ of the Government. Commercially, I should question its having been a paying property, as every day there appeared piteous appeals to the loyal men of Tennessee to support "the uncompromising organ of Union," by sending in subscriptions and advertisements, and thus "to keep the flag of the Union, of law and order, streaming defiantly in the very face of the enemy, as he retires sullenly to the Gulf." One great object of the paper professed to be "to bring to light hundreds of crimes and outrages committed by the rebels during their ascendancy, and which the guilty authors believed would never be brought to light." This part of its program was amply redeemed, for the greater part of its meager reading matter consisted of revelations of Confederate misrule during the last few months.

To the credit of the *Union*, I should state that even in a period of such excitement, and in a paper conducted with such vehemence, there were no personal assaults on private individuals, no denunciations by name of suspected Secessionists. The advertisements were very few in number, and what there were were chiefly official ones. In fact the majority were notices of runaway slaves detained in the county jail. It seemed strange to an Englishman to read a long string of advertisements like the following:

> On the 8th day of May, 1862, I will expose to public sale to the highest bidder, for cash, at the Court House, Yard Gate, in Nashville, one negro boy named William, levied on as the property of Sharp and Hamilton, to satisfy sundry executions in my hands.

Again, amongst the committals to the jail I came across the following:

> April 21, 1862. A negro woman, who says her name is Lucinda, and belongs to William Donaldson, of Davidson County. The said woman is about 28 or 30 years old; dark copper colour.

> April 18, 1862. A negro man, who says his name is Andrew. Says he belongs to R. L. Brown, of Davidson county. Dark copper colour. Scar on the left side of his cheek. About 28 years old. Weighs about 158 pounds, and is 5 ft. 7 in. high.

And at the end of each advertisement the owner is requested "to come forward, prove property, and pay charges, as the law directs." Then there were the advertisements of free Negroes, confined to jail on the suspicion of being runaways. Thus:

> March 16, 1862. A negro man, says his name is George Mosely. Says he is a free man of colour. Says he lives in Indianapolis, in Indiana. About 37 years old. Weighs about 187 pounds. Has whiskers and a moustache, a small scar on corner of left eye. Dark copper colour, 5 ft. 10 in. high.

In fact, if it were not for the "peculiar institution," the advertisement department of the *Union* would be but shabbily provided.

The principles of the *Nashville Dispatch* were, according to the statement of its rival, "as nearly secessionist as it can be to keep out of Johnson's clutches," and the accusation was probably well founded. It was obviously written to suit a public to whom the successes of the Union were, to say the least, uninteresting. It professed no political principles, but it contained no prognostication of Federal victories, and, in fact, seemed disposed to ignore Secession generally. I always believed that the *Giornale di Roma* had an unrivaled talent for conveying the minimum of news in a given number of columns, but I think the *Nashville Dispatch* was no unworthy rival in the same laudable endeavor. What little news it gave was composed of items of Southern intelligence, reprinted from the Northern papers, and, except in the official telegrams, the name "rebel" was never used, but always supplied by that of "Confederate." The leaders were generally on miscellaneous subjects, utterly unconnected with the war, and often consisted of short moral discourses on the benefits of forbearance and strict integrity. The trade advertisements were rather more numerous than those of the *Union*, but it had not the official ones of Negro sales or committals to jail. The space lost in this way was filled with a romantic story of love and seduction. Of the two, there was more "grit," to use a Yankee phrase, about the *Union*.

The whole policy, or rather want of policy, of the Federal government, with regard to the reconquered states, was exhibited at Nashville in its practical working. To suppress the rebellion was the one idea that either government or people had been able to grasp as yet; and, with regard to the future, the only vestige of a policy adopted was a general intention to restore, as much as might be, the *status quo* before the war. As soon as Nashville was retaken, Mr. Andrew Johnson was sent there as military governor. A Tennessee man himself, and a slaveholder, he was selected for the post, not only on account of his unswerving adherence to the Union, but because it was considered that his appointment would be a guarantee to the people of Tennessee that no violent interference with their property was designed. For the immediate purpose of pacification, the appointment was a wise one. Every step consistent with a vigorous suppression of active Secession was taken to win back the allegiance of the people, and, as far as the language of the governor went, nothing could be more satisfactory to a slave-owning state. At the period of my visit, when reviewing a Minnesota regiment, quartered at Nashville (Minnesota, be it remembered, is a Free State), I wrote about what Governor Johnson had said:

"It had been charged by the apostles of treason that the North had come here to set Negroes free. He knew the North, had traveled among her people, and he repelled the charge with scorn. There were abolition fanatics there, it was true—sectionalists, traitors, brothers of Southern Secessionists—but these creatures constituted but a fraction of the great body of the North. The voice of the overwhelming mass of the North, as well as of nine men out of ten who stood before him was, 'We care nothing for your negroes. Manage them as best suits yourselves, but the Union shall be preserved, and you must obey the laws;'" and this enunciation of principles was loudly cheered by the soldiers.

How far this patchwork policy will prove ultimately successful in re-establishing a pro-Union feeling, time alone can show. It had had little time to act when I was at Nashville, and it was hard to judge what progress it had made. There was, indeed, no disguising the fact that the Federal Government had not received the sympathy it counted upon in Tennessee. The belief in the North had been that the Union armies would have been hailed as deliverers by a large portion of the population, but, hitherto, they had met, at the best, with a sullen acquiescence. It should be added that the Union party made no attempt to represent things as more favorable than they were, and confessed the absence of Union sympathy as frankly as they admitted all their other failures and shortcomings. Indeed, the best sign, nationally, I saw about the Americans was the resolute fearlessness with which they looked facts in the face, even when telling against themselves. Thus, in Nashville, the Government party admitted openly that since the occupation there had been no public expression of any love for the Union exhibited in this part of Tennessee. As evidences of returning loyalty, the *Nashville Union* quoted, I remember, with great pride, how one old lady had sent a Federal flag to the Governor, with the request that it might be hung up in some public spot; and how the city council had at last, after nearly a month's deliberation, passed a resolution, that "they cordially thanked the officers and soldiers of the United

States for the unexampled kindness and courtesy hitherto extended to their fellow citizens, and that as men striving in the common work of re-establishing the Government of their fathers, they pledged their most sincere and hearty cooperation."

It was impossible to help feeling that if the Unionists were gratified by demonstrations of such doubtful loyalty, they were easily contented. Of any practical manifestation of Union feeling there was little indication. With East Tennessee and Memphis still in the possession of the enemy, there could be no question as yet about how the Senators and Representatives of Tennessee were to be elected, and therefore, for the moment, this difficult question was postponed; but extreme difficulty had been already experienced in filling up the civil offices with loyal men. The corporation, by rather an arbitrary stretch of power, was required to take the oath of allegiance to the United States; and the greatest reluctance was exhibited by them in acceding to the requirement. For three weeks after Governor Johnson arrived, it was found impossible to induce anyone to undertake the office of postmaster; and a yet longer period elapsed before an editor could be found bold enough to conduct a Government newspaper.

However, this absence of Union feeling was not so strange nor so disheartening as it might appear at first sight. There can be no doubt that the common people of Tennessee, like the inhabitants of all the Southern States, believed sincerely that the "Lincoln hordes" were coming down to destroy their property, burn their houses, and murder their wives and children. Extraordinary as such an illusion was, it could be accounted for partly by the comparative isolation of the South, partly by the extent to which the lower classes received all their intelligence and all their opinions from their leaders, and, still more, by the morbid nervousness which the existence of a slave population is sure to beget amongst the dominant race. By degrees the people of Tennessee were becoming convinced that the Northerners had no intention of interfering with their property, or of treating them as subjects of a conquered country; and that, in fact, life and property were far safer under a Federal Government than they had been under the

Confederate rule. Again, the war was too near at hand, and the danger too imminent for Tennessee to appreciate fully that the battle had been fought and lost. It was easy enough for an indifferent spectator in the North to see that the Confederates were fighting a losing fight in the Border States, and that even a return of fortune to their arms would only prolong a hopeless struggle; but, to men living in Tennessee, it was not so easy to take a wide view of the case. If [Gen. P. G. T.] Beauregard had won the battle of Pittsburgh Landing, or had defeated the Federals at Corinth, it was quite possible, though not probable, that Nashville might have been reoccupied for the time by the Confederates; and their return would have been the sure signal for a reign of terror of which all who had given their adherence to the new Government might reasonably have feared to be the victims. Moreover—and I believe this to have been the chief explanation —as long as the war lasts there can be no cordial restoration of Union feeling in any Southern State. Men may grow convinced of the folly of Secession, may even wish for the triumph of the Union; but their hearts must be, after all, with the side for which their kinsmen and friends are fighting. I suppose there is hardly a family in Tennessee which has not some member in the ranks of the Confederate army. It is this conflict of affections which makes all civil war so hateful. How hateful it is, in truth, never came home to me till I saw it actually. I have known myself of a wife whose husband was fighting for the South, while her father and brother were in the Federal army. I knew, too, of a mother who had only two sons, one in the North, and the other in the South, both fighting in the armies that were ranged opposite to each other in front of Yorktown. So I, or anyone, could name a hundred instances of father fighting against son—brother against brother—of families divided—of homes where there was mourning whenever the news of battle came, no matter which side had won the victory. I have dwelt thus somewhat at length on the reasons why I think the sullen attitude of Tennessee might be accounted for, because I am anxious not to convey the impression that I believe in the Southern or rather the Confederate doctrine of an innate and unconquerable aversion between the North and

South. If once the insurrection were suppressed, and order restored, I have little doubt the Southern States would acquiesce
in what was inevitable. There is no difference in race, or language,
or religion, or geographical position to keep the two divisions of
the Union apart. Whether the difference in domestic institutions
would prove an insuperable cause of disunion, I cannot say. If it
should so prove, the North will suppress or remove this cause
before it consents to the disruption of the Union. This is the only
fact of which I feel positive.

In old English books about travel in Switzerland, it used to be
a stock remark that you could tell whether a canton was Protestant or Catholic by the relative cleanliness or dirtiness of the
towns. How far the fact was true, or how far, if true, it established
the truth of the Protestant religion, I could never determine; but
a similar conclusion may certainly be drawn with regard to the
Free and the Slave States. You may lay it down as a rule throughout America, that wherever you find slavery, there you have dirt
also. Nashville, as I said before, is one of the cleanest and brightest of towns at a distance; but when you come close the illusion
vanishes. There is no excuse there for want of cleanliness. The
position of the town makes drainage easy; the stone used so plentifully is clean of itself; and water is abundant. The only thing
wanting seemed to be energy to keep the place clean. The hotel
where I was stopping was in itself an institution (in American
phrase) of the country. It was the best in the city; and Nashville
was always celebrated as one of the most thriving and prosperous
cities in the South. Hotel-keeping was not suffering, like other
trading concerns, from the depression of the moment. This hotel
was crammed with guests, and had been crammed throughout the
previous winter. Outside it was handsome enough, but internally,
I say without hesitation, it was the dirtiest and worst managed
hotel it had been ever my fortune to stop at. The dirt was dirt of
old standing, and the mismanagement must have been the
growth of years long preceding the days when Secession was first
heard of. The bar, as I mentioned, was closed by order; but the
habitués still hung about the scene of their former pleasures. In
the hall there were a number of broken shattered chairs, and here,

with their legs stretched in every conceivable position, a number of well-dressed respectable-looking persons used to loaf all day long, smoking and chewing. They did not seem to have anything to do, or much to say to each other; but they sat there to kill time by looking at one another. The floor was as dirty as successive strata of tobacco-juice could make it; and, at the slightest symptom of chill in the air, the stove was kindled to a red-hot heat, and the atmosphere was made as stifling as the cracks in the doors would permit it to become. The passages were as filthy as want of sweeping could make them; and dirty cloths, slop-pails, and brooms were left lying about them, all day and every day; the narrow wooden staircases were such as you would hardly see in England leading to the poorest of attics; and the household arrangements were as primitive as was consistent with the dirtiness peculiar to civilized life. As to the meals, their profusion was only equaled by their greasiness, and by the utter nondescriptness of their component victuals. The chicken pie tasted uncommonly like the stewed mutton, and both were equally unlike any compound I ever ate before. I could understand why it was thought unnecessary for the Negroes to waste soap and water on washing; but the same reason could not apply to their jackets and shirts, which I presume once were white. The servants were all Negroes, and all, naturally enough, devoted their minds to doing as little work and taking as long about it as possible. What seemed more odd than all, none of the habitual residents—some of them persons of property—appeared to be aware that the establishment was dirty and uncomfortable. The heat of the house must have been fearful in summer and the smells pestilential; for, with a southern climate, the style of building maintained was that of the small rooms and narrow passages of England. Nor was this a single instance. The other hotels in the city were worse; and some of my friends who have traveled through the Southern States have assured me that, except in the very large towns, the hotels are invariably of the same description. The truth is, that where the whites think it beneath them to work, and where the Negroes will not work unless they are forced, you cannot expect domestic comfort.

Missouri

"IF THE visitor at St. Louis," writes the local handbook, "should chance to be benevolent, or literary, or educational, he will perhaps like to look at"—a number of institutions, which I grieve to say I did not go to see. It is an unpleasing reflection that I did not fall under any one of the above three categories, and must rank among the vulgar herd, for whom the guidebook adds, by way of consolation, that, "Let them seek pleasure as they will, here are the opportunities to find it."

I confess that I sought and found my pleasure wandering about the streets of St. Louis. The place itself was a constant marvel to me. I found myself there, between eleven and twelve hundred miles from New York. Traveling night and day by express trains, you reach St. Louis from the Atlantic in forty-five hours—more than twice the time, and at about the same rate of traveling that you take in going express from Boulogne to Marseilles; and yet there are not two points in Europe separated by a couple of hundred miles, which are not far more unlike each other than New York and St. Louis. It is the capital city of the great West, the frontier town between the prairie and the settled country. Westward, the railways only reach as yet a distance of a hundred and odd miles. The great overland caravans for the Pacific Ocean start from here during their short summer season, which was to begin in the middle of May, about a week after my arrival, and to end in the middle of August. The Indians still come to the city at times to barter; and furs and peltries are stock articles of St. Louis commerce. Yet even in the far West, on the edge of the prairie land, I found myself in a vast city, as civilized and as luxuri-

ous as any city of the New World. The story of its growth is
fabulous. Thirty years ago it had about 6,000 inhabitants. Twenty
years afterward, it had upward of 100,000; and today its numbers
are supposed to be some 30,000 more. The city is worthy, indeed,
of the river on which it stands. The praise is not a low one, for to
my mind the rivers of America are the one grand feature about
its scenery. Here, twelve hundred miles from the sea, the Mississippi is as noble a river as one could wish to see; and yet, for two
thousand miles above St. Louis you can sail up the Missouri, the
true parent stream of the Mississippi River.

When once you have seen the Mississippi, you understand the
feeling of the Western States about the possession of the river.
Union men and Secessionists, Abolitionists and slave-owners, are
all agreed on this one point, that come what may, or rule who
may, the West must go with the Mississippi. You might as well
ask Liverpool to allow the mouth of the Mersey to be held by a
foreign power as propose any arrangement or compromise to the
West by which the command of the Mississippi should pass from
its hands. If the Father of Waters had poured into the Atlantic
where the Potomac does, the Confederacy might have been a
possibility; but the possession of the Mississippi has proved fatal
to the existence of the South as an isolated power.

The waters of the Western rivers were, at the time of my visit
to St. Louis, higher than they had been for years, and for miles
before you reached the Mississippi the railroad passed through
flooded fields, and swamps expanded, for the time, into vast
shallow lagoons. The river was full of great trunks of trees, torn
up by the roots, and broken-down fences and dismembered rafts.
The steamer ferry that carried you across landed you at the long
quays, lined with stores and warehouses. There was not a sailing
vessel on the wharves, as the current is too rapid for sailing craft
to ascend the river; but, for a mile in length, the wharf was lined
with the huge river-steamboats. Trade was slack when I was
there, as it was everywhere along the Mississippi, but still there
were boats enough coming and going constantly to make the
scene a lively one. Up the steep slope of the hillside, on the western bank, the city rises in long, broad streets, parallel to the quay,

and, when it has reached the hill's brow, stretches away far on the other side across the prairie of the "Champ des Noyers," which still bears the name given it by the early French settlers. There is no look left about St. Louis of a newly settled city. The hotels are as handsome and as luxurious as in any of the elder States. The shop windows are filled with all the evidences of an old civilization. In the book stalls you see, not single copies, but whole piles of the last *Blackwood's*, and *Edinburgh*, and *Westminster Reviews*; rows upon rows, too, of handsomely bound library books, such as Humboldt's Cosmos, and Macaulay's and Prescott's Histories. There are numbers of foreign book stores, where, if you liked, you could have bought Varnhagen von Ense's "Correspondence," or "Les Miserables" of Victor Hugo. Eight or nine daily newspapers (three of them, by the way, German, and one French) are hawked about the streets. The street railroads stretch over the town in every direction, but yet there are crowds of handsome carriages standing about for hire. You may ride for miles and miles in the suburbs, through rows of handsome private dwelling-houses. All the private houses are detached, two stories high, and built of Dutch-looking brick. The door stands in the middle of the house, not on one side, and the windows are high, narrow, and numerous, as in our own houses of the ante-Pitt era. In all Western cities, the streets are so broad, and the houses so frequently detached, standing in their own plots of ground, that a Western city of one hundred thousand inhabitants covers perhaps three times the space it would in Europe. There may be poverty at St. Louis, but there is no poor, densely-populated quarter. In Missouri, the smokeless anthracite coal is not to be had, and therefore the great factories by the riverside cover the lower part of St. Louis with an English-looking haze of smoke; but the sun is so powerful, and the sky so blue, that not even factory smoke can make the place look dismal.

Of all the slave-cities I had seen, St. Louis was the only one where I could not observe the outward effects of the "peculiar institution." It is true that the number of slaves in the city is small, that it is almost surrounded by Free States, and that the German population is immensely large; still, to admit the truth,

St. Louis is, in spite of slavery, one of the most prosperous cities I have traveled through in the States. The Attorney General, Edward Bates, a citizen of Missouri, told me, and I have no doubt with truth, that the result of the existence of slavery had been to check the rapidity of the growth of St. Louis, as new emigrants always settled in a Free in preference to a Slave State, but though an Abolitionist himself, he said he was glad of the result, for otherwise the state would have been altogether overrun by foreign emigrants. Certainly there is already a foreign look about St. Louis. The climate, in the first place, is too hot—even at an early period of the year—for men to bustle about as they do in Northern cities. The shops thrown open to the air, the people sitting about the doorsteps beneath the shade, and the closed lattice shutters of the houses are signs of the South. But, more than this, the actual proportion of foreigners is very large. In the names of the suburbs, such as the Carondelet, there are traces of French settlers; but the German emigration has swallowed up every other. In the streets one hears more German spoken than English. In talking to the class of persons—waiters, servants, shop-men, and porters—whom a traveler chiefly comes across, it is quite as well to speak in German as in English. Bock beer, lager beer, and May wine, are advertised for sale at every turning. Americans drink freely, and Germans drink copiously; and when the joint thirstiness of Americans and Germans is developed by a southern sun, it is astonishing the quantity of liquor that can be consumed. I should think, without exaggeration, that one-tenth of all the shops in St. Louis must be establishments where, in some form or other, liquor is drunk on the premises. I know, in the main street, I counted that, out of a line of fifty houses I took at hazard, twenty were barrooms, or wine stores, or lager saloons. German habits, too, have been imported into the city. Even in the lower American theaters, the audiences smoke and drink beer, handed to them by German waitresses. There are public "lust gartens" about the town, where German bands play at night, and where whole families, fathers, mothers, and children, come and sit for hours, to drink beer and listen to the music. Let me add, that in several of these places of entertainment which I visited, the audience was, for all I could see, as well-behaved, though not so quiet, as it would have been in Germany. At one of these summer theaters, by the way, there was a troop of Negro minstrels, who sang a patriotic song, of which the chorus was, "The Union forever, and freedom for all." Considering that Missouri is a Slave State, and the singers were, or were believed to be, Negroes, there was a sort of bathos about the performance which it required an American education *not* to appreciate. I recollect, when Father Prout was in Rome, acting as correspondent of an English newspaper, he was invited to an American dinner, in honor of Washington's birthday. He was said to have been annoyed at finding he was expected to give an account of the festivities; at any rate, he closed his report with the following incident, which the other guests did not happen to remember: "The chairman then proposed the toast of the evening—'Hail, Columbia, the land of freedom!'—and called upon the Vice consul to acknowledge the toast by singing a nigger melody." The story was ben trovato, but here it was more than verified. It is a curious illustration of popular feeling that the great comic song of the evening was one sung by a Negro, and called, "What shall a poor nigger do?" One verse I recollect was loudly cheered, and ran as follows:

> Den dere's de dam' Secessionists,
> And dere's de dam' 'Bolitionists,
> But neiders on 'em right;
> For dey spoil de Union, bof on em,
> And set de country in a fight,
> Den what shall a poor nigger do?

It is possible the Negro minstrels, in spite of their color, were artificially black. One curious circumstance I noted also, that the leader of the theatrical orchestra, most of whom were Germans, was an undoubted and indubitable Negro—a thing which would not be tolerated in the Northern States.

The town, moreover, is crowded, like a Bavarian or Papal one, with the offices of the state lottery. It shows the practical working of the American Constitution, when you consider that the United States Government has no more power to hinder every state in the Union from establishing lotteries than we have to require

Belgium to suppress the gaming tables at Spa; and it shows, too, the wise action of the State Governments, that in only three out of the thirty-six states, and these all Border Slave States—Kentucky, Delaware, and Missouri—are lotteries permitted by the local laws. The system is even more iniquitous for the players than the Papal one, a thing which beforehand I thought impossible. There are 78 numbers, of which 13 are drawn. It is easy enough to see that the chances of your guessing one, two, or three of the numbers drawn are within a fraction, 6, 30, and 273 to 1; yet, if you do happen to win, you only get once, twice and a half, and twenty-five times your stake respectively, and from these winnings 15 per cent is deducted for commission. The lottery is drawn twice a day, instead of once a week, as it is in Rome; and you can stake any amount you please, from a shilling upward. From the number of offices about, the business must be a thriving one; and this fact may possibly account for the state taxes being very light in Missouri, and for there also being a great deal of poverty.

As yet the manufacturing element of St. Louis is little developed. There are great beds of iron ore in the state, and coal mines are within easy access by river. Had it not been for the political troubles, large iron factories would have been set up in the city before now, but for the moment all progress has been suspended. Still, in a few years' time, St. Louis will probably be the great iron manufacturing city of the West and South, if not of the whole Union. For the present, its great trade is as a depot of agricultural produce.

Political feeling, as far as I could learn, has run extremely high in Missouri. Ever since the war broke out, the state has been a battlefield between North and South, and has suffered fearfully. Up to the present day, the Southern part of the State is more or less in the hands of the Confederates, and has been successively devastated by rival bands of guerillas. Amongst the native settlers, the Secession party is very strong, as in all Slave States. The chief St. Louis paper—the *Missouri Republican*—was in favor of neutrality and compromise till after the fall of Fort Sumter. In May last, though a staunch advocate of the Union, it obviously disliked the Abolitionists far more than it did the Secessionists, and kept hinting constantly its desire for such a compromise as would bring the South back with its institutions unimpaired. It deprecated strongly bitter language being used toward the Southerners, and threw doubts (and I believe with truth) on the Northern stories of the atrocities committed by the Confederate soldiery. On the other hand, the party represented by the *Republican* was not the most powerful numerically, though the most influential one. The Germans, who command the elections in St. Louis, are Black Republicans, followers of Frémont and Carl Schurz and [Gen. Franz] Sigel. Their Abolitionism is not dictated by moral feelings, like that of the New England States, but is founded rather on a practical conviction that slavery is a vicious system of labor, than on any absolute regard for the Negro. To do them justice, however, they have much less antipathy to the colored race than the native Americans, and are to a man opposed to the legislation which seeks to exclude free Negroes from the state. Moreover, though their Union feeling is very strong, their reverence for the Constitution is small, and their respect for state rights still less. I remarked that even the native Republican papers were shocked at the irreverence with which their German colleagues spoke of the Constitution, and implored them not to broach the heresy that if the Constitution did not work it must be changed forthwith. It was easy to see how this different "standpoint"—to use a German word—was beginning to work practically in electoral matters. In August, the election for members of Congress was to come on in Missouri, and, in May, the electoral campaign was beginning. Mr. [Francis] Blair, the brother of the Postmaster General, who was supposed to represent President Lincoln's views in Congress, was offering himself for re-election, and the native Republican party was supporting him strongly. He is, and has been for years, an Abolitionist, and, still more, the staunchest of Constitutional Union men. The Germans, however, were dissatisfied with him. They stated, and not without reason, that his Abolitionism was of no practical service, as he was not willing to interfere with the States or with their rights of deciding the question of slavery; and that the scheme of deportation, of which he was supposed to be the chief advocate with the President, was not only impracticable, but unjust, both to the taxpayer and the Negro. Mr. Blair had written a letter to the Germans of St. Louis to try to justify his opinions, but, up to that time, without effect.

Till early in last year, St. Louis had been under military, not martial law, and Secession partisans were supposed to be very active, if not numerous. In all the barrooms you could still see notices, that the license had been granted by the Provost Marshal, subject to the holder taking an oath that he was, and would be, faithful to the Union forever, and that any breach of the oath might be punished by death. At the same time, the evidences of a strong Union feeling were numerous, and St. Louis was the only Slave State city I visited where the Federal flag was frequently hung out of private dwellings.

Southern Illinois

ALL RAILROAD systems are perplexing to a stranger, and the American is about the most. What with state divisions, and the impassable rivers, and competing lines, and the enormous distances you have to travel over, it would be hard to steer one's course aright through the railroad labyrinth, even if you had available local timetables to steer by. But what makes the matter worse is that nowhere except at the railway stations, and not always there, can you find any timetable. There is no evidence of scheduled runs on American railroads, and so you have to base your faith on natural laws, and support it by undesigned coincidences from the reports of hotel-keepers and fellow travelers. Still, as in matters of more importance, knowledge so derived is not conclusive, and you may possibly argue falsely.

I myself was a case in point. On the walls of the Galt House at Louisville, there hung an advertisement, brilliant with all the colors of the rainbow, stating in every variety of type that the shortest route to Cairo, St. Louis, Kansas, and the Pacific Ocean was by the Ohio and Mississippi and Illinois Central, and that the express train started nightly at eight o'clock. The report was confirmed by collateral testimony on the part of the landlord, and trusting to it I set forth on my journey, under the belief that, barring accidents, I should be carried to my destination without unnecessary stoppage. The train was in truth an express one, and throughout the night I slept luxuriously in the sleeping cars, rocked to sleep, not unpleasantly, by the swaying motion of the train as we dashed onward through the level lands of Indiana.

But joy in this instance did not come with the morning. It is not pleasant at any time to be waked up at five A.M.; still less to be tumbled out, chilled, half-awake, and out of humor, on the platform of a lonely roadside junction; and least of all to be then and there informed that the branch train does not leave for fourteen hours. The fact was, that, according to the appropriate American phrase, "I had not made good connections," and the result of my error was that I had to spend a livelong broiling summer day at Odin Junction. In the "Dame aux Perles" of the younger Dumas there is a long account of how the artist-hero, in his hunt after the pearl-clad duchess, was detained (if I remember rightly, by want of funds) for some awful period at a railway junction in the plains of Galicia. The story had well-nigh faded out of my memory, but as I stood there, shivering on the platform of Odin Junction, the whole narrative rose to my mind, and I recalled with dismal distinctness how the luckless Oscar or Adolphe loitered about that dreary, lonely station, where there was nothing to read, nobody to speak to, nothing to do, nowhere to walk, nothing even to watch for except the arrival and departure of the trains. There may seem no great hardship in being kept a day in a strange place, when you can spend some hours at least in strolling about and making yourself acquainted with it; but the fatal peculiarity of my case was that when you had once walked up and down the platform you literally knew the whole country as well as if you had been settled there for years. It is impossible to conceive a country more hopelessly and irredeemably flat and bare and unbroken. As far as the eye could reach, the rich green pasture-lands of Illinois stretched away uncheckered by a single tree, like the surface of a vast billiard-board. I have read somewhere that when you stand on the seashore you can see fifteen miles of water ahead. If so, from the platform of the station, which was raised a foot or so above the ground, you must have seen fifteen miles of plain in every direction. In the far distance, on either side of the line, there rose a gray belt of trees where the prairie ended and the swamps began; but this belt, and the telegraph poles, and a score or two of scattered houses, were the only objects which rose above the dead level. The narrow single track of the railroad seemed to be drawn out like a line of wire till it dwindled out of sight, the two furthest points visible at either extremity being in one straight line with the spot on which I stood, and for miles and miles away you could watch the railway trains after they had left the station.

In half a dozen years there will probably be a large town at Odin Junction,* and already, as the inhabitants told me, the city had made a surprising start; but as yet it required an American's faith in the doctrine of development to foresee the coming greatness of Odin. You could number its houses on one hand. There was the station, the hotel, one settler's house alongside, and two shells of houses—all wooden by the way—in the process of building. Within a walk you could see about as many more scattered over the fields. And this was all. The odd fact, however, about this, as about all new American settlements, was, that it had not to develop from a village into a town; but that it had started into existence as the fragment of a city. So, here in Odin (why the Junction should be named after the Northern god I could not discover), there was a hotel large enough for a town of a thousand inhabitants. The one completed settler's house was as pretty and comfortable a cottage orné, with its snow-white hall and green Venetian blinds and neat outhouses, as you would see in Boston; and the two houses in the course of building will be, when finished, of a like size and appearance. The ground was already marked out for the church and the schoolhouse; and you could see that the buildings were carefully arranged so as to form the main street, with the railroad passing through it. When that is finished, there will run out Walnut and Chestnut Streets parallel to it, intersected at right angles by the numbered thoroughfares, and the houses now built or building will take their places naturally in Odin.

It must not be presumed, however, that the whole of these reflections were made upon the platform. Odin Junction, like many other things in America, turned out better on near acquaintance than at first sight. The hotel, like all hotels in the

---

* Over a century later, the township had grown to fewer than two thousand persons. It is on the road between St. Louis and Vincennes, Indiana.

Free States, was clean and comfortable, and as the owners were Germans the cooking was wholesome. Somehow or other the day passed lazily. We breakfasted at six, dined at twelve, had tea at six, and supped at eight. All these were strong substantial meals, each the counterpart of the other, and consisting of steaks, eggs, ham, cakes, and coffee. Our company at table was composed of one or two travelers detained like myself, of the railway officials, guards, clerks, and porters, of the workmen who were putting up the houses hard by, and of the landlord's family. Eating took up a good deal of time, and the process of digestion occupied a good deal more, and watching the new houses building was a quiet and not laborious amusement. The builder was an Englishman, who had emigrated young, had been an overseer in Alabama, then turned cattle driver in Kansas, had made money there, set up a store in St. Louis and failed, and now, when an old man, was beginning life again as a carpenter. He had not touched a tool for years, as he told me, and had never learnt the trade of carpentering, but he had a knack that way, and when he came to Illinois and found there was no carpenter round about Odin, he turned his hand to the trade, and seemed sanguine of building the whole of the city. He had orders on hand already, he told me, for twelve houses. Most of the inhabitants in Odin were Germans, and preferred talking German to me when they found I understood it, but the children spoke English, and hardly understood their mother tongue.

There was one beauty, and one beauty only about the scenery. On that flat pasture prairie-land, and beneath that burning sun, the shadows cast by the passing clouds swept to and fro in deep dark masses. In our own hilly, wooded, hedge-divided country you never witness the sight of a cloud-shadow projected in its full glory. It is only in the Roman Campagna and in the western prairies that this spectacle is possible. Watching the clouds pass lazily, I speculated on an idea that often crossed my mind in America. What must be the effect on a nation's character of being born and reared and bred in a country where there is nothing old to reverence, and nothing grand about the scenery, where even such beauty as there is, is so protracted and extended that it becomes monotonous by repetition. One obvious effect has been produced already, and, I think, inevitably. The single grand feature about American scenery is its vastness; and so for the American mind, sheer size and simple greatness possess an attraction which we in the Old World can hardly realize. There is much that is absurd about the manifestation of this sentiment, and English critics have taken hold freely of its ludicrous side. But I am not sure that there is not also something grand about it. When a settler at Odin boasted to me of the future greatness of the city, the boast struck me at first as ridiculous, but I reflected afterward that it was this pride and this belief in future greatness which had settled and civilized the New World whereon I trod. And so the day passed by and night came on almost at once, as it does in these southern regions after the sun's setting.

A long night again on the rail, and then another early waking, this time not on a platform, but in the middle of a swamp. Some eight miles above Cairo the whole country was under water, and the line was flooded. However, alongside the embankment, in the midst of a forest standing knee-deep in water, there was a flat, platform-shaped barge, with a steam engine in the middle, which, in some mysterious way I am not engineer enough to explain, propelled the raft, for it was nothing else. We were a long time getting off, as the train was loaded with medical stores, on their road to Corinth, in expectation of a second battle. It was hard work, shoving the unwieldy cases down the steep embankment; and harder still dragging on board the coffins, of which there were numbers, sent by friends far away, to receive the remains of soldiers who had died at Pittsburgh Landing. Whatever may be the faults of Americans, they work hard when they are about it; and, in the course of a short time, the raft was loaded, till it sank flush with the water's edge. Fortunately the water was not deep; and, moreover, I had firmly impressed upon myself the advice which a Northern friend gave me when I set out on my journey, that the one thing needful in American traveling is unquestioning faith. I presume that, in ordinary times, a road runs through the forest over whose track we sailed. At any rate, we followed an opening through the trees. Our raft, which was about as unwieldy in steering as the *Monitor* (judging from what I saw of that much over-vaunted miracle), had a way of jamming herself in between trunks of trees, and then had to be strained round by ropes back into the current. At other times she got aground, and had to be punted off with poles; and when she was clear afloat, she would run foul of floating "snags," and swing round the way she was wanted not to go. Happily the current was so rapid that it carried us over every difficulty, and, somehow or other, dodging our heads constantly, as we passed under the overhanging branches, we made way slowly. It was a pretty scene enough, in the bright fresh morning, when the leaves wore the first green tint of spring, and the shadows of the great trees were reflected in the water beneath the rays of the rising sun. So, winding our way through the forest swamp, we came out on the Ohio River, and there transhipped ourselves and our freight on board a steamer, which bore us down the rapid stream to the point where its waters joined the Mississippi, at the city of Cairo.

There are some places in the world which, when you get to them, your first thought is—how shall I get away again; and of these Cairo is one. A Yankee legend states that when the universe was allotted out between heaven, earth, and hell, there was one allotment intended for the third department, and crowded by mistake into the second; and that to this topographical error Cairo owes its terrestrial existence. The inhabitants boast, with a sort of reckless pride, that Cairo is also the original of the "valley of Eden," in which the firm of Chuzzlewit and Co. pitched their location; and a low hut is pointed out, which is said to be identical to the one that Dickens had in his mind when he described the dwelling where Mark Tapley immortalized himself. The description of the Chuzzlewit journey down the Mississippi is utterly inconsistent with this hypothesis; but I felt it would be cruelty to deprive my informant of the one pleasant reminiscence which his city could afford. The Mississippi and the Ohio meet at an acute angle, and on the low narrow neck of land which divides the two, stands Cairo. The whole town is below the level of the river, and would be habitually under water were it not for the high dykes which bar out the floods. As it is, Cairo is more or less

flooded every year, and when I was there the whole town was under water, with the exception of the high jetty which fronts the
Ohio. On this jetty, the one great street of the town, the railroad
runs, and opposite the railroad are the hotels and stores, and
steamboat offices. On the land side of the jetty there stretches a
town of low wooden houses standing, when I saw them, in a lake
of sluggish water. Anything more dismal than the prospect from
the windows of the St. Charles Hotel, out of which I looked over
the whole city, can hardly be conceived. The heat was as great as
that of the hottest of the dog days with us; and the air was laden
with a sort of sultry vapor we scarcely know of in England. A low
mist hung over the vast waters of the Mississippi and the Ohio,
and stole away across the long unbroken line of forest which
covered their muddy banks. The sun burnt down fiercely on the
shadeless wooden city; and whenever there came a puff of air, it
raised clouds of dust from the dry mounds of porous earth of
which the jetty is formed. The waters were sinking in the lagoon,
and the inhabitants paddled languidly in flat-bottomed boats
from house to house, looking to see what damage had been done.
A close fetid smell rose from the sluggish pools of water, and
fever seemed written everywhere. Along the jetty alone there
were signs of life, and even that life was death-like. Long trains
of empty luggage vans were drawn upon the rails on which the
poorer settlers had taken refuge when they were driven out of
their dwellings by the flood, and in these wretched resting places
whole families of women and children, mostly Irish, were huddled together miserably. The great river steamboats were coming
up constantly from the camp before Corinth, bringing cargo
loads of wounded and sick and disabled soldiers, who lay for
hours upon the jetty, waiting for means of transport northward.
There were piles, too, of coffins—not empty ones this time—but
with the dead men's names inscribed upon them, left standing in
front of the railway offices. The smoke of the great steamboat
chimneys hung like a pall over the town, and all day and all night
long you heard the ringing of their bells and the whistling of their
steam as they moved to and fro. The inhabitants were obviously
too dispirited to do what little they could have done to remedy

the unhealthiness of their town. Masses of putrid offal, decaying bones, and dead dogs, lay within eyesight (not to allude to their proximity to the nasal organ) of the best dwellings in the city. The people in the street seemed to loaf about listlessly, the very shop-men, most of whom were German Jews, had barely energy enough to sell their goods; and in all Cairo there was not a news-paper printed, a fact which, in an American city, speaks volumes for the moral as well as the physical prostration of the inhabitants. The truth is, that the town is a mere depot for transhipping goods and passengers at the junction of the Ohio and Mississippi rivers and the great Illinois Central railroad. There is money to be made there, and therefore people are always found to come and settle at Cairo for a time. But the time, either by choice or stern neces-sity, is always a very short one. At first, the wounded soldiers from the army at Shiloh were sent up to Cairo, but the mortality amongst them was found to be so great, that the hospitals were closed, and the sick shipped up the river to Louisville and St. Louis, far away as they lay from the scene of action.

It had been my purpose to go on from Cairo to the camp of the western army, and the battlefield of Pittsburgh Landing. Shortly, however, before my arrival, I found that very stringent orders had been issued by General [Henry] Halleck, then in com-mand, against allowing civilians to visit the army on any pretense, and an attempt to obtain a pass would have necessitated a refer-ence to headquarters at Washington, and consequently a delay of many days at Cairo. There were ague and fever in the bare idea, and so unwillingly I turned my steps northward to the states of the free West.

Racine City

OF MY journey through Illinois it is not necessary that I should speak. One journey in the West is the exact counterpart of the other, and I have said already all that I have to say on the subject. The point of my destination was the city of Racine, where I happened to have friends settled. It lies just beyond the extreme northern frontier of Illinois, while Cairo is at the extreme south. I traveled straight, almost as the crow could fly, along the line of which General McClellan was chairman not long ago, with even less profit to the unfortunate shareholders than he has afforded to the American people. Yet such are the enormous distances in the West, that traveling almost without stopping, at the rate of some five-and-twenty miles an hour, my journey occupied a day and a half.

Very few of my readers will probably be aware that there is such a city in the world as Racine, still less where it is placed. It must be a map of pretty recent date to have the name inscribed on it. It will be sufficient, however, to say, that it is on the western shore of Lake Michigan, sixty miles north of Chicago city, and if the reader does not know where the lake and the city are, he can find them by referring to his atlas. There is nothing remarkable or worthy of description about Racine, and it is for that very reason—pardon the paradox—that I wish to describe it. Years ago, there was a man who invented a machine which turned out hexameters—real Latin ones, not nondescript ones of the Clough or Longfellow type. There was no meaning in them, but the words placed in the machine were so selected that, in whatever order they happened to turn out, they arranged themselves in hexameters. If you had wanted to give a specimen of a machine-made hexameter, you would not have picked out a line in which, by some strange chance, there was a faint glimmering of sense or poetry, but one with the true standard meaningless monotony. Now all Western cities seem to have been turned out by a city-making machine, warranted to produce a city of any size, at the shortest notice, and therefore, in describing the cities of the West, any average one will stand for all—the more average a one the better. Private circumstances, moreover, caused me to see a good deal of Racine; and, indeed, made my stay so pleasant there, that I shall always think gratefully of the dull little town on the shores of the great inland sea.

Racine stands upon the Root River. Whether the town is named by translation from the river, or the river from the town, is a moot point on which the historians of the place are divided. Some persons suggest that the connection between the names of the town and river is purely accidental, and that the city was named after the great French tragedian. It may well be so. There is no limit to the eccentricities of American nomenclature, and there are probably a dozen towns in the United States named after Racine, Rousseau, and Corneille. Whatever doubt there may be about the reasons to which Racine owes its name, there is as yet no lengendary uncertainty about its birth and origin. There are men of middle age, now living in the place, who have lived through the whole life of the city, and who yet came here as full-grown men. A quarter of a century ago, when General [Andrew] Jackson, as Democratic President, suppressed the State Bank of the Union, which owed its origin to the Whigs, hundreds of new private banks sprang into existence, and deluged the country with an extemporized currency. There followed a period of wild speculation, chiefly in the lands of the North-Western territories. Steamboats were then first coming into full use, and, through the chain of the Great Lakes, hundreds of thousands of emigrants from Europe and the Eastern States were carried by steamboats to the western shores of Lake Michigan. After a time the banks failed; there was a commercial crisis, the speculators were ruined, but the emigrants remained. The prairie-land was fertile, the Indians were few and peaceable, and communication with the civilized world was cheap and expeditious. In a few years, the country was colonized far and wide, and towns sprang up in every direction. It was then that Milwaukee, and Chicago, and Racine were founded. *Veni, vidi, edificavi,* should be the motto of Western settlerdom, so rapid is the growth of cities in the West. From some cause or other, of the three sister cities, Racine has been the least prosperous. Chicago and Milwaukee have gone ahead so fast that Racine has been altogether outdistanced in the race, and bears the reputation in the West of a sleepy, humdrum place. To an Englishman, however, its quarter of a century's growth appears wonderful enough.

Along the shores of the lake there stretches a low, steep, sandy cliff, and upon its summit stands the city of Racine. Looking out on the great lake, there is little at first to tell you that you are not standing on the shore of the ocean. There is no trace of tide, and the breeze brings with it no savor of the salt sea; but the horizon on every side is bounded by water alone. Great ships, with snow-white sails, may be seen passing into the far distance, and when the wind blows from the lake, the waves roll in upon the coast with a deep roar and splash, as though they had been driven across the ocean. The Root River, too, with its docks and warehouses, and schooners and swing-bridges, has a seaport air about it, which, if not the real marine article, is a wonderful imitation. Along the brow of the cliff runs the main street of Racine, and, as usual, a series of streets parallel with, and at right angles to, Main Street, completes the town. The whole place looks very new—newer even than it ought to look after some six and twenty years of existence. Houses in this part of the world are short lived. All Western cities hold to the earth by an easily snapped cable. As fast as a settler makes money, he pulls down his house, and builds up a new one. If a householder gets tired of his position, he puts his house on wheels and decamps to another quarter. The lake has of late made inroads on the cliffs of Racine, and, when I was there, many of the residents on the seashore were moving their houses bodily to a safer locality. What with frequent fires, and a passion for house-building, there are probably few dwellings in Racine which remain such as they were when they were first built; and the settlers are now far older than their houses. Thus the main street of Racine is one of the most straggling and irregular of thoroughfares. Every now and then there is a block of stone office buildings, which would not be out of place in Broadway or in Cannon Street. Next door, perhaps, there is a photographic establishment, consisting of a movable wooden hut; and, in the aristocratic extension of Main Street, a sort of suburban avenue, there is every style and grade of building. The favorite order of architecture is a sort of miniature model of the Madeleine at Paris, in wood. Even the office where the local dentist tortures his patients is entered beneath a Corinthian portico, supported by fluted wooden pillars of six feet in height. But amidst these wooden dwellings, each standing in its own garden, there are to be found stone mansions such as you might see in Palace Gardens, or in the more aristocratic terraces of Upper Westbournia. Then there is a public square, a park, a courthouse, a dozen churches and chapels, and meetinghouses of every denomination. The town is rather at a standstill at present in the matter of internal improvements, as, by different jobs and speculations, the corporation has contrived to run itself about eighty thousand pounds into debt. The street lamps, therefore, as in many of the Western cities, are not lit, though there is a gas factory in the town; and the roads are left pretty much as nature made them. However, better times are expected for Racine. A line was to be opened within a few weeks of my visit, connecting it directly with the Mississippi, and then it is hoped that it will compete successfully, in the grain trade, with its rival Milwaukee, and that the harbor, on which twelve thousand pounds have been expended by the town, may become the great port for the Eastern traffic.

It is curious, as you stroll about the streets of Racine, or for that matter, of any other small Western city, to notice the points of dissimilarity between it and an English county town. The differences are not very marked ones. You never see in England a High Street like the main street of Racine, but each single house might stand in an English street without attracting especial notice. There are some slight features, however, about the place, which would tell you at once you were out of England. The footpath is made of planks; the farmers' carts, with which the street is filled, are very skeletons of carts, consisting of an iron framework supported by high narrow wheels, on which a small box is swung, barely large enough for the driver to sit upon. Big names are in fashion for designating everything. The inns are houses or halls, the butcher's is the meat market, the dentist calls himself a dental operator, the shops are stores, marts, or emporiums, and the public-houses are homes, arcades, exchanges, or saloons. There is nothing indeed corresponding to the old-fashioned English public-house. The barrooms, of which there is a plentiful supply, are, externally, like common shops, except that the door is covered by a wooden screen, so that the drinker is not exposed to the gaze of the passers in the streets. Here, by the way, as everywhere in the States, you never see a woman even in the poorest of barrooms. The shops themselves are about as good or as poor as you would find in a town of the like size (Racine has 12,000 inhabitants) at home. What is un-English about them is the number of German labels and German advertisements exhibited in their windows.

The amusements of Racine are about as limited as if it stood in our midland counties. Judging from the posters of ancient date which hung upon the walls, a passing circus, an itinerant exhibition of Ethiopian minstrels, and an occasional concert, were all the entertainment afforded to the inhabitants. Some of the street advertisements would have been novelties to English townsfolk. A Mrs. Francis Lord Bond was to lecture on Sunday evenings on spiritualism; a fancy fair was to be held for the Catholic convent of St. Ignatius; and a German *choralverein* was to meet weekly for the performance of sacred music. Then, even in this remote and far away corner of the States, there were the war advertisements. The Mayor announced that a great battle was expected daily before Corinth, and requested his townspeople to provide stores beforehand for the relief of the wounded. The Ladies' Aid Committee informed the female public of Racine that there would be a sewing meeting every Friday in the Town Hall, where all ladies were requested to come, and sew bandages for the Union soldiers, every lady to bring her own sewing-machine. Then, too, there was the requisition of the Governor, calling for recruits to fill up the gaps in the ranks of the Wisconsin regiments, who were cut to pieces on the field of Shiloh.

Of course, a town of the importance of Racine must have a press. In more prosperous days there were three dailies published there; but times were bad, and the dailies had collapsed into weeklies. These were the *Advocate*, the *Press*, the *Democrat*; and a German paper, the *Volksblatt*. As a sample of a Western country newspaper, let me take a copy I picked up of the *Racine Advocate*. It is of the regular unwieldy English four-page size, and costs six shillings annually, or five halfpence a single number, and is headed with a poetical declaration of faith, that

> Pledged but to truth, to liberty and law,
> No favours win us, and no fears shall awe.

The advertisements, which occupy two of the four pages, are chiefly of patent medicines, business-cards, and foreclosure sales. The local news, as in all American country papers, is extremely meager, and there are no law reports or accounts of county meetings. There were letters from the war, copied out of New York papers, and lists of the killed and wounded in the Wisconsin regiments; but fully one page of the paper was occupied by short tales and poems. When I say that their headings were, "How the Bachelor was Won," "A Girl's Wardrobe," "Gone Before," and "Katie Lee," the reader will have no difficulty in realizing what the intellectual varieties afforded by the *Advocate* consisted of.

Society in Racine is still in a primitive stage. Dinner parties are unknown, and balls are events of great rarity; but tea parties, to which you are invited on the morning of the day, are of constant occurrence. Probably there is as much scandal and gossip here as in an Old World country town; but there are not, as yet, the social divisions which exist with us. If you inquire the names of the owners of the handsomest houses in Racine, you will find that one, perhaps, began life as a stable boy, another was a waiter a few years ago in a hotel of the town, and a third was a bricklayer in early life. On the other hand, some of the poorest people in the place are persons who were of good family and good education in the Old World. A short time ago, the two least reputable members of the community were an ex-member of a fashionable London club and a quondam English nobleman. This very mixture of all classes which you find throughout the West gives a freedom, and also an originality, to the society in small towns, which you would not find under similar circumstances in England. If I were asked whether I would like to live in Racine, my answer would be an emphatic negative; but if the choice were put to me, whether I would sooner live there, or in an out-of-the-way English county town, I am afraid that nothing but patriotism would induce me to decline Racine.

The Prairie and the Mississippi

In COMPANY with the friend at whose house I was stopping in Racine, I went out into the prairie to visit the town of Lanark, situated on the extreme northwestern frontier of Illinois. It is no good referring to any map of the United States to ascertain the locality of this city. It had not then completed the first year of its existence, and was inscribed on no chart or map as yet designed. Probably, beyond the circle of twenty miles round Lanark, there were not a score of people who knew that there was such a place in the world, still less that it was a rising locality. In the far West, cities start into existence like Aladdin's Palace. You read of this mushroom growth in books of travel, but it is hard to realize it without seeing it on the spot. You pass through the vast city of Chicago, along its splendid streets and quays and avenues, and are told that thirty years ago no buildings stood there except an old mud fort, raised to keep off the Indians, and that the first child ever born in the city was only married the other day. You are told so, but you hardly believe it, or, at any rate, you form no idea of how the solitary fort grew into the mighty city. To understand the process of development, you must take a baby-town just beginning to stand alone, and not the full-grown giant of a metropolis. It is for this reason, and because, in French phrase, I have "assisted" at the birth of Lanark City, that I have taken it as the specimen of a Western settlement.

Between Lake Michigan and the Mississippi River lies the prairie-land of Illinois. From the river to the lakes there run a host of railroads, and amongst them there is one, now in process of construction, called the Racine and Mississippi Railroad. If you

take any map of the West, and draw a straight, or what the
Americans call an "air-line," from Racine to the nearest point of
the Mississippi, you will have before you the exact course of the
railroad in question; and twenty miles or so from the river lay the
then terminus of the line, Lanark City. It was in company with
Mr. George Thomson, the English projector of the railroad and
the founder of the city, that Lanark and I made acquaintance
with each other. The course of emigration, naturally enough,
caused the borders of the great river and lake highways to be first
occupied by settlers; and it is only slowly, as population increases,
that the inland districts of the Western States become settled.
Thus the interior of Northern Illiinois is still a great prairie
country, dotted here and there with new cities. Railroads are not
constructed there to connect existing towns, as much as to open
out new ranges of country; and if the Racine and Mississippi had
to depend upon the custom of the inhabitants settled along its
route before the line was made, its chance of profit would be
a small one. For miles and miles our road lay along the silent, almost deserted, prairie—every now and then a low cutting through
a hillock, sometimes a short embankment over a hollow, and then
a flat bridge carried on piles across a marshy stream, but as a rule,
a long level track, scarcely raised above the ground, and stretching
without curve or bend for miles before and miles behind you.
Right in the middle of the prairie, the rail came to an end at
Lanark.

Alongside the depot there stood a sort of railway caravan, which
had been the first house of Lanark. When the rail was finished,
there was not a hut or covered dwelling of any kind on the spot,
and so this caravan was sent down there as a shelter for the railroad servants. By this time it had served its purpose, and I heard
the order given for its transmission back to Racine, in order to be
used elsewhere for a like object. Close to the station there was a
hotel built already, not a pot-house or a roadside tavern, but a
genuine, well-ordered inn. Of course, being in America, it had a
barroom, a public room with long tables, and public meals at
fixed hours. It was clean too, and neatly furnished, as hotels in
the Free States mostly are. The only national institution in which

it was deficient was a gong. The first landlord—there had been three already—had levanted, taking that inevitable deafening instrument of torture with him on his departure, and happily it had not yet been replaced. There was a piano in the house, belonging to the wife of a gentleman employed on the line, and in his room I found copies of Macaulay's History, and of Gibbon's "Decline and Fall." The hotel was the property of the Company, and had been built by them to induce settlers to come to the place, and it seemed to be doing a good business. Meanwhile, the town was fast growing up around it.

Lanark, like all Western cities, is built on the simplest of plans. The owners or projectors of the settlement buy a certain number of acres, draw out a plan of the town, dividing it into streets and lots, and allow any purchaser to build any sort of dwelling on his lot he likes. The houses may be as irregular and unlike as possible; but, as the spaces allotted for the streets are not allowed to be encroached upon, the general plan of the town must correspond with the chart. The map of the city had been drawn out by a Scotch clerk in the service of the railroad, who had undertaken the task of naming the streets. To display his nationality, he had given Scotch names—Bute, Argyle, Forth, Moray, and Macs innumerable—and had only condescended to American prejudices so far as to permit of there being a Main and a Chestnut Street. Most of these streets, however, were still streets of the future, and the influx of population had as yet only called Main and Bute Streets into existence. The first of these is the commercial thoroughfare of Lanark, and in it there were some twenty shops already established. I noticed two competing ironmongers and tinmen, whose stores seemed plentifully stocked, two or three rival groceries, two saddle and harness makers, and a couple of beer and oyster saloons—a tailor's, a shoemaker's, and a lawyer's office. Besides these, there were two large stores building, one of which was to be a furniture warehouse, and the other, I think, a dry goods shop. Bute Street consisted of private cottages. A number of shanties, too, were scattered round the place, but not close enough yet to one another to form streets. Every house in the place was of wood, many of them two, or even three, stories high. The majority of the houses had curtains and green veranda shutters, and even the poorest I looked into were far superior in comfort to an ordinary English laborer's cottage, not to mention their being clean and airy. The streets were mere tracks of prairie-land, hardened by the wheels of teams, of which the town was full; but there were planked footpaths raised along Main Street.

The object, indeed, for which Lanark has been founded is to form a depot for agricultural produce. The fertile plains of the vast prairie will produce boundless supplies of wheat and corn. There is no clearing to be done before these plains can be cultivated. For some cause or other, which nobody appears to me to have explained as yet satisfactorily, trees do not grow spontaneously upon the prairie, fertile as it is; and for miles on every side of Lanark there was scarcely a tree to be seen. A New England farmer, who had lately removed there, told me he should never feel at home until he had brought some rocks from the Pilgrim State, and planted trees between their crevices, so as to form a miniature Massachusetts of his own. The richness of the soil is something marvelous. You have but to turn it up some three inches deep, and the land will yield crops year after year without rest or manure. An acre will bear from thirty to forty bushels, and wheat fetches from half-a-crown to three shillings a bushel. Indian corn, or "corn" as it is called there, is so plentiful that in many winters it is burnt for fuel. With such prices the only thing which stops the cultivation of wheat is the difficulty and expense of bringing it to market; and as fast as the railroad removes this difficulty, the cultivation extends rapidly. On one day, within a few weeks of the railroad being opened, three hundred teamloads of wheat were brought to the single station of Lanark. The population of the city therefore consists of farmers, and of dealers who have come to provide for their wants. There is, of course, a great deal of luck about Western towns, as about all other speculations in a new country; and it is impossible as yet to say whether Lanark will succeed in becoming the depot of its district; but its prospects are flourishing. Its population, as far I could gather, numbered already about 300 persons. There was no church yet built, but every week there came some minister or other, who preached in a room at the hotel. The people were already making arrangements for establishing schools. One of the chief settlers, with whom I had some conversation, talked of raising 1,000 dollars in the town for this purpose, and said that he hoped to get as much more from the Education Fund of Springfield, the county town of Lanark district. The first public meeting in the town was to be held the week following my visit, to consider the school question, as the railway company had offered to give land for the school buildings at unusually low prices. The site of a church was, I understood, fixed upon, and I had pointed out to me a long square of prairie-land, which is to be hereafter the park of Lanark. If, a dozen years hence, the park were to be surrounded by stone mansions, the growth of Lanark would not be more surprising than that of other Western cities.

The railroad was pushing on fast toward the Mississippi. It was strange to anyone who, like myself, had seen a good deal of European railroad-making, to watch the rough-and-ready way in which this line was carried forward. The low mound of earth, on which the single line of rails was placed, was heaped up hastily from a trench cut on either side. You would have fancied that the weight of the engine would crush down the embankment, and break through the flat bridges supported on the slender wooden piles. But, somehow or other, American railroads work well and serve their purpose. The cost of construction was low enough to make the mouth of an English shareholder water, being under two thousand pounds a mile. This, however, is unusually cheap even for America; and I believe the cost of the Illinois Central, over as easy a country, was about eight thousand pounds per mile. What makes this cheapness of construction the more remarkable is that wages were high. The rate of pay for common unskilled laborers varied from four to six shillings a day; and the teams, gangs of which were brought in to the work by farmers settled in the neighborhood, were paid for at the rate of ten shillings daily. It is probable, moreover, that the farmers worked at a low rate, as the funds for the line were chiefly provided by promissory notes given by them, and secured by the mortgage of their farms. A very large proportion of the workmen were Irish; and the meadows along the line were covered with shanties and Gypsy-tents, where Irish women and children huddled together, in as close a proximity to their state of native dirt as the fresh air of the prairie would permit. The sale of whiskey or intoxicating liquors was prohibited, by a sort of extempore lynch-law; and I was struck by hearing the American overseer go round to the different shanties and tell their inmates that if he heard of their having liquor on the premises he would pull down the huts over their heads. From what I saw of my friend Mr. Smith, I have not the slightest doubt that, though the most good-natured man in the world, he would have kept his word to the letter.

In this out-of-the-way spot, as everywhere in the West, the war was the one subject of talk. It was too far North for Secessionism, and the people to a man were staunch Unionists. A report came while I was at Lanark that Richmond was taken. There was a flagstaff in the main street, and at once the Stars and Stripes were hoisted in honor of the supposed victory. It was striking, too, to observe how thoroughly all these farmers and settlers were "posted," in American parlance, on the events and politics of the war. To most of them, as Illinois men, Lincoln and McClellan (from his connection with the Illinois Central) were known personally, and their merits, as well as those of other American statesmen, were discussed freely and often ably. Mr. [Secretary of War Edwin] Stanton seemed the most popular of the public men of the day, chiefly on account of his anti-slavery views. Indeed, in these Northern States of the West, popular feeling appeared to me to be more genuinely Abolitionist than in any part of the Union. There was little sentiment expressed about the Negro's wrongs; but there was a strong feeling that slavery is a bad system, and a disgrace to the country; and, still more, there was a bitter hostility—almost a personal antipathy—to the slaveholding aristocracy of the South. Half-measures, or patched-up compromises, found little favor with those plain matter-of-fact Western men: "The slave-owners have made the rebellion, and they ought to pay for it. The North has been half-ruined by the South, and the South is rightly punished if she is ruined altogether.

Compensation to rebels is absurd, and loyal men ought not to be called upon to pay for the property of rebels. If the South chooses to burn its cotton, and produce a famine in its own territory, so much the better. The more slave-owners are ruined, the better for the Union."

Such was the purport of the sentiments I heard expressed; the form of expression was, in general, a great deal too emphatic to be repeated literally. McClellan, with his supposed pro-slavery views, was looked on with open distrust, and spoken of, even at that period, with undisguised contempt. Lincoln, with his compensation scheme, was thought not to be up to the mark; and the policy which seemed to please this village public best was that of General [David] Hunter, which gave a knockdown blow, for once and for all, to slavery and slave-owners.

Still, in this Western world of the North, it was only the rumor of war, not the war itself, that the traveler came across. The great tide of the civil war had not spread so far northward. Illinois and Wisconsin regiments there were in the fight, and plenty, but the states themselves had been but little affected directly. According to the popular English view, the whole country is in a state of revolution, trade is bankrupt, and the entire progress of the nation stopped for years to come; yet here, in the West, in the very heat of the war, there was a great country growing into existence by rapid strides. The great march of civilization was still, as ever, tending westward, building railroads, clearing forests, reclaiming wild lands, raising cities, and making the wilderness into a fertile country. This progress westward across the prairie is the great fact of American history; and those who want to understand the real character of the present civil war, must remember that this progress is still going on without ceasing. The growth of Lanark is one little incident in the history of the West, and it is as such I have dwelt upon it.

It was near Lanark that I first caught a real glimpse of the prairie. We have all laughed, or by this time ceased laughing, at the story of the Irishman who brought a brick from the Pyramids, to show his friends what the Pyramids were like. Yet I know not that the prairie could be described better, to those who have never

seen it, than by bringing home a spadeful of prairie-sod, and telling the spectators to multiply that sod in their minds by any
multiple of millions they choose to fix upon. In truth, there is
nothing to describe about the prairie except its vastness, and that
is indescribable. I suppose most of us in our lifetime have dreamt
a dream that we were wandering on a vast boundless moor, seeking for something aimlessly, and that in this dreary search after
we knew not what, we wandered from slope to slope, and still
the moor stretched before us, endless and unbounded. Such a
dream I, for my part, remember dreaming years ago; and as I
drove for a mile-long drive across the prairies of Northern Illinois,
it seemed to me that the dream had come true at last.

East, west, north, and south—on the right hand and on the
left—in front and behind, stretched the broken woodless upland.
Underneath the foot a springy turf, covered with scentless violets
and wild prairie roses; overhead a bright cloudless sky, whence
the sun shot down beams that would have scorched up the soil
long ago but for the fresh soft prairie-breeze blowing from across
the Rocky Mountains; low grassy slopes on every side, looking
like waves of turf rising and falling gently. Not a tree to be seen
in the far distance; not a house in sight far or near; not a drove
of sheep or a herd of cattle; no sign of life except the dun-colored
prairie chickens whirring through the heather as we drove along
—nothing but the broken woodless upland. So we passed on,
coming from time to time upon some break in the monotony of
the vast dreamlike solitude. Sometimes it was a prairie stream,
running clear as crystal between its low sedgy banks, through
which our horses forded knee-deep, and then again the broken
woodless upland; sometimes it was a lone Irish shanty, knocked
up roughly with planks and logs, and wearing a look as though it
had been built by shipwrecked settlers, stranded on the shore of
the prairie sea. Farther on we came upon a herd of half-wild
horses, who, as we approached, dashed away in a wild stampede;
then upon a knot of trees, whose seeds had been wafted from
the distant forests, and taken root kindly on the rich prairie soil;
now upon an emigrant's team, with the women and children under the canvas awning, and the red-shirted and brigand-looking

miners at its side, traveling across the prairie in search of the
land of gold; and then again the silent solitude and the broken
woodless upland.

These scanty breaks, however, in the monotony of the scene,
were signs of the approach of civilization—warnings, as it were,
that the days of the Lanark prairie are well-nigh numbered. The
railroad in which my companions were interested went right
through the heart of the district. To my English ideas, the line
looked like the realization of the famous railroad which went
from nowhere in general to nowhere in particular. But American
experience has amply proved that a railroad in the Far West cre-
ates its own constituency. In three or four years' time the prairie
over which I traveled will be enclosed; the rich soil will be turned
up, and bring forth endless crops of wheat till, as a settler told me,
the wide expanse looks at harvest-time like a golden carpet; and
large towns may very likely be raised on the spot where the Irish
shanties stood when I passed. Every year the traveler in search
of the prairie has to go further and further west; but its extent
is still so vast, that generations, perhaps centuries, must pass
away before it becomes a matter of tradition. Settlers in the country tell one that it is necessary to live for some time upon the
prairie-land in order to feel its charm, and that, when its charm
is once felt, all other scenery grows tame. It may be so. I believe,
without understanding it, that there are people who grow to love
the sea, and feel a delight in seeing nothing but the wide expanse
of the ocean round them for days, and weeks, and months together; so, for some minds, the endless sameness of the prairie
may possess a strange attraction. For my own part, the sense of
boundless vastness hanging over the scene was overpowering
rather than impressive, and I plead guilty to a feeling of relief
when we got out of the open land into the tilled fields and green
woods, and cheerful villages which spread along the banks of the
Mississippi River.

Of many pleasant river sails it has been my lot to make in different parts of the world, my two days' sail up the great Western
river is, I think, the pleasantest. I came upon it some sixteen
hundred miles from its source, and nearly the same distance from

its mouth, far away in the North West, where it forms the frontier line between the states of Wisconsin and Iowa. The spring freshets had been unusually high, and the floods were only beginning to subside, so that the expanse of water was grander even than it is in ordinary times; the flat shifting mud-banks, which the river forms year by year from the deposits of its rich alluvial soil, were covered with the flood, and in many places the water spread from bank to bank for a distance of three miles and upwards. How the steamer found its way amidst the countless channels and between the thousand islands, all covered with the rich rank forests, and all the counterparts of each other, is a mystery to me still. If ever there was a river worthy of the name of the "silent highway," it is the Mississippi. The great saloon steamers, with the single wheel placed at their stern, glide along so noiselessly, that to me, used to the straining and creaking of an English steamboat, it seemed difficult to believe that the vessel was in motion. The vast shallow flood rolls along without a swell, almost without a ripple. The silence of the great forests along the banks is unbroken by the sound of birds or of any living thing. For miles and miles together not a village or house is to be seen, and the river flows on as silent and as solitary as it must have flowed when De Soto first struck upon its course two centuries ago, and hailed it proudly as the "Father of Many Waters."

On either side of the river rise high cliffs or "bluffs" as they are called there, of reddish sandstone. At a distance the great masses of rock, twisted into all sorts of fantastic shapes by the action of the water, ages and ages ago, look like the ruins of some old Norman castle. Sometimes the Mississippi rolls at the very foot of the overhanging cliffs; at others, a low swampland, covered with close-set forest trees, lies between the river and the cliff. But to me the great beauty of the scene lay in the richness of the coloring. The woodlands of England are tame and colorless compared with the green forests of the Mississippi in the first burst of summer, and the towering masses of rock, the patches of bare sandstone, and the hillsides of the steep gullies that run down to the river, shone out with a depth and gorgeousness of color that I had fancied was not to be found under a northern sun. As for sunsets, you should see them on the Mississippi, when the river, in one of its hundred twists and turnings, bends for a space westward. Then you seem to be floating down the current toward a vast canopy of fire and flame and golden glory. There, indeed, you behold a sunset such as the fancy of Turner alone might have pictured, and sought in vain to realize.

Trade was dull on the Mississippi. At this early summer season the boats would have been crowded only two years ago by hundreds of Southern families flying from the deadly heats of New Orleans, but now we had scarce a score of passengers on board. There was but little life upon the river; two or three times a day we passed steamers bound for St. Louis; and sometimes we came upon a string of huge lumber-rafts punted cautiously along by gangs of wild-looking red-shirted boatmen. But this was all. Every couple of hours or so, we touched at some small town on the riverside, to take up passengers, of whom there were few forthcoming. These towns are all alike, differing only in size. A long street of low houses, stores, and wharves fronting the river, a large stone building, generally a hotel which has failed, a few back streets running toward the bluff, perhaps a row of villas on the hillside, and very often a railway depot; these are the common characteristics of a Mississippi town. The one beautiful thing about them is their position, nestling as they do at the foot of the cliffs, and this is a beauty which even the ugliness of the towns themselves cannot destroy.

There are still many traces in this part of the Mississippi of the early French settlements. Prairie du Port, Prairie du Chien, and Dubuque are names which bespeak their own origin. Along the river there are several French villages, or rather parts of villages. The inhabitants are a queer race, "jumbos," as the American settlers call them—part French, part Negro, and part Indian. In this admixture of half-breeds the French element has kept the mastery, and they still speak a broken French and are all devout Catholics. They also retain the passion of the French peasant for his land. No price will induce a half-breed to part willingly with his land, but he is content to possess it without seeking to improve it. Indeed, the development, physically as well as morally, of this mixed breed has not been such as to strengthen the cause of the advocates of amalgamation between the white and the colored population. They are a wild, handsome, Gypsy-looking race, though not of sturdy growth. As a rule, they are an inoffensive people, but are dirty, ignorant, and indolent. They live chiefly by fishing and hunting, and die away gradually in the villages where they are born. As far as I could learn, there is no particular prejudice against them amongst the Anglo-Saxon settlers any more than there is against the Indians. Both races, half-breeds as well as Indians, are so obviously dying out that the feeling of the Americans toward them is one rather of pity than of jealousy. At Prairie du Chien, or "Prare doo Shane," according to the popular Western pronunciation, stand the ruins of large barracks. It seems strange in this land of railroads and steamboats and great cities to learn that these barracks were erected only thirty years ago, in order to protect the soldiers of the United States against the Indians in the famous Black Hawk war. The barracks are useless already, for the Indian has retreated hundreds of miles away. By these ruins I came upon the first party of genuine Indians I had seen. There were four of them, two men, father and son, and their squaws. They were very dirty, very ragged, and painted with all kinds of colors. They had bows and arrows with them, of the rudest kind, but their chief livelihood, I suspect, was derived from begging. They told us, in broken English, that they were very miserable, which I have no doubt was true; and the only trace of dignity I could see about them was that they took the small alms our party gave, with absolute apparent unconcern. The one piece of luggage belonging to the tribe was carried by the younger squaw, and that—alas! for Mohican romance!—was a teapot of Britannia metal.

Chicago and the West

OF ALL American commercial cities, Chicago is, to my mind, the handsomest. Thirty years ago, not a house was standing there. Now, with its miles of wharves and warehouses, its endless canals and docks, its seventy churches, and its rows of palace-like mansions, Chicago is probably, both in size and importance, the third or fourth city in the States. There is an unusual uniformity about the buildings, from the fact that they have all been built almost at the same time, and the monotony of the straight rectangular streets is somewhat relieved by the Dutch-looking canals which intersect them in every direction. When, however, you have made the stock remark that, within a quarter of a century, a trans-Atlantic Liverpool has been raised upon the swampy shores of Lake Michigan, you have said pretty well all that is to be said about the metropolis of the West. If a poor neighbor becomes a millionaire, you think it a remarkable occurrence, and possibly you regard him with envy; but I don't think, judging from my own ideas, that you are struck with a reverential awe. So, in like manner, when you have once realized the idea of how Chicago has grown out of nothing in no time, you have about exhausted the subject. Barges, and drays, and steamboats, and factories, are much the same all the world over. Goethe is constantly reported to have said (though I own I never came across the saying in any of his writings), that there was more poetry in a spinning jenny than in the whole Iliad of Homer. It may be so, but Goethe never tried to write a poem about a factory, and so I defy anyone, except a land agent, to expatiate on the beauties and glories of Chicago. To me it is remarkable and noteworthy chiefly as the center of the New World, which is growing up with a giant's growth in those Free States of the North West. A commercial panic, a change in the route of traffic, might destroy Chicago, but no human power could destroy the great corn-growing region of which, for the time, it is the capital.

At the period of my visit, Illinois was undergoing one of those periodical revolutions which seem so strange to English politicians. The whole state was about to throw off its Constitution as a snake casts its slough, and Chicago naturally enough was the headquarters of the agitation, such as there was. Politics run high in Illinois. It is the state, by birth or by adoption, not only of President Lincoln, but of Stephen Douglas, his great Democratic rival in the late Presidential contest. The struggle in Illinois was a bitter and a close one. Lincoln polled 172,161 votes against 160,215 for Douglas. It is very hard for an English student of American politics to understand the meaning in which party names are used in the North, and probably most Englishmen who were asked to define the difference between American Republicans and Democrats would state that the former were anti-slavery men and the latter pro-slavery. At best, this is a half truth. In our English sense of the words, Republicans and Democrats approach much more nearly in politics to Liberals and Conservatives. When an Englishman reads, as he does in all American political discussions, that the Slaveocracy of the South supported itself by an alliance with the Democracy of the North, his impression is that the Democratic party advocated all that class of measures which would be in favor with an Old World Democracy. The impression is erroneous, because the demos of the New World (I am speaking especially of the Western States) exists under essentially different conditions from the demos of the Old World. Where everybody is a voter, and where every voter is a man of some property, and generally of some landed property, the ruling demos will be a demos of small landholders, and both the prejudices and principles of such a class are essentially conservative in many ways. A love for local institutions, a dislike of government interference, a jealousy of any privileged class, an ignorant aversion to taxation, a strong regard for the rights of property, and bitter national prejudices and vanities, are pretty sure to be amongst their distinguishing characteristics. Political parties must be judged by their relative, not by their actual, principles. Still, for all that, there is in each country a distinct Liberal and Conservative party. Thus, in reality, the Republicans are the Liberals, and the Democrats the Conservatives of America. It is hardly fair to the Northern Democracy to allege that it tolerated slavery simply for the sake of Southern political support. Any national interference with slavery was an interference with state rights, and the essence of Democratic Conservatism is to support vested rights and local independence against the action of the Central Government. *Stare super antiquas vias,* "the Constitution as it is, and the Union as it was," is thus the rallying cry of the American Democracy. If the reader can picture to himself what the politics of England would be if there was no unrepresented class, and if the vast majority of the voters were small householders or landholders, he will have little difficulty in seeing what would be the politics of the party which bid highest for the support of the majority. Free trade would be attacked as vehemently as the game laws. Toleration would be as unpopular as tithes, and a demand for tenant-right would be accompanied by a cry of "England for the English." Under very different conditions, a somewhat similar state of things exists in America.

Thus, even if the slavery issue were removed tomorrow, the struggle between Republicans and Democrats would continue, possibly under different names, and new party organizations, but still the same in principle. The struggle then going on between the two parties in the State of Illinois had little directly to do with slavery, and illustrated the tendency of American politics, as well as the working of State Government.

The West is so vast a region, and comprises states of such different physical and geographical conditions, that ultimately the different portions of the district will doubtless exhibit distinctive features of their own. At present, the fact that each Western State has been colonized much at the same time and much in the same manner, has given a temporary character of uniformity to their systems of politics. As years go on, new forms of society will doubtless develop themselves there. The West is preeminently the country of the future. When Prince Napoleon traveled, at the outbreak of the war, through the Western States, he remarked to an acquaintance of mine that, in not many years to come, the valley of the Mississippi would be the center of civilization. The remark was probably dictated in part by the natural desire of a Frenchman to say something gratifying to his entertainer, but in part also by the farsightedness of a Napoleon. It must be an unobservant traveler who goes through this region without having the conviction forced upon him that the West is destined to play a part, and that no insignificant one, in the world's history. Everywhere railroads are building, towns are growing up, and, above all, the wild soil of the prairie is being turned, almost without an effort, into the richest corn-growing country. Rapid as the progress of railroads is, the growth of the soil is more rapid still. In many parts of the West there are said to be three years' crops of wheat stored up, waiting only for delivery till the means of transport are provided. Indian corn is so plentiful that it is burnt for fuel, and on the prairie there is pasture-land for all the herds of cattle which the world can boast of. Centuries well-nigh must pass, even with the astonishing increase of population, before absolute want is known in the West by any class, or before it ceases to be the granary of the New World, if not of the Old also. These are the economical conditions under which the West is rising into national existence; the political conditions are not less remarkable. All the Northwestern States have been founded by individual enterprise: they owe nothing to Government aid, or support, or patronage. Every farm and town and state has been created by the free action of settlers —doing as seemed best in their own sight. The West, too, more than any part of the Union, has been colonized by one uniform class. There have been no aristocratic families amongst the first colonists, as in Virginia or Maryland, and even, in some measure, in Kentucky and Tennessee; no original Dutch settlement, as in New York; no dominant religious leadership, as in the New England States. In the West all men are equal as a matter of fact, not at all as a matter of abstract theory. The only difference between man and man is, that one man is richer than another. But fortunes are made and lost so easily in this part of the world that the mere possession of wealth does not convey the same power or importance as it would in an older and more defined civilization. I quite admit that this dead level of society has its disadvantages. For a man of refined tastes, and imbued with the teachings of Old World culture, the West must be a wearisome residence. It would be so, I think, for myself. As the undergraduate said, when he was asked to describe the structure of the walls of Babylon, "I am not a bricklayer." Not being a bricklayer of any kind, social or political, I have no taste for living in brickfields; and the West is nothing more as yet than a vast political and social brick-field, upon which, and out of which, some unknown edifice is to be raised hereafter, or, rather, is being raised now. Still, there are some lessons which may be learnt already from the young history of the West, and chief amongst them is the force of self-government. There is little power to compel obedience to law, still less is there any superintending authority to tell men what they ought and ought not to do; but, somehow or other, there is a general security, a respect for law, and a peaceable order, which seemed to grow up without any forcing process. Wherever you have slavery, you have rowdyism also; but, in the Free States of the West, the rowdy proper is as unknown as the slave.

But the more pressing question with regard to the West is what its influence will be on the war. We in Europe look upon the struggle as solely one between North and South, and can scarcely realize the fact that the West will, in a few years, be more powerful than the North and South put together, and is virtually the arbiter of the struggle between the two. As Mr. Hawthorne once remarked to me, "We of the Old States are nothing more than the fringe on the garment of the West." Now, about one fact there is no doubt whatever, and that is that the West has thrown its whole power into the cause, not of the North, but of the Union. Two essential conditions are required for its development—one, that it should have free access through the Great

Lakes to the Atlantic; the other, that it should hold the Mississippi to the Gulf of Mexico: and the only way by which both these conditions can be satisfied is, by the whole country between the lakes and the river being held by one Government; while the only Government which can so hold it, as a matter of fact, is one which more or less resembles the old Union. So much for the present. The future of the West, which is not a dream, but an unfulfilled reality, requires an extension of the same conditions. During the present generation the great Pacific railroad will become an accomplished fact. Then the whole influence of the growing states of the Pacific seaboard will be thrown into the scale of the West, and will enable it to demand even more imperatively than at present that free access to the Atlantic which can only be secured by the whole country between the two oceans being subject to one Government. It requires no great amount of thought or education to understand these conclusions, and the Western men are sufficiently educated by the free-school system and the more important teaching of political self-government to appreciate them fully. The West means to preserve the Union, and is as determined as the North—perhaps more so, though on different grounds. It was curious to note the difference of tone about the war in the West and in the North, as expressed both in the press and in conversation. There was much less of regard for the Constitution as an abstraction, much less of sentimental talk about the "fathers of the country," or the wickedness of Secession. On the other hand, there was a greater regard for individual freedom of action, and a greater impatience of any Government interference. The truth is, the enormous German element in the Western population has produced a marked effect upon the state of public feeling. To the German settler the fame of Washington inspires no particular reverence. The names of Franz Sigel and Carl Schurz and John Frémont carry more weight than those of Jefferson and Hamilton and Madison; and the traditions of the War of Independence are not so vivid as those of '48 and the campaign of Schleswig-Holstein. They are attached to the Union because it secures the prosperity and development of their new country, and because it has proved a good Government to them, or rather, has allowed them the unwonted privilege of governing themselves. The German element, it is true, is modified with wonderful rapidity into the dominant American one; but still, in the process of absorption, it modifies the absorbent.

In like manner it is easy, as I have remarked before, to trace an essential difference of feeling with regard to the question of Abolition in the Free West and in the North. With the New England States, Abolition is a question of principle and of moral enthusiasm. In New York and the great Central States, the Abolitionist feeling is checked and hampered by the national reverence for the Constitution. Even amongst the most ardent Abolitionists in the North there are few logical or sincere enough to admit that the maintenance of the Constitution *may* prove incompatible with the abolition of slavery; and Wendell Phillips is the only Abolitionist who faces this dilemma boldly, and asserts that, if it should arise, then the sooner the Constitution perishes the better. Now, in the West, Abolitionism is practical, not sentimental. Two propositions with regard to slavery have established themselves firmly in the Western mind. The first is that slavery in the West is fatal to the progress of the country; the second, which has been adopted chiefly since the outbreak of Secession, is that the existence of slavery at all is fatal to the peace and durability of the Union. Given these propositions, the West draws the conclusion that slavery must be abolished; and, if emancipation should prove inconsistent with the Constitution, then the masterwork of Washington must be modified. To do the Germans justice, too, they are, with the exception of the poorer Catholics, anti-slavery on principle. In the school in which they learnt democracy, the doctrine of the rights of man was not qualified by a clause against color.

These remarks of mine must be taken as expressing rather the general tendency of what I saw and heard in the West, than as a description of the exact state of public feeling either then or at the present day. Like all America, the West, though in a less degree perhaps, is in a state of political upheaving. Politics and parties and principles vary from day to day, with the events of the war. The one point on which all Western men seemed agreed was that the insurrection must and should be suppressed; and the war, in every railway car and tavern and house you entered, was the sole topic of talk and interest. You could not forget the war, even if you had wished. Every carriage on the railway trains was laden with sick or wounded soldiers, traveling homeward to be nursed, and, if I could judge their faces rightly, to die. So far, the West had done the hardest part of the fighting, and still appeared ready to fight on to the end. With this mention I must pass on from the West. I trust it may never be my fortune to settle in a new country; but, if it should be, my prayer is that it may be in the Free West, on the country watered by the Mississippi River.

Boston

"THE OLDEST house in all Boston, built MDCLVI." This was the notice over a mercer's shop in Washington Street, which caught my eye in entering Boston. The shop was one of those little wooden pillbox houses you see about seaport towns at home, which might as well have been built yesterday or a thousand years ago. In itself it contained nothing noticeable; but what rendered it remarkable was that, in this new world, age should be considered any recommendation. It is, I think, Swift who suggests that in an ideal State, all citizens who attained to the age of sixty should be removed as public nuisances. Throughout the West there is a like feeling with reference to inanimate objects. If a hotel is old, travelers cease to frequent it; if a house is old, the owner begins to rebuild it; if a tree is old, it is cut down at once. It is not that the Americans have no reverence for antiquity; but that, settlers in a new hemisphere, they bear with them, unconsciously perhaps, the traditions of the old. Methuselah would not have attached much value to an heirloom bequeathed by his great grandson to *his* great-great grandson; and, in like manner, the Americans, whose language and whose race is that of Hengist and Horsa, can hardly consider it a point of great interest whether a building is two, or twenty, or two hundred years old. In fact, the feeling of Americans toward England is a mixed and often a contradictory one. An American is almost always offended if you tell him that America is very like England. He has a conviction—not altogether I think an absurd one—that his country ought to have a separate individuality, which makes the idea of his nation being the copy of another almost

237

repugnant. At the same time he has an opposite conviction, which I would not gainsay, that, equally with the native-born Englishman, he is the descendant of the England of Shakespeare, and Hampden and Bacon. It is this conflicting state of sentiment which causes half the difficulties between England and America. America is at once proud of England and jealous of her; and I see little prospect of a state of stable equilibrium in the matter of friendship between the two countries till America has got what she is fast getting, a literature and a history and a past of her own.

This, however, is rather a roundabout manner of coming to the conclusion I wish to draw from my observation of the mercer's shop in Washington Street, Boston, which proclaimed its antiquity as a recommendation to the public. Here, in New England, alone perhaps in all America, is such an inscription possible. Coming, as I did, to Massachusetts from the Far West, my prevailing feeling was, all along, that I had got back to an Old World civilization. Having reversed the ordinary route of European travelers—having made Boston my terminus, and not my starting-point—I was perhaps more struck with the oldness of New England than with the characteristics which belonged to it as a portion of the New World. Montalembert said once that when he was weary of despotism, he came across the Channel to take a bath of freedom. So, if I were settled in the Western World, I should come to New England from time to time, to take a bath of antiquity. Old and new are relative terms, and the change is as great in coming from Chicago to Boston as it is in passing from England to Massachusetts. Be the cause what it may, I felt, and felt pleasantly, that I was getting home. One must have wandered, as I did for months, through new cities and new states and new locations, to know the pleasure of coming back to a country where there is something older than oneself. The olive-leaf which the dove brought back to the ark was welcome as a token of the older world rising above the dull level of the flood; and so this one inscription of a building that dates from two centuries ago was welcome as a memory of the past to one who was well-nigh weary of the promises of the future.

But, indeed, it needed no Western training to find Boston
pleasant in the month of June. After six weeks' residence there,
I was unable to discover on what plan the city was built, if, which
I doubt, it was ever built on any plan at all. The very names of the
streets are good English names, which tell you something about
their several histories—nothing about their relative location.
There is no such address in Boston as "No. 1000A Street, between 100 and 101z Street." The street cars do not take you, as
elsewhere in America, to Pekin, Peru, Paris, Constantinople, and
Jerusalem; but to old-fashioned English suburbs—Cambridge
and Charlestown, and Roxbury and Watertown. So State Street
—it used to be King Street—Tremont, Beacon, Leveret, Mount
Vernon, and a hundred other streets, run in and out of each
other at all kinds of angles, up and down all kinds of slopes, in
a perfect chaos of disorder. Somehow or other you always keep
coming upon the sea in all sorts of unexpected places; and,
whichever way you strike out, you always get back to Washington
Street. This is all that I could learn as to the topography of Boston. But even though you do lose your way, it is pleasanter to an
ill-regulated European mind to go wrong in Boston than to go
right in St. Louis or Chicago. There is even a pleasure (I make
the confession with a sense of humiliation) in being received at a
hotel where the waiters wear white neckties and are pompous
as well as civil. There are no mammoth hotels, no rows of commercial palaces, no stores of gigantic height, resplendent with
marble facings; but, on the other hand, there are streets upon
streets of solemn, cozy Dutch-brick houses, looking as though a
dozen generations had been born within their walls and carried
out from behind their doors. Before each house there are little
patches of grass-plot gardens hemmed in by iron railings of substantial respectability. At the corners of the streets, perched
in the most inconvenient localities, there are old stone-built
churches which must have heard our King Georges prayed for on
many a Sunday. There is a State House with a yellow gilt dome
of the Brighton Pavilion order of architecture, which it could
have entered into the head of none but an English architect to
conceive. In quaint nooks, right in the city's heart, stand old-

fashioned English graveyards, looking as if they had been brought over from the city in the days while city trees still were green; and, in the very center of Boston, there is a fine old park full of ups and downs, and turf and knots of trees, which must have been the especial charge of the King's forester, whose house you can still have pointed out to you not far from the city.

Putting aside the dreary six months' winter of ice and snow, I would choose Boston for my dwelling-place in the States. The town itself is so bright and clean, so full of life without bustle; and then the suburbs are such pleasant places. Bunker's Hill, I own candidly, I did not go to. Talking of Bunker's Hill monument, there is a story told in Boston which is worth repeating. An English nobleman, who visited America not long ago, was taken to see the stock sight of Boston. "It was here, my lord," said his American guide, "that Warren fell." "Dear me!" replied the peer, staring at the monument in blissful ignorance of who Warren was, "I hope he did not hurt himself." Let me add that during my stay at Boston, I learnt two facts about the battle of Bunker's Hill, of which, to judge from myself, I think the English public are completely ignorant. The first is that the battle was fought on the same day as the battle of Quatre-Bras. The second is that it ended in a British victory, though a victory of the Cannæ kind. On learning this, I felt absolved from the necessity of visiting the monument.

The truth is, there are so many pretty places about Boston that it is hard to choose among them. On every line by which you enter the city, you pass for miles by hundreds and thousands of pleasant country houses, sometimes grouped together in villages, sometimes in knots of two or three, sometimes standing alone in their own gardens. There is no superstition in New England about the neighborhood of trees being unwholesome, and in the early summer the houses are almost buried beneath the green shade of the overhanging foliage. Out of the city itself the houses, with few exceptions, are built of wood. Stone is more plentiful there than timber; in fact, the whole State of Massachusetts is little more than a great granite boulder covered over with a thin layer of scanty soil. Wood, however, is preferred for house building, partly because a wooden house requires less labor in construction, and labor is expensive and far from plentiful, partly because wooden dwellings dry more quickly, and are more habitable than stone ones. To show how scanty skilled labor is still in New England, I may mention that some friends of mine, who live a few miles from Boston, wanting in last May to have a store-closet fitted up with shelves, sent for the only carpenter within reach. The man was quite willing to undertake the job, but could not find time to *fix it up* till the following August; and so it being Hobson's choice, my friends had to wait till he was disengaged.

It can only be the high price of labor which hinders Massachusetts from being a very poor country. I have never seen fields elsewhere at once so picturesque and so barren. They are very small for the most part, sometimes surrounded with stone fences built up laboriously, at others divided off by hedge-rows reminding me of Leicestershire, rich in stones beyond description, and bearing the meagerest of crops. Great masses of rock rise up in their midst, and the plows seem to have turned up three handfuls of stones to one of earth. The system of agriculture, I should say, was very primitive, but painstaking. Indeed, the life of New England farmers is no easy one. They rise early, work hard, and toil year after year with bare returns for their labors. Why a man is a farmer in Massachusetts, or, for that matter, anywhere, is a mystery. I can only account for it by the, to me, unintelligible passion for the possession of land. The farms in the country districts have many of them remained in the same family from the earliest days of the colony. Property, as in almost all parts of America, is divided equally by custom, not by law. Any man is at perfect liberty to make whatever disposition of his estate he thinks fit. As a rule, the eldest son of a New England farmer takes the farm, mortgages it deeply, to pay off his brothers' and sisters' shares in the estate, and then toils on, throughout his life perhaps, to clear off the incumbrances which eat up his scanty profits. Whenever the struggle becomes too hard, the great West is always open to give the settler a new start in life under kindlier auspices, and therefore real poverty is almost unknown in New

England. As long, however, as the Massachusetts yeoman can make both ends meet in any way, he prefers to drag on his life at home.

Yet with all this, I saw nowhere the trace of poverty. I drove for miles along the pleasant country roads, with their broad roadside strips of turf and their English hedge-rows; I passed through villages without end; and yet I never saw a cottage about which there was the unmistakable stamp of want. It is true that white paint conceals a good deal of dirt, but still I saw no single cottage in which I should think it a hardship to have to live. Most of them had gardens, where wild vines and honeysuckles and roses were trained carefully. Through the windows you could see sofas, and rocking chairs, and books, and lamps—all signs evidencing some degree of wealth, or at least of comfort. The poorest cottages were always those of the raw Irish emigrants, but still there was hardly one of them which was not a palace compared with the cottage of an ordinary English laborer, to say nothing of Ireland. It is curious, by the way, that there is a great deal of the old English prejudice against the Irish in New England. Intermarriages between the poor Irish and the poor New Englanders are almost unheard of, and it is a most unusual occurrence for an Irishman to be elected to any office in the state. However, the Irish make and, what is more, save money; and for the most part lose race and language and religion in the third generation. The German element seems to be very small. A German name over a shop door is a rare sight in the New England villages, and the names that catch a traveler's eye are good old English ones, such as Hurst, Bassett, College, Thompson, and Packard.

Of all country houses I have been in, some I know of near Boston seem to me about the pleasantest. There is no style, and very little pretension of any kind about them. There are none but women servants, and but few of them. There are no luxurious carriages, and if you want riding-horses you must hire them. There is no display of plate or liveries; and you dine at two o'clock, and do not dress for dinner. Possibly for this cause you are all the more comfortable. At any rate, you have everything that, to my mind, a country house ought to have. There are pleasant gardens and shady walks, warm rooms and large old grates, easy chairs without number, portraits of English ancestors who lived and died before America was ever heard of, good libraries, and excellent cookery. Added to all this, you are in an English atmosphere—very welcome to an Englishman. You find English books about you, read English newspapers, and are talked to with English talk. The latest English criticisms, the gossip of the English book world, the passing incidents of English life, "Essays and Reviews," and the Kennedy law case, are topics about which your hosts know as much, and perhaps care more, than you do yourself. Indeed, it often struck me that my Boston friends knew more about England than they did about America. I say this in no depreciation of their patriotism. It may seem strange to English critics—who are wont to assume, as a self-evident axiom, that America is a hateful country, and that the system of American Government is repulsive to every educated and refined mind—to discover, as they would do by a short residence at Boston, that men of genius and men of letters—men whose names are known and honored wherever the English language is read—feel as proud of their own country and as proud of their own institutions as if they had been Englishmen. I do not say, that the feeling toward England is more friendly in Boston than elsewhere in the States; perhaps it is even less so. The community of feeling, and sentiment, and literature, between New and Old England has caused the New Englanders to feel more bitterly than other Americans what they consider, justly or unjustly, the sins of England toward the Union; but, in spite of themselves, the old love for England still crops out, in the almost touching cordiality with which an Englishman is welcomed here. Just as the artist world of Europe, willingly or unwillingly, turns to Italy as the home of Art, so the mind, and culture, and genius of America turns, and will turn for many long years yet, to the mother country as the home of her language, and history, and literature. That this should be so is an honor to England, and, like all honors, it entails a responsibility.

The New England Abolitionists

DURING THE early part of June, when I first came to Boston, the Army of the Potomac had advanced beyond Yorktown, and the North was expecting daily to hear of the capture of Richmond. Toward the middle of June, in the weeks that just preceded the Chickahominy battles, there grew up, for the first time, a feeling of popular anxiety about the issue of the campaign. The national hopes, though they had not yet begun to waver, were not very vivid. Even the New York papers were at their wits' ends to produce sensation paragraphs, and contented themselves with oracular statements, that "a gentleman of intelligence, recently returned from Richmond, was convinced that McClellan's plans must be crowned with ultimate success." The long-suffering patience, I may remark, with which the American people awaited McClellan's action was a remarkable trait of the national character. With the exception of the *New York Tribune,* and its namesake of Chicago, there was not a paper of any eminence in the North which was openly hostile to him. With ten times the provocation, there was not one tithe of the invective poured by the American press on General McClellan for his unaccountable inaction that was heaped by our own newspapers upon Lord Raglan, for the tardiness of his movements in the Crimea. When I first came to America I believed it was impossible that, under a Democratic Government, popular impatience would leave General McClellan a long lease of power unless he justified his claims by some brilliant action. Further experience showed me that I undervalued the good sense of the people. After the first few months, there never was any great popular enthusiasm about

McClellan. It was not likely, indeed, that there should have been any. Throughout the spring, there was a growing conviction that the General commanding-in-chief was not strong enough for his post. An old Democrat, and a political partisan of McClellan's, in speaking to me, at the period of which I write, about his military capacity, remarked, "If McClellan was a great general, we should not be discussing, a year after his appointment, whether he really was so or not." This impression seemed to me, though expressed less openly, to be the prevailing one; and yet there was no public outcry for his recall. The broad sense of the matter was, that to have removed McClellan at this moment, in the midst of the campaign, and in front of the enemy, would have been so great an evil that it could only have been wise to incur it if it became clear that the General was not merely relatively but absolutely incapable. There was no evidence as yet that this was the case, and therefore the people were content to wait. Possibly it may seem a paradox to the English reader to talk of the patience of popular government. I can only say, without entering on a theoretical discussion, that taken as a whole, the self-restraint, the moderation, and the patience of the American people in the conduct of this people's war, were in themselves facts worth noting.

The one circumstance, however, which in my belief contributed toward keeping McClellan in power was the vehemence with which the Abolitionist party assailed him. It is not that the Commander-in-Chief was popular with the vast majority of the North *because* he was a pro-slavery General, but there was a general and not ill-founded conviction that the attacks made upon him were due more to his politics than to his strategy; and therefore these attacks helped him more than they hurt him. Indeed, the position of McClellan threw considerable light on the *active* want of strength of the Abolitionists. The truth is, that the Anti-slavery party had, as it were, two creeds, the exoteric and the esoteric. According to the former, the popular faith, slavery is a great evil, a calamity to any country addicted to it; and, like every other national evil, should, as far as possible, be checked by legislation, and still more by the force of public opinion; but, above all, should in no way be promoted by any act of the Government. This is substantially the Republican creed; and owing chiefly to the exertions of the Abolitionists, this Republican creed became practically the creed of the North. But amongst themselves the Abolitionists, pure and simple, have an esoteric creed, more logical perhaps, but less accommodating. With them slavery is an absolute sin—not an evil, but a crime. Slavery being thus in itself a crime, the nation is bound to suppress it at all costs and all dangers; and if that should be found impossible, the nation has no choice but to put away the accursed thing, and to renounce all partnership in the profits of iniquity. This esoteric faith was held by a very small and, I suspect, at the moment, a decreasing party. New England was the headquarters of the Abolitionists, and yet the outward evidences of their power—I might almost say of their existence—were few indeed. In all Boston, with its shoals of papers, there was not one Abolition daily newspaper. The *Courier*, the most largely circulated of any Boston paper, reprinted every morning at the head of its articles the resolution passed by the House of Representatives in February, 1861, with a view of averting the danger of Secession: *"That neither the Federal Government, nor the people or Governments of the non-slaveholding States, have a purpose or a constitutional right to legislate upon, or interfere with slavery, in any of the States of the Union."* From this text the *Courier* preached regularly against the Abolitionists, and especially against Wendell Phillips, whom it pursued with a bitter personal animosity. The Boston *Herald*, a halfpenny paper, which has a large popular circulation, was still more fiercely anti-Abolitionist. Writing of the gradual emancipation project of President Lincoln, it stated that the scheme "meets with no favour, and is not acceptable to even the Border Slave States. Emancipation, as advocated by Mr. Sumner and others, is condemned by all the States South, and by one half of the public in the Free States." The *Post*, which was a moderate Republican paper, and is perhaps the best-written and most respectable of American newspapers, used to declaim against bringing forward the question of emancipation at all, till Secession was suppressed.

Its text was, "that the people everywhere ought to insist that partisanship shall stop, and that congress shall cooperate with the President in the one simple object to restore the national authority." The official organ of the anti-slavery public in New England is the *Liberator*, a weekly newspaper of which Lloyd Garrison is the Editor. I should gather its circulation to be entirely a class one, as I never by any chance saw it offered for sale in the shops or streets. Besides this, there is a paper published in Boston called the *Pine and Palm*, which is supposed to be addressed to the free Negroes. It has the regular tract-newspaper air of the quondam *True Briton* and the modern *Friend of the British Workman;* and like every paper in search of a public, has a debilitated tone about it. There has lately been a monthly review published in Boston, the *Continental*, which is well written, and avowedly Abolitionist in politics; but as yet I should judge its circulation to be extremely small. The *Atlantic Monthly*, the great New England Review, is very catholic in its politics, staunchly Unionist, and more or less anti-slavery; but still it is decidedly not Abolitionist.

On the whole, I should say that the tone of Boston society is very like that of the press. To advocate pro-slavery doctrines would be decidedly unfashionable; to advocate immediate Abolition would be hardly less so. Moderate anti-slaveryism is obviously the correct thing. Till within the last few years, to avow the Abolition creed in Boston was to exclude yourself from society. A person who openly advocated the voluntary system in a cathedral town, or who spoke against the game laws in a fox-hunting county, would have about as much chance of being well received in the local society as an Abolitionist would have had in Boston. With the "John Brown year," as the report of the Anti-Slavery Society termed the year 1860, a change came. For the first time almost, American Abolitionism emerged from the sentimentalism of the *Uncle Tom* phase, and became a living fact and a stern reality; and its professors won that respect which society always accords to power. At the present moment, a prominent Abolitionist would be somewhat of a lion in Boston, like a foreign patriot or a renowned spiritualist medium; and it would hardly now as formerly be made an objection to meeting anyone at dinner, that he or she was an Abolitionist. Still, even yet the fact of being known to hold anti-slavery opinions is not a pass to society, but, if anything, the contrary. The different religious communions in New England still ignore to a great extent the question of slavery. The Episcopalians and the Methodists, the two sects which have the greatest following in the South, have always decried any discussion of slavery as tending to produce schism in the Church. No denomination that I am aware of ever succeeded in passing a resolution to exclude slaveholders from its communion; and the Unitarians are, I believe, the only religious sect who offer up prayers in their chapels for the over-throw of slavery. The question how far the Churches in America were at liberty to enter on the topic of slavery is a very difficult one. Every allowance should be made, if their final decision was, as I think, wrong. It certainly has proved unfortunate. All parties agree that the clergy, who, twenty or thirty years ago, possessed immense power in New England, have now no political influence whatever. It is clear, too, that the date of their decline in authority coincides with the period when the question of slavery became the dominant question of the day, and the Church decided to abstain from its discussion. The great influence probably both of Ralph Waldo Emerson and Theodore Parker is due to the façt that their teaching grappled with subjects the Church was, and is, afraid to speak out upon openly.

The rural districts are, I suspect, the stronghold of New England Abolitionism. In the country, much more of the old Puritan feeling is to be found than in the towns. During the access of the temperance mania, which had power to pass the Maine liquor law, but not power enough to carry it into effect, the Massachusetts farmers in many places cut down their apple trees with their own hands, in order to hinder the possibility of cider being manufactured again. The same uncompromising spirit undoubtedly prevails still; and wherever Abolition sentiments have made their way in the country villages, the descendants of the Puritans are for cutting down slavery, root and branch, without stint and without mercy. In the towns the feeling about or against slavery is much less strongly developed. Their trade interests were opposed to any collision with the South, and trade interests in America are even more powerful than they are with us. Besides all this, a very large majority of the New Englanders were hostile to the Abolition movement, not from love of standing well with the fashionable "upper ten thousand," or even from pecuniary interest, but in a great measure from honest conviction. I don't think that we in England have at all done justice to the distinction between the Anti-slavery and the Abolition party. Every Englishman almost, I suppose, would say, if he were asked, that he disapproved of slavery. Yet, I suppose, also, that there is not one Englishman in a hundred, or in a thousand, who would admit that England was countenancing slavery by buying slave-grown cotton. The answer would be, and perhaps with reason—"England has nothing whatever to do with the internal institutions of her customers. We disapprove of slavery, and do not hesitate to say so, but we are not bound by this disapproval to break off all commercial or social relations with slaveholders. It is enough for us that we have done our own duty." Now this, with little alteration, is exactly the language of the New England Republicans. "We disapprove," they say, "of slavery; we have abolished it everywhere within our own jurisdiction; we have opposed any extension of the system for which we could be considered responsible; but we are not bound to exclude ourselves from all fellowship and connection with other states in which slavery is established." Now, Abolition means, if it means anything, that any union or partnership with slaveholding communities is a sin. If the North is in duty bound to suppress slavery in the Slave States, at the risk of breaking up the Union, I am not clear that, by the same rule, England is not bound to decline the purchase of slave-grown cotton. The whole question is a most difficult and a most painful one; and I should be sorry to condemn either the Abolitionist or the Anti-slavery party. It is, however, to my mind, most unjust to accuse the latter of want of sincerity because they do not and cannot endorse the creed of Abolitionism. That the result of this war may be the overthrow of slavery is my most earnest hope and prayer;

but I cannot blame those who, hating slavery, and resolved to
check its extension, are not prepared to extinguish it in other
states, unless the necessity is forced upon them by the instinct
of self-preservation.

With the public, the press, the Church, and society hostile to
them, it is not surprising that the progress of the Abolitionists
proper should have been small. The society which represents
them significantly enough does not bear the name of the "Abolition Society," but has adopted the more moderate, though less
appropriate, one of the "Anti-slavery." The direct influence of
this body I take to have been small. During the "John Brown
year," when the popular excitement about slavery was at the
highest, the whole receipts of the society were under three
thousand pounds—a scanty allowance in this most charitable of
states. In the list of the vice-presidents and committee you will
not find one single name of public note, except that of Lloyd
Garrison, and Wendell Phillips. The men whose names we know
best in Europe, in connection with the anti-slavery cause—
Charles Sumner, Ward Beecher, [Owen] Lovejoy, [Benjamin]
Wade, and [John] Frémont—are not members of the committee. The explanation of this is obvious. The fundamental
tenet of the Abolitionists is that slavery is a crime with which an
honest man can hold no communion. Now the whole of the
United States' Constitution rests upon the assumption that
slavery, even if an evil, is not a crime which the Government is
called upon to deal with. It is very difficult, therefore, for any
man to be an Abolitionist, in our English sense of the word, and
yet to take part in American public life. The Ultra-Abolitionists
say that the Republicans have solved the problem of serving
both God and mammon. Certainly, the creed of the Republicans
consists in being as hostile to slavery as is consistent with loyalty
to the Union and the Constitution; while the Abolitionists hold
the converse doctrine, and are as loyal to the Union as is consistent with hostility to slavery. Between the holders of these
conflicting doctrines there may be sympathy, but there cannot
be cooperation.

Amongst the Abolitionists themselves there are different sections. The party, of which the Stowes and Beechers may be considered the representatives, approximates most closely to the outer world. The marvelous and almost unparalleled success of "Uncle Tom's Cabin," raised this section to a temporary predominance. For my own part I was not impressed favorably by what I heard and saw of the Beecher-Stowe Abolitionists. They seemed to me to represent the sickly sentimentalism which is sure to attach itself to any cause however good. I believe that "Uncle Tom's Cabin" did as much harm, by removing the question of emancipation from the domain of fact into that of fiction, as it did good, by calling public attention to the evils of slavery. It is possible that Mr. Ward Beecher's oratorical theology may really influence a large class of semi-educated persons. To me it bore an appearance of affectation and want of earnestness, mixed up with a kind of undignified jocosity, which I found hard to reconcile with a belief in the preacher's real depth of feeling. It may be that I judge them hardly; but it always seemed to me that the Anti-slavery cause would have fared better without the services of the Beecher connection. They labored under the fatal objection that, wishing the end, they were afraid to assert their approval of the means. They professed certain doctrines which entailed inevitable consequences, and yet they shrunk perpetually from admitting the logical deduction of their own professions. Teaching a creed which was subversive of the Union, they had not courage to pronounce distinctly against the maintenance of the established order of things, and thus both friends and enemies looked upon them as half-hearted, and not altogether without reason. Then there was another section, which might be called the "Mountain" of Abolitionism, which went even further than the recognized leaders of the party. This section, of which Mr. [Moncure] Conway, the author of "The Rejected Stone," was the most prominent member, repudiated all connection whatever with persons who did not hold their extreme views, and regarded men like [Wendell] Phillips and [James Russell] Lowell as traitors to the cause, because they conceived that they might lawfully accept the assistance of others, who, not holding their own opinions, were still willing, up to a certain point, to assist in carrying them into effect.

But both these sections of the Abolitionists were insignificant and uninfluential, as compared with that led by Wendell Phillips and Lloyd Garrison. Of the whole phalanx, the former was the tower of strength. Gifted with great talents, with untiring energy, and, above all, with an eloquence which I have never heard equaled, he might have risen to any height in public life. But, for conscience's sake, he refused to enter on a career which necessitated, to say the least, an outward acquiescence in the sin of slavery. He has labored for years past, amidst ridicule and abuse and obloquy, to awaken the nation to a sense of their duty. It is difficult for an Englishman to conceive the amount of moral courage required by an American who preaches the doctrine that the venerated Constitution of Washington and Hamilton is in itself a compact with sin, an evil to be abolished. His friends say, that he is the Aaron of the party, while Garrison has been the Moses. It may be so, but the words and voice which have stirred up the hearts of the New Englanders for long years past have been those of Phillips. Whatever your opinions may be, I defy you to listen to that scathing burning eloquence of his, and not be carried away, for the time at least. Most of us have a heart somewhere about us, and the great Abolitionist orator has an unrivaled talent for finding that heart out, and working upon its chords. When you once have heard him, agreeing or disagreeing, you cannot doubt the fact of his courage; pro-slavery, or anti-slavery, you cannot question the power of his eloquence. And his labor has not been in vain.

It was my good fortune, while in New England, to see a great deal of the Abolitionist party, and I have never come across a set of people whom I have admired and respected more. I should be sorry, therefore, if these remarks should convey an impression that in my opinion the influence of the Abolitionists has been small. It is to them in great measure, to their unceasing testimony as to the truth of the "higher law," that the existence of the Republican party is due. Directly, I should doubt the Abolitionists having increased of late, either in numbers or in influence. It is impossible to say how long it may be before the American people come to the conclusion that slavery is a crime which, like robbery, must be suppressed, and which no Christian government can permit. It is doubtful to my mind whether the people ever will come, as a nation, to this conclusion. But every day the conviction is spreading throughout the North that slavery is an evil to be tolerated at the utmost. This may not be the whole truth, but still it is a very large half of it, and from that conviction to the extinction of slavery the step is not a long one. When once slavery is abolished, Abolition principles will, of course, become fashionable, but I question whether the early Abolitionists will even then be personally popular. There are prophets whose prophecies are scouted at the time, and not appreciated when fulfilled, and I think that men like Wendell Phillips belong to this class. Happily their reward will be in the success of their labors, not in popular applause. The last two years, however, have already raised the social and political position of the Abolitionists. They are now advocates, instead of enemies, of the Union. As the nation became more and more convinced that the Abolitionist maxim is true and that the Union is incompatible with slavery, the men known hitherto as the bitterest opponents of slavery, came in popular idea to be regarded as the stanchest friends of the Union. Indeed, the recent policy of the Abolitionists is explained better by a saying of Wendell Phillips, than by any elaborate explanation. Someone asked him how he, who had been proclaiming for years "that the Union was the fruit of slavery and of the devil," could be now an ardent advocate of this very Union. His answer was, "Yes; but I never expected then that slavery and the devil would secede from the Union." So it is; Secession has brought the Abolitionists and the Republicans into the same camp, but the Abolitionists are still a distant outpost, a sort of *enfants perdus* of the army of the Union.

The Church in America

THE FIRST thing almost which strikes a newly arrived traveler in the United States is the immense number of churches. Every village has its half-dozen churches and chapels, Episcopalian, Unitarian, Presbyterian, Universalists, Calvinists, Independent, or any other sect you like to name. The country is dotted over with the wooden steeples, whose white painted sides, I must own, sparkle in the bright sunlight uncommonly like marble. Sunday is kept with a Scotch propriety; not a shop or tavern is open; the railroads are closed for the day; and the omnibuses cease running. Happily with an inexplicable inconsistency, the horse-railroads are allowed to run, though omnibuses and steam-engines may not; and therefore, there are some means of locomotion still left on the Sabbath. The churches are apparently crowded, and the number of churchgoers you see about the streets is larger in proportion to the population than it would be in London. In fact, if you used your eyes only, the first attribute you would ascribe to the Americans would be that of a church-going people.

Yet, if you used your ears as well as your eyes, you would soon become aware of a second fact, equally remarkable, and apparently inconsistent with the first, and that is that you never hear anything about religious opinions or discussions. Throughout the whole period of my residence in America I never met, in any newspaper, with any allusion to the religious opinion of any public man, nor have I ever seen any question connected with religion discussed in the press. I don't suppose one American in a hundred ever asked, or thought of asking, what Church Mr.

Lincoln, Mr. Seward, Mr. Stanton, or General McClellan, belonged to. I *believe* the first to be a Baptist, the second an Episcopalian, and the last two Unitarians, but I am by no means sure that I am correct in my impressions; and as nobody I met was likely to know anything about the matter, I had no means of discovering with certainty, even if I had wished it, what denomination these gentlemen, or other public men, were members of. As far as I could gather, in public life, it is better for a politician to belong to some Church or other. The mere fact of doing so, like being married, or having a house of your own, is a sort of public testimony to your respectability and morality; but which Church you select is a matter of absolute indifference to anybody but yourself. The only sect against whom there seems to exist any popular prejudice is the Catholic Church; and this prejudice I take to be derived partly from the traditions of the Old Country, partly from an impression, not altogether unsupported by evidence, that the power of the Papacy is hostile to the institutions of a free country. When Frémont was standing for the Presidency, an unfounded charge of being a Catholic was brought against him, and the fact of its being so brought, and deliberately disavowed, shows that some importance was attached to it. In private society religion—by which I mean controversial religion—does not seem to be a topic of general interest. It would be almost impossible for an American to mix much in English society without becoming aware whether his acquaintances were Episcopalians or Unitarians, High Church or Low Church. Now, of the hundreds of people I knew, to a certain extent, intimately in the States, I am not aware to what denomination more than a couple of them belonged, and in their case I only happened to become acquainted with their religious creed because I learnt accidentally what Church they were in the habit of attending. If I had chosen, I might, no doubt, have discovered—just as any man curious in such matters might discover the family history of his acquaintances in this country. But, unless you take a special trouble to acquire the information, it is not of the sort which comes to you unconsciously. Toleration, apparently, is absolute, not only in principle, but in practice.

What Church you belong to, whether you change from one Church to another, or whether you belong to no Church at all, are questions which your own conscience alone has to settle. Anybody who is intimately acquainted with country life in England must be aware that a well-to-do family would cease to be respectable, and would probably be looked upon unfavorably by the neighborhood, if none of its members ever went to any place of worship. In America, dissent from the ordinary modes of faith entails no social disabilities. This state of things is not caused by public indifference as to religious matters; on the contrary, a direct profession of religion is much more common amongst men than it is with us.

I remember, when I first came to America, being astonished at hearing a young man say that, under certain eventualities, he should "join the Church." I questioned him as to which Church he intended to join, and found that he had no idea as yet. He was perfectly serious, however, and contemplated joining the Church in order to relieve himself from a *liaison* in which he was entangled, exactly as I might propose to join the bar in order to relieve myself from the necessity of serving on juries. Gradually, the meaning of the expression "joining the Church" became intelligible to me. In all the American Churches, with the exception of the Catholic and the Episcopalian, the fact of being born of parents belonging to any sect does not constitute you ipso facto a member of it. The child of Methodist parents, for instance, can be christened, if they desire it; but he does not become a Methodist, nor is he admitted to their communion until he has formally announced his intention, after arriving at years of discretion, of joining the Church. So it is with the other denominations. Every sect has a number of half-members, who attend its services, but have never formally joined the Church, and do not share its communion. These half-members have a vote, and pay rates equally with the full-members. What spiritual privileges they possess, or are supposed to possess, is an open question. Of late years, the American Churches have looked unfavorably on their non-professing members, whose number has much decreased in consequence. The calculation is that of the whole

American adult population about one-fifth are professing members of some church or other. Probably the fact that the Episcopalian Church alone, amongst Protestant sects, does not require a distinct profession of faith is one of the chief causes of its comparative increase. In many of the sects, the act of joining the Church is not supposed to be necessarily preceded by spiritual conversion, but is simply taken as a declaration that the member is a professedly religious man. The result of this system is that the relative proportion of avowedly religious persons is larger than in England, while the proportion of persons who belong to a Church without any distinct profession of religion is infinitely smaller. How far this system works favorably, in a religious point of view, is a question on which I have no wish to enter. There is one social aspect, however, of the system which is remarkable. I mean the impulse it has given in America to spiritualism, and similar forms of delusion.

At home, ninety-nine men out of a hundred, who have no particular opinions on religious matters, belong naturally to the faith their fathers belonged to; and such religious wants or aspirations as they may have are satisfied by the National Church. In America, the contrary is the case. Any man who has no pronounced religious opinions belongs to no Church; and therefore whatever wants he may have of a spiritual nature remain unsatisfied. Thus any new faith, false or true, has an unappropriated public to work upon in America which it has not in a Catholic country, and to a very limited extent in England. But, on the other hand, it is clear that spiritualism has obtained a hold on the popular American mind which it has not on our side the Atlantic. What English paper, London or provincial, would contain advertisements of astrologers, clairvoyants, and mediums? Now, with the exception of some few of the New York and Boston journals, there is not a newspaper in America which does not contain astrological and spiritual advertisements. In every paper almost you can pick out advertisements similar to the following, which I quote from the *Boston Herald:*

"Mrs. Leonora Smith, clairvoyant Medium, No. 15, La Grange Place, gives sittings daily for communications from the spirit-world, seeing and describing spirits." Again, "Madame Lagon, natural Astrologist and Medium, will give to the public a fore-knowledge of all the general affairs through life, seeing and describing spirits."

All this information is offered at the moderate price of one shilling for ladies and two for gentlemen. There is no town I have been into where a medium or astrologist, chiefly of the female gender, did not advertise herself in the local papers. In the West especially astrology is a flourishing trade. During my travels in the Western States I visited several of these mediums out of curiosity, in the hope of witnessing some exhibition of skill which might explain their success. I found most of them to be German Jewesses, sharp, shrewd women enough, but in no single instance did I see any exhibition of clairvoyance or spirit-rapping remarkable enough to bear description. If any of my readers ever consulted the hermit at Beulah Spa, or at any suburban tea-gardens, they will know exactly what was told me by these spiritual mediums. It was the old, old story of a dark lady or a fair woman, or a long journey, or a letter arriving with money, or any other piece of rigmarole nonsense. The curious fact was that the waiting-rooms of these imposters were often crowded by well-dressed persons, chiefly women.

I do not suppose that the higher class of Americans would visit fortunetellers of this description. A charge varying from one to five shillings is not sufficient to attract wealthy inquirers after spiritual mysteries. As fashionable amusements, spirit-rapping and table-turning have a good deal died out. Still spiritualism, as a creed, numbers many believers in America. Commodore Foote, in his address to the people of Memphis, after the capture of that city by the Federals, based his arguments against Secession on Swedenborgian doctrines, and told them that "the Civil War had been produced out of the inner life." People smiled at the announcement, but nobody seemed to think it odd that a distinguished public man, holding an important position, should be a Swedenborgian, or adhere to any other faith, however eccentric. As far as I could discover, the popular American judgment about spiritualism is much the same as our English one. A certain number of clever, if not sensible men, believe in it heartily. The great majority of Americans consider the whole outward manifestations of the creed to be delusions or impostures, and its internal doctrines to be detrimental to elevated morality. Still with regard to spiritualism, as to every other "ism," there is absolute toleration, and if President Lincoln chose to consult the spirits (as for all I know he may do), on every occasion of his life, no one would consider it a ground for objecting to his fitness as President.

I have dwelt somewhat at length upon this tolerance of spiritualism, because I consider it an important feature in American life. Even the most liberal of ordinary English critics seem to me to have adopted a parrot-cry about the tyranny of the majority in America over the minority, without ever considering whether the cry was true or not. Now all history shows that there is no subject on which people are more apt to tyrannize over a minority than on religious matters; and anyone who knows America must see that religious sentiment is extremely strong there. The doctrines of spiritualism are naturally offensive to all established creeds, as they tend to destroy the whole theory of modern religion with regard to a future state. Yet there has been no attempt whatever to tyrannize over the spiritualist minority. With the exception of the Mormons, whose case was, in many respects, a peculiar one, there has been no instance in America of religious persecution. And what is still more remarkable, under the rule of a democracy, deep national religious convictions have been proved to be consistent with complete freedom of opinion on religious matters. There is no such thing in the North as social persecution, or loss of political standing, on account of your religion, or want of religion. How far this is consistent with the theory of the tyranny of majorities, I much question personally.

Cambridge, U.S.

SOME FOUR miles or so from Boston lies the university town of New England—the Cambridge of the New World. There are few places in the States of which I have carried away with me brighter memories. The kindness of new-made friends caused Cambridge to be a sort of home to me during my stay at Boston. But even without personal recollections, my impressions of the university town, and above all of its class-day, as the annual commemoration is called, would be very pleasant ones. Let me speak of it as I found it.

It is by the street-railroads that you go to Cambridge, U.S. The idea may not be academical, but the reality is wonderfully pleasant. If I had no other reason for not liking George Francis Train, I should find cause enough for my dislike in the fact that he has discredited the street-railway system in England. I know, indeed, of no pleasanter mode of traveling for a short distance; and of all American street-railroads, the Cambridge ones are the best. It is true that the cars are overcrowded at times. Nothing is perfect in this bad world of ours. It is true, too, that gentlemen are expected to leave their seats when ladies have no place to sit down in; but then so many of the Boston ladies are young and pretty, and always smile so pleasantly when you make room for them, that I wonder how Mr. Trollope found it in his heart to grumble at the custom. It is undeniable also, that if, as I trust my readers do, you drive your own mail-phaeton, you find the street-rails hinder the high-road from being as smooth as it would be otherwise. Still, even from the summit of a mail-phaeton you cannot help perceiving that the number of people who do not possess carriages of their own considerably exceeds the number of those who do; and, therefore, on the whole, street-railroads are a gain to the community at large. Putting aside these slight objections, your ride to Cambridge, especially on a summer evening, is all that you can desire. Your fare is only threepence: low as the fare is, a dirtily dressed passenger is almost unknown; and even if you are sometimes crowded, it is pleasant to see colored women and children sitting or standing among the other passengers on terms of perfect equality. You travel as smoothly as you would in the softest of spring carriages. You go as quick as you would in an Eastern-Counties express, and you pay as little as you would in a London omnibus.

The road itself is a very pretty one. Up and down the old-fashioned hilly streets of Boston, with their quaint red brick houses, then over a long wide bridge across the Charles River, or rather, across the sea creek into which the Charles River runs— a creek famed in the annals of Boston for the fact that the tea was thrown into its waters in the days of the Revolution; then through the long straggling suburb of Cambridge Port, then through rows after rows of wooden villas, standing each in its own gardens, and so on into the little quiet town of Cambridge. Of town or streets there is but little; what there is, is grouped around Harvard College. Three low blocks of buildings, built two hundred years ago, looking for all the world as though the Pilgrim Fathers had transported them ready made from Trinity Hall or Emmanuel College, and called Hollis, Stoughton, and Massachusetts, form two sides of a college quad. On the third stands the college library, a cross in architectural fashion between King's Chapel and the brick church in Barnwell, with the same dumpy pinnacles on the roof, like the legs of a dinner table turned upside down. The square is completed by a block of lecture rooms, of the plainest structure. Hard by the college, there are a row or two of shops, university book stalls, groceries, and the like; and round about, in every direction, there are pleasant shady streets, lined with trees and quickset hedges and old-fashioned country houses. Indeed, the whole place had, to my eyes, an academic air, for which I was not prepared. One of the professors told me, that after Arthur Clough had resided here a short time, he said that "he felt himself back in Oxford." Indeed, strolling through the grounds of that sleepy, quiet university, it seems hard to realize that you are in the country of New York and Chicago and the West.

The students are quieter, apparently, than our English ones; or, at any rate, you see less of them about the streets. Once or twice in the evenings I heard snatches of noisy songs, as I passed the college buildings, which, coupled with the jingling of glasses, called back recollections of college supper-parties. Otherwise I saw or heard but little of the students, and those I did meet with had none of that air of being the owners, possessors, and masters of the university precincts, so peculiar to the undergraduates of Oxford and Cambridge. The age of the students is about the same as in our own universities. Twenty-one is, as with us, the average age at which students take their degree, or rather, close their college course, for taking one's degree is, at Harvard College, by no means the usual termination of the university career. There is no particular reason why students should take a degree; and, as a rule, when they have studied as many years as their finances or their inclinations will allow them, they leave the university without undergoing the formality of graduating. The fact that there are no fellowships to be obtained makes an academical degree of little comparative value. There is no distinctive dress worn now either by students or professors. The college discipline is very like our own, except that the students are treated more like men than schoolboys, and, I should gather, with success. The undergraduates may or may not live in the college rooms, according to their own choice. There are many more students than rooms; and, at the commencement of each year, the vacant rooms are distributed by lottery amongst the freshmen. If the lucky winners like to sell their privilege, they are at liberty to do so; and, practically, the poorer students generally make something by the sale of their right to rooms. Why men should wish to live in the smallest of old-fashioned college rooms instead of in comfortable lodgings in the town is a mystery that no man can comprehend after the age of one-and-twenty; but the wish prevails in Cambridge, U. S. as well as in Cambridge, England. Of late years, the system of "commons" has been given up, and the students take their meals in clubs, or at boarding houses. The undergraduates are obliged to attend lectures and chapel in the morning. The prayers, which are very short, are worded so as to contain nothing offensive to the tenets of any Christian sect, and must, I fancy, in consequence be curious specimens of moral commonplaces. On Sundays, there is service held at college, according to the orthodox form, as the Calvinist faith is called in New England, and students who do not go to church elsewhere are expected to attend it. Parents, however, may fix what form of worship their sons shall frequent; and the majority of the undergraduates who come from near Boston pass their Sundays at home. In glancing over a list of the students, I saw that they belonged to some dozen different religious denominations, and that some three per cent of the whole number avowed no preference for any particular form of religion. Of those who belonged nominally to the several sects, about a fifth or sixth were Church members. The average expense of the university course varied, as I was told, from £150 to £250 per annum; but, in many instances, I suspect, this latter estimate must be much exceeded. At the class-day I was present at, four students kept open house for all their friends, and I was told they had ordered refreshments to be provided for a thousand persons. Considering the style of the entertainment, it must have cost a dollar a head, at the very least; and a thousand dollars (£200) is rather a large sum, even for our own university swells, to spend on an entertainment. Though the outlay was talked of by the professors as absurd, it did not seem to me to be regarded as anything very unusual.

But, at this rate, I shall never get to Cambridge class-day. It was a glorious hot summer day, hotter than we often have in England; and the chimes of Cambridge rang out merrily, and the little town was full of ladies with the brightest of bonnets and the prettiest of faces. Class-day is the last day of the Academic course, at least for the fourth-year students, or senior sophomores, as I think they are called; and on this day these students give a sort of farewell festival to the rest of the college, and to their friends. By the kindness of one of my friends—Professor Lowell—I was invited to be present at the ceremony. Under a broiling sun, on the twentieth of June last, we strolled, in the forenoon, across the college grounds, past Washington's elm, to the house of the President, or rather the acting President—for at that time the office was vacant.

At the house of the acting President, the professors and the students were collected. It so happened that on that morning the news had reached America of the death of Mr. [Arthur Hugh] Clough; and it was pleasant to me, as it would have been to any Englishman who appreciated the high talents of that scholar-poet, to see how kindly and how highly his memory was cherished by his brother professors who had known and loved him. The fourth-year sophomores, who were the heroes of the day, were all assembled, arrayed in the glossiest of new black dress clothes and with the whitest of kid gloves. Evening dress somehow takes more kindly to American youths than to our own, and the students seemed to me a set of as good-looking gentlemanlike young men as it has been often my fortune to see. We formed a line, and marched two-and-two together through the grounds, with a band of music leading the way, and a sympathetic crowd of by-standers gazing at us, and following in our wake. I am afraid, as I think of it, that my friend and I must have rather marred the appearance of the procession, by being in colored clothes. However, black is not a cool color to wear in the dog days, and so I hope we were pardoned. Our walk ended in the Unitarian church of Cambridge, which the University has a right to use for public ceremonies. Thanks to my being with the dons' party, I got a seat upon the raised platform at the end of the chapel, and sat there in glory and comparative coolness. The moment we were seated there was a rush of students through the doors, and a perfectly unnecessary fight was got up with the constables who guarded the entrance, which reminded me of wrestlings I had witnessed upon the staircase of the theater at the Oxford Commemorations. In fact, the whole scene had an Oxford air about it. There were the ladies with bonnets of every color, blue, white, and pink, fanning themselves in the crowded seats. There was a host of bright young faces, and the orations were strings of appropriate platitudes and decorous *facetiæ* of the mildest character, such as most of us have heard oftentimes in college halls, and under no other circumstances. Of the speakers, I would only say that they were two young men of six feet high and upward—one the stroke of the Harvard boat—and as fine specimens of manhood as you would desire to see. We had a band, which played the overture to *Martha,* and other operatic music, with remarkable precision; a prayer full of the most apposite commonplaces; and an ode of a patriotic character. There were allusions to the war in plenty throughout the proceedings, but everything was too decorous for the exhibition of any ardent patriotism. Amongst the crowd, however, there was one poor lad, pale, worn, and limping upon crutches, who had lost his leg in the battle of Balls Bluff, and who had come to witness the gala day of the class which he had left to join the war. He was the hero of the day, and at every patriotic sentiment all eyes were turned toward him, as though he were the living embodiment of the country's struggle and defeats and victories. I have no doubt, according to the Yankee phrase, he had "a good time of it" that class-day at Cambridge, amongst his old friends and fellow students; but I could not help feeling that there was a long hereafter before him, when the war is over, and the excitement has passed away; and when I, for my part, would sooner have both legs than have been a hero and be a cripple.

Then, when the orations were over, we strolled through the old college rooms, where the students had prepared luncheons for their friends, and where every stranger who came was welcomed with that frank cordiality which seems to me so universal a characteristic of American hospitality. Then, having eaten as much ice cream and raised pies and lobster salads as our digestions would permit of, we wandered off through the pleasant college grounds; and, in defiance of academical decorum, in full view of the public road, smoked cigars upon the lawn of a college Professor, who invited us to the act by his own example. Let me say, that of all academical dignitaries whom I have known—and

I have known a good number—I should say that the Professors of Harvard College were, as a body, the pleasantest. They are all men of scholarly education, some of them of European repute, and yet, in one sense, they are also men of the world. There is nothing amongst them of that pedantry and that exaggerated notion of their own importance which is almost an invariable characteristic of our own University dons. Living near a great city, almost all of them married men, with moderate incomes, they form a sort of family of scholars, such as I never met elsewhere.

Later in the afternoon there was dancing for the students and their friends in the College Hall, on whose walls there hung quaint pictures of old-fashioned Puritan benefactors, and in whose midst was suspended the famous six-oar outrigger boat of Harvard College. The dancing seemed to me very good, but the hall was overpoweringly hot, and for my part I preferred the open green, where there was music also, and where all the world was allowed to dance. The scene was in itself a curious instance of American freedom, and also of American good behavior. The green is open to the high-road, and the whole of the Cambridge world, or of the Boston world for that matter, might have come and danced here. Probably everybody who cared to dance did come, but the dancers were as well-behaved, as quiet, and as orderly as they would have been in a London ballroom. I could not help asking myself, without a satisfactory reply, whether such a scene would be possible at the backs of the Cambridge Colleges, or in the Christchurch meadows; and whether, if it were possible, our young university students would dance as freely in the midst of any of the Oxford or Cambridge towns-people who chose to come there accompanied by their sweet-hearts and sisters. The dancing was followed by a sort of farewell romp of the departing students round an old oak tree, wherein the chief amusement seemed to consist in the destruction of each others' hats. Then in the evening there was a reception of the students and their friends at the President's house, and an exhibition of Chinese lanterns and rockets on the college green; where, judging from the look of the groups I met strolling about in the dim evening light, I should say that many flirtations of the day must have been ratified by declarations and vows of eternal fidelity. *Chi lo sa?* And after the guests, and relations, and ladies had gone home, I rather suspect the students made a night of it, over the debris of the cold collations. This, however, is mere suspicion. They may have gone to bed when I did, or have quenched their thirst with the lemonade they provided for the ladies, but I own I doubt it.

Concord

I HAPPENED, while in Boston, to see a good deal of the literary society of the place. Let me say something of the men whose writings I, in common with most Englishmen, had learnt to know long ago; and whose faces then, for the first time, became as familiar to me as their names.

I am afraid that to most English readers the name of Concord will recall no national reverses. We have a remarkable talent as a nation for forgetting what is unpleasant to remember, but still the fact remains that at Concord a British regiment *did* run away before a rabble of American volunteers. Our loss consisted of two men killed, whose names have been long forgotten. This was the first armed resistance raised by the Colonists against the imperial troops, and a little obelisk has been erected beside the nameless graves of these two British privates to record the first blow struck in behalf of American independence. A low stunted avenue leads from the Boston high-road to the bank of the Concord River. Along this avenue the British troops advanced and retreated, and on the bank of the river stands a squat dumpy obelisk of the Georgian era. Close to the avenue is the Old Manse, from which Hawthorne culled the mosses. Sitting one summer day by the side of that lazy stream, the author of "The Scarlet Letter" told me a story of the battle which was new to me. When the galling fire of the enemy from the opposite bank caused our troops to retire, the two British soldiers who fell at Concord were not both killed. One of them was only wounded, but in the hurry of the retreat was left for dead on the field. As

268

the British troops withdrew, a farming lad, employed at the Old Manse, came out to look at the scene of the battle. He had an axe with him, and, holding it in his hand, he stole alongside the wounded soldiers, whom he believed to be dead. Just as he got near, the one who was still alive raised himself upon his hands and knees, and began to look about him. The boy in an agony of fear fancied that the man was going to fire, and, striking at him with the axe, cut open his skull, and then fled in terror. Shortly afterward, some British soldiers, returning to carry off the wounded, found their comrade with his head split in two, and raised the cry that the Americans scalped the dead. The cry spread through the regiment and created a panic, under whose influence the soldiers took to their heels and fled. The boy grew to be a very old man, and died not many years ago, and, as he grew infirm and old, the thought that he had killed a wounded man in cold blood haunted him to his grave. If the village tradition be true, it is a curious instance of what great events are produced by the smallest causes. The American revolution sprang into being from the defeat of the British troops at Concord; the British were defeated because our soldiers were struck with panic; and the panic was caused because a timid lad happened to have an axe in his hand.

But Concord has nearer and dearer claims to the thoughts of all English-speaking people than the memory of an obscure battle. It is the home of Emerson and Hawthorne. An old-fashioned, sleepy, New England village; one broad, long, rambling street of wooden houses, standing, for the most apart, and overshadowed by leafy trees; a quiet village green or two; shady, dreamy-looking graveyards, filled with old moss-covered tombstones of Colonists who lived and died subjects of the Crown of England; a rich, marshy valley, hemmed in by low-wooded hills; and a dull, lazy stream, oozing on so slowly through many turnings, that you fancy it is afraid of being carried out to the ocean that awaits it a few miles away; these are the outward memorabilia of Concord. Passing through the village, you come to a roomy country house, buried almost beneath trees, and looking the model of a quiet

English parsonage; and then, entering it, it must be some fault of your own, if you are not welcome at the kindly home of Emerson.

His is not a face or figure to which photographs can do justice. The tall spare form, the strongly-marked features, and the thin scanty hair, are all, to the English mind, typical, as it were, of that distinct American nationality of which Mr. Emerson has been the ablest, if not the first exponent. In repose, I fancy, his prevailing expression would be somewhat grave, with a shade of sadness; but the true charm of his face can be learnt only if you hear him speaking. Then, when the "slow wise smile," as someone well called it, plays about that grim-set mouth, and the flow of those lucid sentences, so simple and yet so perfect, pours forth in calm, measured sequence, the large liquid eyes seem to kindle with a magnetic light, and you feel yourself in the presence of a living power. You may sit at his feet or not—that is a matter for your own judgment, but a Gamaliel is there. Hearing him thus speak, I understood, better than I had learnt from his writings, the influence which Mr. Emerson had wielded over the mind of America, and how Concord has become a kind of Mecca, of which the representative man of American thought is the Mahomet.

Some quarter of a mile further on, hidden almost by the overhanging hill at whose foot it stands, out of sight and hearing of the village-world, you come to the home of Mr. Hawthorne—a quaint, rambling, pleasant house, which appears to have grown no one knows how, as some houses do, and to have culminated mysteriously in an Italian campanile tower; so that it is rather a tower with a house attached, than a house surmounted by a tower. It is a fitting place for a romancer to have fixed his dwelling in. Right above the house there stretches a pine wood, so quiet and so lonely, so full of fading lights and shadows, and through whose trees the wind sighs so fitfully, that it seems natural for all quaint fancies and strange memories to rise there unbidden. As to the tenant of the turret and the pine wood, I could not, if I wished, describe him better than by saying that he is just what, not knowing him, you fancy the author of "The Scarlet Letter" ought to look like. I suppose that most persons form an idea to themselves of the outward look and aspect of any author they have learnt to care for; and I know that, as far as my own experience goes, the idea is but seldom realized. The author, when at last you meet with him in the flesh, may be better than your idea, but he is not the person you had pictured to yourself and dwelt on fondly. Now, if you were to place Mr. Hawthorne amongst a thousand persons, I think any one that had read his writings would guess at once, amongst all that crowd, which the author was. The grand, broad forehead; the soft wavy hair, tangling itself so carelessly; the bright dreamy hazel eyes, flashing from beneath the deep massive eyebrows; and the sweet smile, so full at once of sad pathos and kindly humor, all formed for me the features one would have dreamed of for the author, who, more than any living writer, has understood the poetry of prose. It is a fancy of mine —a fancy inspired, perhaps, by the atmosphere in which I formed it—that Nature, when she began to make Mr. Hawthorne, designed him for a man of action, and then, ere the work was done, she changed her mind, and sought to transform him into a poet, and that thus the combination of the two characters—of the worker and the dreamer—came out at last in the form of the writer of romance. Well, if Concord had been the scene of an English Waterloo, I am afraid I should still think of it with the kindliest of memories—should, indeed, remember it only as the dwelling-place of men who have won fresh triumphs for English words, triumphs to me far dearer than those of English arms.

It was my fortune, too, to see—though but for a short period— the great poet of America. Of all pleasant summerhouses, the houses around Boston seemed to me the pleasantest; and of such houses I know of none pleasanter than the one standing on the Mount Auburn Road, where General Washington used to dwell, and where Longfellow dwells now. The pleasant lawn, the graceful rooms, filled with books and pictures and works of art, formed the fit abode for the poet who has known so well how to use the sweet stately rhythm of the English hexameter; and of that abode the host, with his graceful manners, his refined and noble countenance, and his conversation, so full of learning and poetic diction, seems the rightful owner. But of this I would say nothing further, for I felt that, if I was in the presence of a great poet, I was in the presence also of a greater sorrow.

I have said thus much of the three great American writers whose names are best known in England. Like all men of genius, they are in some sense public property; and the public has, I think, a right to know something of how they look and live. Genius has penalties as well as privileges. Of the many other men of talent and writers of note whom it was my pleasure to meet with in America, and especially in New England, I say nothing, because I doubt whether I should be justified in so doing. A private has a right, perhaps, to criticize the Commander-in-Chief, but I doubt if he is entitled to sit in judgment on the Colonels. Like any other Englishman who has visited America with any sort of credentials, I was received into the intimacy, and I trust I may add, the friendship of many literary men in that country. I feel that if, as there seems too much likelihood, it should become the custom for an English visitor to give a sort of moral auctioneer's catalogue of the houses, establishments, habits and customs of his hosts, then this friendly welcome must be dispensed with ere long. I have therefore made it my endeavor, in these pages, to quote nothing which I learnt in the character of a visitor, not of a spectator. There are two American writers, however, of whom I would say one word in passing, and they are James Russell Lowell, the author of the "Biglow Papers," and Oliver Wendell Holmes, the creator of "Elsie Venner." When America has completed her great mission of settling the New World, I cannot doubt that the wonderful energy and power of her people will produce a characteristic national literature worthy of herself, and, I say it without boasting, of the mother country also. In the works of these two gentlemen, I think you can discover the first commencement of a distinct era of American literature. The first has created a new school of poetry—the poetry of common Yankee life; the second has opened out a new vein of romance in the relations of physiology to the development of character. Both these writers have—at least so I fancy—a greater career before them than they have yet accomplished.

Let me say also, in concluding these scattered remarks on the literary men of Boston, that what struck me most about them collectively was the degree of intimacy and cordiality on which they lived with one another. To anyone who knows anything of the literary world in England, it will seem a remarkable fact that all men of intellectual note in Boston should meet regularly once a month, of their own free will and pleasure, to dine with each other; and still more so, that they should meet as friends, not as rivals. No doubt, this absence of jealousy is due, in great measure, to the literary field of America being so little occupied that there is nothing like the same competition between authors as there is with us; but it is due, I think, chiefly to that general kindliness and good nature which appear to me characteristic, socially, of the American people.

New England and the War

My SOJOURN in New England enabled me to appreciate the truth of an observation I have heard made by many intelligent Americans, that the effect of this civil war will be to consolidate the country. If it were not for the common interest in the war, it would have been hard to realize that Boston formed part of the same country as Chicago, and St. Louis, and Nashville. There, as elsewhere, the war seemed to me the chief bond of union and identity between the different states of the North. Nowhere indeed, in my own observation, was the ardor for the war greater than in Massachusetts. It had come home, perhaps, to those New England States more closely than to any other which were not actually the scene of the war. Wherever I went, I stumbled on traces of the great war, in which the nation was pouring out the life-blood of its children without stint or measure. Day after day, whilst sitting on the lawn of a friend's house on the Mount Auburn Road, I used to see the funerals of soldiers who had died in the campaign, passing by on their way to the cemetery. Nobody, I noticed, paid any heed to the occurrence. A servant-girl or so went to the gate to look at the procession, but no excitement was created by the sight. How, indeed, could it be otherwise? The spectacle, melancholy to me, had grown such everyday work in Boston—it was only one death the more out of so very many. In one house, I recollect, I found the family in distress, because a report had just been received that the regiment in which the eldest son of the house was serving had been under fire, and had suffered heavily. In another, the parents were uneasy, because their only son, a mere boy, wanted to be off to the war. In a third, a photograph lay upon the table of a gallant manly lad, proud of his new uniform. I asked who he was, and was told, as if it were an everyday matter, that it was the likeness of a near and dear relative who had fallen in the war—and so on. I could mention scores of such incidents. I have only picked out these, because they occurred to me at the houses of men whose names are well known in England. I went by hazard into a village church, and there I heard thanks offered up for an exchanged prisoner, who had that day been restored to his home after months of captivity. I suppose there is scarce a household in Massachusetts, which the war has not associated with some hope, or fear, or sorrow of its own.

There is much, too, left in Massachusetts of the Puritan, or rather of the race to which the Puritan gave birth. Life itself is a hard and laborious matter in that stony, barren country. There is about the New Englander a strong marked individuality, a religious zeal bordering on intolerance, a steady attachment to his own state, a passion for land, and a love of labor—qualities which have been handed down, with little change, from the Pilgrim Fathers. Amongst a people with such characteristics, it is not strange that there should be an earnestness, possibly a ferocity, about the war one hardly comes across in the more modern states. In the West, it is probable that if you could persuade the inhabitants that Secession was advantageous to their interest, the Union feeling would die away in great measure. In New England, the sense of personal interest has little, if anything, to do with the passion for the war. These causes operate to create a very different kind of public sentiment in the East from that which prevails in the West. The name of compromise is hateful to the New Englander; and, to the Puritan mind, there is but one issue to this conflict, possible or permissible, and that is the victory of the Union. I have spoken already of the status of the Abolitionist party in New England. As I have there shown, the popular mind was not prepared for a raid on the property and the institutions of other states. The reverence for the Constitution, the respect for law, and the strong attachment to local independence, which are marked features in the New England character, all tended to paralyze the active power of the anti-slavery sentiment. Notwithstanding this, the moral power of the Abolitionists must have been very great indeed. In the hymn-books you found at this period anti-slavery psalms; in the free schools, the teaching was anti-slavery in tone; and the public feeling toward the free Negro had avowedly grown a kindlier one than it had been hitherto.

That even in New England the war for the Union was in any sense a national crusade for the suppression of slavery I do not believe, but I do believe that, *next* to the desire for the preservation of the Union, the national antipathy to slavery is the strongest feeling of the New England heart. In a certain measure, the love for the Union and the hatred of slavery were conflicting forces, which counteracted each other; but, as the belief gained ground that the way to preserve the Union was to destroy slavery, the power of these forces, when combined, became overwhelming.

At the period of my sojourn in New England, the conviction that the Union could not be preserved consistently with slavery, was beginning to make way rapidly; a great impulse had been given to it by the incident of General Nathaniel Banks' defeat in the Shenandoah Valley, which formed the first warning of the approaching disasters in the Peninsula. The North had become so accustomed, at this time, to the idea of victory, so wedded to the conviction that the downfall of the rebellion was close at hand, that the intelligence of a Federal army having been disastrously defeated fell like a thunderbolt on the Northern States. I would add, however, that the manner in which this intelligence was received gave me a stronger impression of the resolution and power of the North than anything I had yet witnessed. From no party, or paper, or person I came across, did I hear anything but the one expression of opinion, that the war must be pushed on with redoubled energy. Within a week, a hundred thousand volunteers had enlisted, and the services of probably as many more had been declined. To judge of the importance of this fact, you must remember who these new volunteers were. The scum and riffraff of the towns had been long ago worked off into the army; every man who had no particular work to do, or no special ties to keep him at home, had been already drafted off. The hundred thousand who volunteered on this occasion were all men, who, as a class, had counted the cost of war, and found that, on the whole, their cares or duties or ties had been too important hitherto to allow them to join the campaign. Yet the moment the cry was raised that the cause of the Union was in peril every other consideration was thrown aside. So it had been all along, and so, I believe, it would have been to the end, if miserable mismanagement, worse generalship, and a half-hearted policy, had not paralyzed for a time the force of popular enthusiasm. The brag and bluster and rhodomontade of a portion, and that the noisiest portion of the American press and public, were, in Italian phrase, as "anti-pathetic" to me, while I lived within sound of it, as they could be to any Englishman. But still, I could not have avoided seeing the deep, passionate, resolution which underlay it all. If Englishmen would once make up their minds that the Anglo-Saxon race is much the same on both sides of the Atlantic, and that the resolution of the North to suppress the insurrection at all cost and all hazards, and, must I add, at the price of all severities, was much the counterpart of our own feeling with regard to the Indian Mutiny, the conviction would be a valuable one for both England and America.

The words which I have just written, "At the price of all severities," represent my impression of a change of feeling which I had observed, with more regret than wonder, to be coming over the Northern mind. When I reached America at the commencement of last year, my prevailing impression was one of astonishment at the extraordinary absence of personal animosity toward the South displayed by the North. Since that period, I noted a marked, though gradual, change. The belief that there existed an influential, or at any rate a numerous Union party in the South, was dispelled by the stern evidence of fact. The old fond delusion, that, when once the Confederate army was defeated the *Union as it was* would be restored, was fast vanishing, and had given place to a conviction that, even if the war was over, the Union would still have to deal with a bitter and an inveterate enemy. Then, too, the stories of the barbarities and cruelties inflicted by the Confederates on Federal prisoners had inevitably soured the Northern mind. For a long time I believed that these stories of brutality were as unfounded as the similar accusations, which in all wars, and especially in civil wars, are bandied about between the contending parties. I had heard, during the Garibaldian campaign, scores of such anecdotes related both of the Revolutionary and of the Royal troops. I had had occasion, however, to investigate a good number of these narratives, and had found them invariably to be grossly exaggerated. Very reluctantly, however, I came to the conclusion that there was, at any rate, a considerable amount of truth in these stories of Southern horrors. I suspect, indeed, that there is something in the whole system of slavery, in the practice of treating men as brute beasts, which deadens the feelings of a slaveholding population and renders them singularly callous to the sight of human suffering. Be this explanation right or wrong, I cannot now doubt the fact. I may mention two small incidents which came to my own knowledge on reliable evidence. One is that on the scarf of a Confederate prisoner captured at Williamsburg, there was found a ring formed from a human bone; another, that in a letter, picked up at Roanoke Island, and written by a Southern gentleman well known in New England, to his brother in New Orleans, the writer stated that he had got the skull of a —— Yankee, and wished to know if their mother would like it as an ornament for her sideboard. In these stories there is little in themselves, but they tend to render more credible, to my mind, the thousand tales of horror which were circulated at this period in the Northern papers. At any rate, the belief in the truth of these narratives was universal in the North, and produced painful and personal bitterness toward the South.

Still the desire for revenge was, undoubtedly, developing itself in the New England States. Out of evil there comes good; and one good of all this was, that the anti-slavery sentiment was daily growing stronger. Governor John A. Andrew, about this time, expressed, though perhaps prematurely, the popular instinct of Massachusetts when he stated, in reply to the Government demand for fresh troops, that the East would fight more readily if men knew that they were fighting against slavery. It is the pressure of this growing earnestness, of this resolution to sacrifice everything to one end, which at last forced the Government at Washington to make the war for the restoration of the Union a war also for the abolition of slavery.

Independence Day in New York

"You should go to New York for the Fourth—before then we *must* have grand news from Richmond—and you will see a sight that you ought to witness—a regular noisy, rowdy, glorious, Fourth of July." So an American friend of mine said to me in the latter days of June, and I followed his advice; but, according to the French proverb, "Man proposes, God disposes," and though I saw the Fourth, instead of being glorious, it was the gloomiest Independence Day that the Empire city had known during the present century. It was only on the preceding day that the full truth concerning McClellan's retreat had become known. The bitter suspense, indeed, was over, and people were beginning to look the worst fairly in the face. But the half-stunned feeling of dismay had not yet passed away; and even the public mind of America, with all its extraordinary elasticity, was still unable to brace itself to rejoicing and self-glorification. It was under such auspices that the last Independence Day was celebrated.

As to the day itself, it was a glorious one, with a sky bright and clear as that of Italy. The city was again gay with flags, and its shops were closed, and the streets were filled with holiday people, and the bells rang, and the cannon fired, and what was better than all, the news from the Peninsula was more encouraging; but still there was no spirit in the day, the life of the festival was gone. The one stock amusement of Independence Day consists in making as much noise as possible. From twelve o'clock on the previous night to midnight on the Fourth, the whole energies of the children and boys of New York are devoted to letting off as many crackers, firing as many pocket-pistols, and pelting passersby with as many detonating balls as their own or their friends' purses can afford. All day long, in every street from Fifth Avenue down to Bowery, there is a never-ending discharge of this mimic artillery. You are lucky if you pass through the day without getting your hair singed, or your face scorched, or holes burnt in your clothes; and in fact prudent people keep much at home during the Fourth. Anybody who ever passed a Christmas at Naples, and has run the gauntlet of its squibs, and rockets, and pistols, will sympathize with me when I say that it was some consolation for the national calamity to find that it checked the discharge of fireworks. It was bad enough as it was, but if McClellan had won a victory instead of being defeated, half the city would have been maimed and deafened. Some thirty people were taken to the hospitals in the course of the day from injuries inflicted by the fireworks. Like Oyster Day too in London, this annual Saturnalia, though professedly coming only once a year, lingers on in practice for days afterward.

This discharge of fireworks was the one genuine exhibition of popular rejoicing throughout the day. Things must be very bad indeed before boys leave off throwing crackers in consequence of a national disaster; but with the grown-up population it was little of a holiday time. In the cool of the morning what few troops there were left in the city marched down Broadway; but most of them were boys, or old men, or raw recruits, and the show, in a military point of view, was a very poor one, and excited little interest. At ten o'clock there was a meeting in celebration of the anniversary held by the Common Council in the Cooper Institute. The meeting was announced for ten, but the proceedings did not begin till near eleven. The great hall, which I should say could hold between two and three thousand people, was never a quarter full, and a third of what crowd there was stood on the speakers' platform. The Mayor, Mr. George Opdyke, was in the chair, and delivered a short address, in which he stated, amongst other things, that "with the loyal people of America, come what may, be the nations banded in arms against us, nothing shall be successful in overthrowing our cherished institutions." A long prayer was offered up by the select preacher to the Corporation, containing a statement novel to a New York audience as coming from such lips, that this rebellion had been inflicted by Heaven on the people of America on account of their sins, because they had fallen away from the faith of their fathers, and had extended, protected, and perpetuated by their legislation, the abominable sin of slavery. An oration was next spoken by a Mr. Hiram Walbridge, more calm and dignified in its language than American declamations are wont to be. After dwelling on the popular resolution to do all and suffer all, rather than succumb, he gave vent to the grievances of the people in words such as these: "Our lives, our money, our hopes, our destiny, our all, are at the service of the Government in upholding the Constitution and the Union. We, however, feel that we have the right to know every incident which marks the varying fortunes of the struggle, for it is our own chosen sons who are falling in defense of liberty. We also earnestly desire, if any foreign mediation is meditated, it may be met with firmness and without complaint." Then followed a patriotic poem of interminable length and fatal fluency, some verses of which, perhaps, are worth reciting as specimens of American popular poetry:

> Loftier waved the flags of freedom,
>   Louder rolled the Union drums,
> When th' inspiring shout went upward,
>   "Old Manhattan's army comes!"
> Washington once more invoked us,
>   And we rose in columns grand;
> Marching round the flag of Sumter,
>   Grasped within his sculptured hand.
>
> Then Manhattan's loyal legions
>   Shook the earth with martial tramp,
> And she kissed her noblest children,
>   Hurrying down to Freedom's camp.
> And the sundered coils of treason
>   Writhed upon her loyal shore,
> When she flung her gallant "Seventh"
>   In the scales of righteous war.

Besides this, there were some national glees sung without much spirit; a few patriotic airs played by a brass band; and a recital of the "Declaration of Independence," in which the narrative of poor old George the Third's offenses and shortcomings sounded strangely out of place in the midst of the dread struggle of the passing hour. But the whole affair was tame and spiritless to a strange degree. All hearts and thoughts were far away on the banks of the James River.

Early in the morning placards were stuck over the town, headed, "To the People," and signed "By many Union Men," calling for vengeance on the Abolitionists, on Greeley and Beecher, and others, who had brought on this reverse of McClellan's army by their diabolical machinations; and summoning a public open-air meeting for the afternoon, in the City Park, to denounce Abolition. The *Tribune* office faces the park, and if a mob could have been collected, the intention of the ringleaders was to storm the office. The placards, however, were all torn down in an hour's time; no crowd whatever assembled, except a score or so of rowdies and a dozen policemen, and no one was found bold enough to ascend the hustings, which had been erected expressly for the meeting.

There was no general illumination at night; the fireworks exhibited by the municipality were very poor, and the day closed tamely and quietly.

The Case of the North

"WHAT ON earth is the North fighting for?" is a question which I have often heard asked in England. If you were to put it to an American, he would doubt your asking it seriously; the answer seems to him so very simple and obvious. The Americans are not a reflective people; they look at facts much more than at theories, and, like ourselves, act rather from general convictions than on any logical system of reasoning. Their answer, therefore, to such a question is often indistinct and illogical enough. But having talked with scores of Northern men of all states and all classes on the subject, I should say that the general chain of argument, which forms the basis of the different answers you receive, is easy to explain and understand. In considering it, it should be borne in mind that the merits or demerits of the Northern cause are entirely independent of the issue of the war. Before the war commenced, the North had no doubt, whether right or wrong, that it possessed the power to suppress the insurrection by armed force. The present question, therefore, is not whether the North was wise in going to war, but whether her motives were sufficient to justify her in so doing? I am not going to enter upon the questions, whether war is ever justifiable except in self-defense, or whether any nation is ever at liberty morally to coerce another against its will. The arguments against aggression and coercion are very strong ones, but they are not ones which an Englishman can use; and I wish to speak of this question from an English point of view.

The answer, then, would be much after this fashion—"We will put the slavery question aside. On that point we are divided among ourselves. We do not claim to be carrying on a war of emancipation; we are not fighting for the blacks, but for the whites. Universal emancipation may come, probably will come, as one result of our war; but *the* object of the war is to preserve the Union. We allowed perfect freedom to the Southern States —freedom as full and as untrammeled as we enjoyed ourselves. Not only did we not interfere with their peculiar institution, but we granted them every facility they claimed for its maintenance. We permitted the South to have more than its full share of power and to fill up the Government with Southern men. There was one thing only we objected to, and that was to having slavery forced upon the Free Territories of the North. We objected to this legally and constitutionally; and by legal and constitutional measures we expressed the will of the nation. Our whole Government, like all free governments, rests upon the principle that the will of the majority must decide. The South revolted at once, because it was defeated by the vote of the majority. If we had acquiesced in that revolt, the vital principle of our Government was overthrown. Any minority whatever, either in the Union or in the separate states, which happened to be dissatisfied with the decision of the majority, might have followed the example of the South, and our Government would have fallen to pieces, like an arch without a keystone. The one principle of power in a Democracy is the submission of the minority to the will of the people; and, in fighting against the South, we are fighting for the vital principle of our Government. You call a man a coward who will let himself be robbed of all that makes life valuable without making an effort to resist; and what would you have called a nation that submitted placidly to its own dismemberment?

"We are fighting too," so the Northerners would urge, "not only for abstract constitutional principles, but for clear matter-of-fact interests. Our Government was at any rate a very good one in our own eyes. As a people we had prospered under it. We had enjoyed more of freedom, order, and happiness beneath the Union than, we believe, any people had ever enjoyed before. From the Atlantic to the Pacific, from Maine to the Gulf of Mexico, we were one people, dwelling under one Government, speaking one language, without custom-houses, or passports, or frontier lines to separate us; without the fear of invasion and war; without the need for standing armies, and camps, and fortified cities—free to carry on unmolested our great mission of reclaiming the vast wilderness. We are asked to abandon all this, and you wonder that we refuse to do so without striking a blow in defense of our rights.

"It is not only our present, but our future, that is at stake. Supposing we had acceded to the proposals of tame submission, what would have been the inevitable result? We should have had upon our frontier a hostile power, to whom our free institutions were a standing menace, and to whom extension of territory was a necessity of political existence. War must have come sooner or later, and in the interests of our future peace it was better to fight at once. Even if a peaceable and durable separation had been possible, and if terms of compromise could have been devised, where was the process of disunion to end? If once the South goes, the Union is dissolved; the Western States would inevitably part company before long with the seaboard States; California would assert its independence, the Border States would fall away from the Central States; and the Union, the great work of our forefathers, would give place to a system of rival republics, with mutual enmities, antagonistic policies, foreign alliances, and intestine wars. We have seen the whole of Europe applauding Italy for endeavoring to become one people, under one Government, and are we to be blamed because we decline being reduced to the same political condition that Italy was in before the revolution?"

Such in substance would be the answer of any average Northerner. In speaking to a foreigner, he would not dwell much on the national dream of the golden future, to whose realization Secession is absolutely fatal; but I believe that in the heart of most Americans this feeling is uppermost. That dream of the possible future was not so unreasonable or so chimerical a one as we are apt to fancy. It was the one great beauty of the Federal Constitution that it was adapted to an almost indefinite expansion of territory. Such complete and absolute liberty was granted to the individual states by the Federal compact; the Central Government conferred so many advantages, and demanded so few sacrifices, that it was really possible for state after state to have joined the Union, as civilization pushed further westward, without the necessity of change or revolution. It was within the bounds of possibility, almost of probability, that the dream might have been realized, and that the whole of that vast continent might have been occupied by a hundred states, each ruling itself as it thought best, and all living under one common free Government. The idea that Washington should one day be the seat of Government of the whole of North America was not a more absurd one than that the little island of England should rule over India and Australia and Canada. Be the idea reasonable or not, it was at least a very grand one, and one consonant, too, with that admiration for sheer magnitude which is peculiar to the American mind. It was an idea palpable to all understandings, and shared by all classes.

It would be very difficult for the writer, or probably for the reader, or for ninety-nine Englishmen out of every hundred, to show in what single respect, financial, commercial, or political, they were one atom better off from the fact that the British flag waves over a thousand colonies; and yet every Englishman must feel that our colonial empire adds somehow or other to his personal dignity and happiness. So, in like manner, if an American feels that his pride and sense of dignity are involved in that possible empire of the future, it is not for an Englishman to ridicule the idea. It happened that early in this war I had the pleasure of being introduced to General Winfield Scott. With that frank cordiality of manner which gives a charm to the conversation of well-bred Americans at home, he began talking to me about England, expressing his keen desire to see our country again after an absence of forty years; and he wound up by saying, "England, sir, is a noble country—a country worth fighting for." What the old hero said of England, I think, any candid Englishman, who knew the country, would say of America. The North has a cause worth fighting for; and, successful or unsuccessful, it will be better for the North, better also for the world at large, that a great cause has been fought for gallantly.

I admit freely, on the other hand, that the South also has fought gallantly. I can understand the sympathy that bystanders inevitably feel for the weaker party fighting against great odds, and holding out manfully against defeat and discouragement. Anyone who knows the facts must be aware that the odds in favor of the North were not nearly so strong as they looked at first sight. I suppose, too, the most ardent of revolutionists must admit that every revolution should be justified by some act of oppression; and the most eager of Secessionists would be puzzled to find any one act of oppression which the South had endured at the hands of the North before Secession, with that one single exception, which Southern partisans always keep in the background, namely that the North objected to the extension of slavery. "I do not like you, Dr. Fell," may be a very good argument for a schoolboy; but when a nation can give no better "reason why" for revolution, I confess that my sympathies are with the established Government. It is curious, indeed, to hear Englishmen, who stand aghast at the notion of the Repeal of the Union, and who look on the Indian Mutiny as an act of unparalleled ingratitude, advocating the sacred right of revolution with regard to the South. Still, to my mind, the right of every nation, wisely or unwisely, to choose its own Government is so important a principle, that I should admit its application to the case of the South if it were not for the question of slavery.

"Qui veut la fin veut les moyens," according to the French proverb; and a large party in England are so anxious for the disruption of the Union, that they are disposed to look very tenderly on the peculiar institution whose maintenance is essential to the success of their hopes. Still, happily, we have as yet had no party cynical enough to advocate openly the merits of slavery. Everybody still professes to disapprove of slavery. "Of course," so the cant of the day runs, "slavery is a very dreadful thing, and everybody—the South above all—would be glad to see it abolished; but slavery has nothing to do with the present war. The North dislikes the Negro even more than the South does; and whichever side conquers, the Negro has nothing to expect from the war. He is out of court, and any attempt to get up sympathy on his behalf is irrelevant to the present question."

Now, in answer to this sort of talk, I grant that the North has not gone to war for the idea of emancipation, and is not fighting for it now. Nations very seldom do fight for an idea. There has been one war for an idea in the last half-century, and we have never left off deriding it, and sneering at it, till the present hour. Very few great causes in this world are fought for on abstract principles; and if one out of many motives for which the North is fighting is a dislike to slavery, it is as much as you can reasonably expect. In any great question, you must look much more to the principles at stake than to the motives of the actors. The race-horse who runs for the stake does not know or care a straw about your betting-book, but you feel as much interest in his success as if he was running for your sake alone. I would impress on my readers that the issue of slavery is really involved in the present struggle. Soon after the return of the Comte de Paris, he said to an informant of mine: "The thing that surprises me most in England is to be told that slavery has nothing to do with the American war. Why, from the day I set foot in America to the day I left it, I never heard of anything except the question of slavery." Every English traveler must confirm this opinion. During my whole stay in the United States, I never took up a newspaper—and Heaven only knows how many I did take up daily—without seeing the slave question discussed in some form or other. If the war had done no other good, it would have effected this much, that the case of the slave has been forced upon the conscience of the North, and that the criminal apathy which acquiesced tamely in the existence of an admitted evil has received its death blow. More than this, however, the one *casus belli* has been, throughout, the question of the extension of slavery. Stories about tariff grievances, about aristocratic incompatibility to put up with democratic institutions, about difference of race, and political government, are mere inventions to suit a European public, which their authors must have laughed inwardly to see swallowed so willingly. It would be as well, by the way, if the persons who

talk so much of the aristocratic character of Southern institutions
would take the trouble to study the constitutions of the Slaveholding States. They would find that, with the single exception
of South Carolina, the institutions of the South are founded on
the most advanced democratic principles. It was my fortune to
see a good deal of Southern men and newspapers in the States,
and the one cause of complaint against the North was always and
alone the slave question. If slavery were not the cause of Secession, it is impossible to explain the limits of the Secession movement. Massachusetts is not more different from Georgia in geographical position, commercial interests, and social character,
than Tennessee is from Louisiana, or Virginia from Alabama.
Every Free State, without one exception, is loyal to the Union.
Every Slave State, with the single exception of Delaware where
slavery is nominal, has been disloyal openly or covertly. The inference is obvious, and to my mind, undeniable. Now, the Southern leaders have shown too much acuteness to make it probable
that they risked everything to avoid an imaginary danger. They
seceded from the Union, solely and avowedly, because slavery
was in danger from the North; and it is more probable that they
knew the real state of affairs than their enthusiastic partisans on
this side the water, who assert that slavery had nothing to do with
Secession. I believe myself, from their own point of view, they
were right in seceding. They understood the position better than
the North did. They knew perfectly that the Republican party
had no intention of interfering with slavery as it existed; they
knew that the peculiar institution was as safe under Lincoln as
it had been under Buchanan; but they knew also that to the
permanent existence of slavery in the Union, two things were
essential—the supremacy of the slave power in the Central Government, and the faculty of indefinite expansion. Another election might restore them to the seats of office in Washington; but,
if once the extension of slavery were prohibited, as it was by the
adoption of the Chicago program, slavery was doomed. The system of cotton production under slave labor exhausts the soil so
rapidly, that slavery would be starved out without a constant supply of fresh ground to occupy. I hear constantly that the South

only wants to establish its independence. If the European Powers could offer tomorrow to guarantee the independence of the Gulf States, the offer would be rejected without hesitation, unless the Confederacy could be secured also the possession of the vast regions that lie west of the Mississippi, whereon to ground new Slave States and Territories. The North is fighting against, the South is fighting for, the power of extending slavery across the American continent; and, if this was all that could be said, it is clear on which side must be the sympathies of anyone who really and honestly believes that slavery is an evil and a sin.

But this is not all that can be said. The present war is working directly for the overthrow of slavery where it exists already. If you look at facts, not at words, you will see that, since the outbreak of the war, the progress of the anti-slavery movement has been marvelously rapid. Slavery is abolished once for all in the District of Columbia, and no Senator can come henceforth to Washington, bringing his slaves with him. With a free territory lying in their midst, slavery becomes ultimately impossible in Maryland, as well as in Virginia. For the first time in American history, distinct national proposals have been made to emancipate the slaves. The proposals are impracticable and unsatisfactory enough, but still they form a solemn avowal of the fact that slavery is to be abolished. The slave trade has been finally suppressed, as far as the United States is concerned, and, after half a century of delay, Haiti has been recognized. These measures are no unimportant ones in the world's history; but what renders them more important is that they are due, not to popular enthusiasm, but to the inexorable logic of facts. Stern experience is teaching the North that slavery is fatal to their own freedom, and it is beneath the growth of this conviction that these blows have been dealt against the system.

At last, this growing conviction has terminated in its inevitable result, the Emancipation edict of President Lincoln. It is useless to speculate on what the effect of this measure may be upon the fortunes of the war. One single battle may reverse the whole position of affairs. It is possible that this great act, which was the inevitable result of Secession, may have been performed too late.

But this does not affect the question of abstract justice. I, myself, plead guilty to a faith in the *higher law,* and hold that the Federal Government would have done more wisely and more justly if it had abolished slavery throughout the whole of the Union on grounds, not of temporary expediency, but of eternal justice. Still, I cannot condemn Mr. Lincoln, or his advisers, for their almost servile adherence to the letter of the law, as they construed it. By virtue of *the war power,* the Government has, or believes it has, authority to emancipate the slaves in the insurgent states, since it has power to perform any other act necessary for the preservation of the Union. But, by the Constitution, it has no more power to interfere with slavery in any loyal state, than England has to interfere with serfdom in Russia. By the proclamation, the Federal Government has done everything that it could do legally with reference to slavery. That it has not done more is a complaint that cannot be brought justly.

It is no answer to statements such as these to vapor about the inhumanity of the North toward the free Negro. Anybody who knows England and Englishmen must be aware that if we had an immense foreign population among ourselves, belonging to an ignorant, half-savage, and inferior race, too numerous to be objects of sentimental curiosity, too marked in form and feature to be absorbed gradually, our feeling toward them would be very much that of the Northerner toward the Negro. The sentiment which dictates the advertisement, so common in our newspapers, of "No Irish need apply," is in principle very much the same as that which in the North objects to the contact of the Negro. Moreover, in all the Northern States, after all is said and done, the Negro is treated like a man, not like a beast of burden. In half the New England States, the black man has exactly the same legal rights and privileges as the white, and throughout the whole of the older Free States the growth of public opinion is in favor of a more kindly treatment of the Negro. Somehow or other, the men of color in the Free States prefer their treatment, however inconsiderate, to the considerate care of slave-owners. There is nothing easier than for an emancipated or runaway slave, who has experienced the vanity of freedom, to recover the joys of slavery.

He has only got to appear as a vagrant in a Slave State, and the
state will take the trouble of providing him with a master free of
expense; yet, strange to say, slaves are not found to avail themselves of the privilege. But, admitting the very worst that could
be said of the condition of free Negroes in the North, a humane
man must, I fear, conclude that, on the whole, it is better for the
world that the American Negroes should die out like the Indians,
than that they should go on increasing and multiplying under
slavery, and thus perpetuating an accursed system to generations
yet unborn.

Southern friends, whom I knew in the North, used to try hard
to persuade me that the best chance for Abolition lay in the establishment of a Southern Confederacy. I do not doubt they
were sincere in their convictions, but, like most Secession advocates, they proved too much. When you are told that the slaves
are the happiest people in the world, and that slavery is the best
institution ever devised for the benefit of the poor, you are surprised to learn, in one and the same breath, that the main object
and chief desire of the Secessionists is to abolish slavery. Whatever may be asserted abroad, I have never seen any address or
proclamation of the Southern leaders, in which the possibility of
emancipation was even hinted at—in which, on the contrary,
the indefinite extension of slavery was not rather held forward
as the reward of success. That a social system, based on slavery,
must fall to pieces ultimately, I have little doubt myself; but,
"ultimately" is a long word. The immediate result of the establishment of the Southern Confederacy is obvious enough. A new
lease of existence will be given to slavery; vast additional territories will be added to the dominions of slavery, and the cancer
of slavery will spread its roots over the width and length of the
New World. Those who wish the South to succeed, wish slavery
to be extended and strengthened. There is no avoiding this conclusion; and, therefore, as I hold that the right of every man to
be free is a principle even more important than the right of every
nation to choose its own government, I am deaf to the appeal that
the South deserves our sympathy because it is fighting to establish its independence. If the North had but dared to take for its

battle cry the grand preamble of the Declaration of Independence: "We hold these truths to be self-evident, that all men are created equal; that they are endowed by their Creator with certain inalienable rights; that amongst these are life, liberty, and the pursuit of happiness"; then it might have appealed to the world for sympathy in a manner it cannot now. That this cannot be, I regret bitterly. The North still ignores the principles contained in its great charter of freedom, but it does not repudiate them like the South. And, in the words of a homely proverb, "Half a loaf is better than no bread."

Facts, however, not words or sentiments, will decide the contest between North and South. The *causa victa* may be better than the *causa victrix*, but after all the real question is which side will conquer, not which side ought to conquer. It would be absurd to enter in these pages on prognostications as to the military issue of the war, but there are certain broad features in the struggle which are too much lost sight of over here. Ever since the attack on Fort Sumter, the Northern frontier has advanced, and the Southern receded. The progress of the Federal armies has been slow enough, but all they have gained they have kept. No single town of any importance has been permanently recaptured by the Confederates; no single victory has ever been followed up, and no Southern army has ever succeeded in occupying any portion of Free State soil. Still Southern partisans would reply, with some show of reason, that these considerations, important as they are, do not affect the vital question of the possibility of the North ever subjugating the South. This is true; and, if the South was really fighting only to secure its independence, and to establish a Confederacy of the Gulf States, the answer would be conclusive. But, in reality, as I pointed out before, the struggle between North and South is, which party shall obtain possession of the Border States and the territories west of the lower Mississippi; which party, in fact, shall be the ruling power on the North American Continent? So far the successes of the North are fatal to the hopes of Southern Empire. The South would not value, the North would not fear, a Confederacy confined within the Gulf States; and yet the result of the campaign has been to render it most improbable that the Confederacy, even if successful, will extend beyond its present narrow limits. So far the North has gained and the South lost.

The war will be decided, not by any single defeat or victory, but by the relative power of the two combatants. Now, as far as wealth, numbers, and resources are concerned, it is not worth the trouble of proving that the North is superior to the South. As far as mere personal courage is concerned, one may fairly assume that both sides are equal. Anyone who has, like myself, been through the hospitals of the North, where Federal and Confederate wounded are nursed together, can entertain no doubt that the battles of the war have been fought on both sides only too gallantly. The one doubt is, whether the South may not be superior to the North in resolution, in readiness to make sacrifices, and in unity of action. If it is so, the chances are in favor of the South; but there is no proof as yet that it is the case. Much, and as I think undue, stress has been laid on the slow progress of enlistment in the North. It is very easy to talk glibly about what England would do in case she was at war, but if England did as much relatively as the Union States have done, it would be a grand and a terrible effort. There is no evidence that the South has done as much, but the contrary. More than a year ago the volunteering energies of the South were exhausted, and though the enemy was actually invading the sacred soil, it was necessary to resort to conscription, in order to raise soldiers for the war. By this time the Confederacy must have as many men under arms as she can raise in any event. Her armies have suffered fearfully in battle, and still more fearfully from disease. Moreover, all the defects inherent to irregular troops, which tell so much on the North, tell doubly and trebly upon the South. Southern papers, which I saw while in America, were full of complaints of the misconduct of their troops, the want of patriotism of their citizens, and the incompetence of their generals. Of course these stories were exaggerations, or only partial truths, otherwise the South could not have held out so long, but they serve to show that there is disorder, and jobbery, and maladministration, and discontent, South as well as North. At any rate, before we offer up a Te Deum for the success of the Confederacy, it would be well to wait a little while longer.

"But granting all this," I hear my intelligent objector—my moral ninepin, whom, disputant-like, I put up for the sole purpose of bowling down—conclude by saying, "if the North should win, how is it possible permanently to hold and govern the South?" Now this is a question that I bored all my American acquaintances, ministers and Senators amongst the number, with asking, and I own that very few of them seemed to be able to answer it satisfactorily. The nation is too much wrapped up in the immediate issue of the war to trouble itself much with speculations on the future. Moreover, the plain fact is that the vast majority of Americans cannot realize the idea that the Southerners really do not like the Union. To themselves the Union appears so natural, so liberal, and so good a government, that it is impossible that anybody who has lived beneath its rule should leave it willingly. Secession in Northern eyes is still an unaccountable and inexplicable act of madness. If the Southern States were, some fine morning, to lay down their arms, say they had been mistaken, and reunite themselves of their own accord to the Union, I believe that half, or more than half, the Americans of the Federal States would declare, with truth, that they had expected it all along. The belief in the existence of a strong Union party in the South has survived every refutation. The influence of this belief has diverted the popular mind from contemplating seriously the difficulties of reconstitution. Once conquer the South, suppress the armed insurrection, and all, according to the popular Northern faith, will be well. The leaders and promoters of Secession will be exiled, ruined, or reduced to insignificance; the great mass of the army will acknowledge that resistance is hopeless, and will make the best of their position: and then, somehow or other, it is incredible that the people of the South should not return to the belief that they are better off under the Union than under any other possible government. There is a good deal to be said for this view. All American politicians I have spoken to have assured me that in the South, even more than in the North, public opinion changes with a degree of rapidity we cannot realize in Europe. There is no doubt, also, that, as a rule, nations do not resist without a chance of success. Between North and South there is no barrier of race, or religion, or language; and, if once the supremacy of either side was indisputably established, I think the weaker of the two would acquiesce in the rule of the stronger, without great reluctance or coercion.

The reason why the great majority of the Northern people are unwilling to interfere unflinchingly with the system of slavery is because any interference destroys the possibility of reconstituting "the Constitution as it is, and the Union as it was." But there is a powerful party in the North, who are opposed to this Micawber-like policy. According to their views, slavery is an inevitable source of hostility between North and South. To them, any peaceable restoration of the *status quo ante bellum,* unaccompanied by a settlement of the slavery question, would appear a national calamity. Slavery, they argue, has caused the war. There can be no peace till the cause of war is removed. The South must be reorganized and reconstituted. The slave-owners—some three hundred thousand in all—must be virtually removed, whether by ruin, exile, or confiscation, matters little. Their place must be supplied by capitalists from the free North. Slavery once abolished, labor will cease to be dishonorable in the South. Emigration will pour in. A social revolution must be accomplished, and a new system of society constituted in the South, in which slavery has no part or share. To my mind, this view is really more rational than the popular one.

Very rapidly this view is gaining strength in the North. The people of the North, as a body, have no love for slavery, care very little about the slave, but have an intense attachment to the Union. The Abolitionists were unpopular at the commencement of the war, because it was believed their policy retarded the restoration of the Union by embittering the South. As it has grown apparent that there is no chance of conciliating the South, the policy of Abolition has become popular, as the one best adapted for preserving the Union.

If the war continues, it must continue as a war for emancipation. This is a fact it is useless ignoring. As long as emancipation does come, it can matter little to any true enemy of slavery by whom, or through whom, it does come; and, of all countries in the world, England is not the one to retard such a consummation. Whenever the partisans of the South are unable to deny the probability of emancipation being brought about by the war, they begin at once to lament the horrors of this wicked contest, to moan about the brutality of the North, and to hold up the bugbear of a servile war.

Now, that all war is an awful thing, and that a war amongst kinsmen, speaking the same language, is the most awful of wars, I admit most fully. But supposing war is justifiable when your cause is good, and supposing the cause of the North, as I have endeavored to show, is good, it is mere cant to maunder about the inevitable miseries and horrors of this particular war, as if every war had hitherto been exempt from them. As to the brutality of the North, that is a question of fact, not of sentiment; and if anybody can show me another instance in the world's history of a civil war having raged in a country for a year without one traitor being executed, it will be matter of surprise to me. That individual acts of barbarity have been committed I cannot doubt, because such occur in every war; but there has been no national demand for vengeance, such as was raised in England at the Indian Mutiny. Ex-President James Buchanan lives at Wheatlands, unmolested and unnoticed. Avowed Secessionists reside in New York and Boston with as much security as though they were in Paris or London, and the policy of confiscation has been forced upon the Government by Congress without the support, if not against the wishes, of the people. If the slaves are so contented with their position, so attached to their masters as we are told they are, there can be no danger of their butchering their masters' families at the first opportunity which offers. There is, indeed, little prospect of their rising. I should think more highly of the Negro race than I do, if I believed there was any probability that, unarmed and unassisted by white men, they would rise against their owners. The slaves on the plantations will not rise till they are supplied with arms, and the Federal Government has steadily refused to supply them with arms. Even if they should be armed, they will fight, if at all, in company with white men. Now, the feeling of race is so strong amongst the whites, so much stronger than any other feeling whatever, that, however grievous the provocation given to the black man might be, no American would look on and see a Negro butchering a fellow white man without interfering on the side of the white. Even in Canada, the volunteers refused, the other day, to be drilled in company with a colored regiment; and from a kindred feeling, only bitterly intensified, no slave would be permitted to wreak his vengeance on the white man as long as he was fighting under the orders of American soldiers. If ever there should be a servile war, it must be carried on by black men alone against the whites, not by blacks aided by whites.

If, then, the North succeeds in subjugating the South, the one clear result is that slavery must be abolished. What else will follow it is idle to speculate on now, but this conclusion is sufficient to make me desire that the North should succeed.

It is, so I am told, unpatriotic to desire the success of the North, because the continuance of the war causes such bitter misery in Lancashire, and because the restoration of the Union would lead inevitably to a war between the United States and England. With regard to the first of these objections, I feel its force strongly. Every Englishman must care more about his own countrymen than he does about either Yankees or Negroes. I could not, indeed, wish the distress in Lancashire to be removed at the price of a great national sin; and such, in my judgment, would be the interference of England to establish a slave power in order to procure cotton. But if the war *could* be terminated without any action on our part, I own I should less acutely regret what I consider a misfortune to humanity if I thought it would bring permanent relief to our manufacturing poor. But I do not think so. If the Confederacy were established now, there would be no chance of cotton being procured elsewhere; the supremacy of Southern slave-grown cotton would be reinaugurated all the more firmly for the sufferings we have undergone; and England would be virtually dependent on the South, entangled in her alliances, involved in her wars, and liable for her embarrassments. Moreover, it is a delusion to suppose that the South would prove a good customer to English manufacturers. The South can never be a maritime power. For years to come she must be afraid of Northern invasion. For the sake therefore, of her own safety, she cannot rely upon England to supply her with manufactures, and must encourage manufactures of her own. The only way to do this in a poor half-civilized country like the South, is by a high prohibitive tariff; and such a tariff will certainly be adopted by the South whenever her independence is established. By the establishment, therefore, of the Southern Confederacy, our manufacturing districts would purchase exemption from present distress at the price of much heavier and more permanent loss in future.

As to the danger of war between England and America, it is idle to deny its existence. There is a state of feeling on both sides the Atlantic which is only too likely to lead to war. Both nations believe that they are entirely in the right, that they have given no cause of offense. Which is most right or the most wrong there is no good in discussing now. It is enough that a feeling of hostility exists. But the danger of war is far greater in the event of the failure of the North than in the event of its success. If the North should subjugate the South, a generation must pass away before the South is really reunited to the North; and, until the South is reunited, the Union *cannot* make war upon any foreign power. The necessity of keeping down insurrection in the South would render impossible aggression in the North. But take the other alternative. The North will be for a time a homogeneous, powerful, and prosperous nation of twenty millions of white freemen. As a nation, it will be burning under a sense of disgrace and defeat. The necessity of cementing together what remains of the Union will render a foreign war politically desirable. No war will be so gratifying to the national pride as a war with England. The neutrality of the Southern Confederacy will be purchased easily by acquiescence in its designs on Cuba and Mexico; and a war with England for the Canadas will be the inevitable result of a divided Union. Those who wish for peace, then, must desire the success of the North.

This, then, is the upshot of the conclusions I formed during my journeyings through the Federal States, that in the interest of humanity, in the interest of America, and in the interest of England, the success of the North is the thing we ought to hope and wish for.

Homeward Bound

Of my voyage home I have to say but little. The moment I had stepped upon the deck of the good ship *Europa*, which was to bear me back, my connection with the New World was severed. In truth, the first walk up and down the quarterdeck of a homeward-bound Cunard steamer, lying alongside an American quay, affords a curious and, to an Englishman, not an unpleasing sensation. A couple of steps across the narrow gangway and you have passed from the New World into the Old. America is still in full view, almost within arm's reach. The great steam ferries are ploughing through the waters round you; the street-railroads are bringing down their heavy loads close to the wharves; the old-fashioned hackney-coaches are lumbering along, loaded with trunks of trans-Atlantic volume; the air is filled with the shouts of Yankee newsboys; the quays are crowded with sallow American faces, and, perhaps, if you are lucky, amongst the crowd you may see the countenances of kind friends, who have made the New World feel like home to you. The day is hot, as only American days are hot, with a dull, dead heat; and the sky is blue, as English skies never are blue. And yet, in spite of all this, you are in England; you are lying, it is true, in American waters, you are subject still to the laws of the United States, and three thousand long, dreary, watery miles stretch between you and home; but you are as much in England as if your vessel was a floating island, just detached from the Land's End or the North Foreland. The stewards treat you with that admixture of obsequious politeness and chilling indifference peculiar to English waiters. The officers of the ship, down to the boatswain, regard the natives with a supreme and undisguised conviction of superiority, not given to anyone not born within the four seas to attain to. And the captain—well, any country might be proud of him—but by no human possibility could he have been produced anywhere except in England! So by the time you have got out to sea, you begin, almost before the low coast of the eastern seaboard is out of sight, to doubt whether you have ever been away from home, and whether the receding vision of the New World is not a dream. Especially when the vessel begins to roll, an impression grows upon you that America itself is a sort of "Fata morgana," and that it is an open question whether Columbus really did discover anything beyond that waste of waters.

That impression has often come over me again in writing these pages. I experience a good deal of that kind of feeling which most of us, I dare say, have felt when we jump off a bathing-machine, and happen to turn the wrong way, so that when the salt water has got out of our eyes, we cannot see the machine we imagined to be close to us. It has struck me frequently since my return, that what I recollect, or fancy I recollect, seeing, must be a delusion of the mind. I saw a country rich, prosperous, and powerful, and am told that I have returned from a ruined, bankrupt, and wretched land. I saw a people eager for war, full of resolution, and confident of success, and learn that this selfsame people has no heart in the struggle, and longs for foreign interference to secure a humiliating peace at any price. I saw great principles at stake, great questions at issue, and learn that in this contest there is no principle involved. These are matters of opinion, in which I may be mistaken; but so much I do know for a fact, that I saw vast armies, composed of as fine troops as the Old World could show —not Irish, nor Germans, but native-born Americans; that I came across the track of great battles, and learnt, by only too palpable an evidence, how bloody and how hard-fought had been the contest; that I knew myself of hundreds and thousands of men of wealth, and station, and education, who had left home, and family, and business, to risk their lives for the cause which, right or wrong, they believed to be that of their country. And yet I am still informed that I must be mistaken, because it is notorious that the Americans do not fight at all, that their soldiers are hired mercenaries, and that such qualities as courage and love of country do not exist north of Mason and Dixon's line. I am constrained, therefore, to think, that, as my objectors are wrong in matters of fact, they may be wrong also in matters of opinion. If the impression left upon my mind as to the outlook of the war should differ from the one popularly received in England, I trust I may be excused, on the ground that things look very differently near at hand from what they do at a distance; which view is more likely to be the correct one, I do not presume to say.

Of this I am convinced, that the one thing required to keep America and England on friendly terms is that each country should know the other better. It is rare to find an Englishman, who has lived long in America, or an American who has passed much time in England, who has not a feeling of affection for the country which was for a space his home. I lived long enough in the States to understand this feeling. I was prepared, when I went there, to find a great country and a powerful people; but I was not prepared to find a people so kindly and easy-natured, or a country so like our own. I should, indeed, be ungrateful, if my recollections of the North were anything but pleasant ones, or my wishes for her welfare not very heartfelt. I know that on the pleasant banks of Staten Island, in the dusty streets of Washington, in the wooded suburbs of Boston, in quiet New England villages, on the banks of the Mississippi, and on the shores of the Western lakes, there are households where these pages will be read, and where the readers, I trust, look upon the writer as a friend. To the inmates of those dwellings, and to all the multitude of persons from whom I received kindnesses in the States, I would take this opportunity of expressing my kindly recollections. Owing in great measure to the assistance I thus received, I was enabled to see the North under more favorable circumstances than falls to the lot of ordinary travelers. It was thus my fortune to behold a great country in a great crisis of its history. The longer I lived there, the more clearly I learnt to see that the cause of the North was the cause of right, and order, and law. Very fast, too, rather by the workings of God's laws than by man's wisdom, it is becoming the cause of freedom and of human rights. There is much, I grant, to offend one in the language of the North—not a little to dishearten one in what has not been done, something to condemn also in what has been done. Still, in this world, you must take the greater good with the lesser evil; and those who believe in freedom and in human progress, must, I think, wish the North Godspeed.

The End.

Index

Abolition: necessity of, to Union, 78–79, 192; views of Northerners regarding, 52; views of Republican party regarding, 84; views of Westerners regarding, 222–223, 235. *See also* Abolitionist party; Emancipation.

Abolitionist party, 55, 88; as advocates of the Union, 253; creeds of, regarding slavery, 245; in New England, 246–253; opinions of, regarding England's attitude toward slavery, 118–119; opinions of, regarding slavery, 53; progress of, 77–78, 250–253; reaction of, to McClellan, 245; in rural areas, 248–249; sentiments against, 283; social and political position of, 253; various factions of, 251–252

Agriculture, 220, 241

Alexandria, Virginia, 150–151

America: impressions of, in England, 303–304 (*see also* England); relations with England, 304 (*see also* England); unreality of, 303; vastness of, 194, 206 (*see also* Prairie).

American affairs, English opinions about, 116–117. *See also* England.

Americans: appearance, 10–11; behavior, as compared with English, 266; effects of scenery on character, 205–206; feelings toward antiquity, 237; generosity, 173; honesty, 189; kindness, 304; lack of logic, 284; openness, 173; opinions, *see* individual topics; patience, 244–245; pride, 206, 243; principles of, in Civil War, 303–304; similarity, 39–40; social habits, 273. *See also* National character.

Amusements: in New York, 12; in Racine, 214; in St. Louis, 197–198; in Washington, 63. *See also* Harvard College, entertainment at.

Antietam, 163

Anti-slavery. *See* Abolition; Emancipation; Slavery.

Anti-slavery party, 55

Anti-slavery Society, 250

Appearance of Americans, 10–11

Architecture: of Boston, 230, 240–241; of churches, 176; in New York, 9; in Racine, 213; in St. Louis, 196; in Washington, 61–62

Arlington Heights, Virginia, 146

Arlington Park, 146–147

Cities—*Continued.*
ark, Illinois); Western, similarity of, 210–211. *See also* Mississippi River, towns on.

Civil War: effects, 16–19, 182–183, 184, 214–215, 274–279; issues in, 44–45, 284–292 (*see also* Abolition; Emancipation; Secession; Slavery); motives of North in, 284–292; reaction of Americans to, 17–18, 143–144, 145, 222–223; reaction of English to, 144–145; role in consolidating U.S., 274; role of emancipation in, 297–298; slavery as an issue in, *see* Slavery; unfamiliarity of, to Americans, 139, 141; unpreparedness of Americans for, 114–115. *See also* Confederate Army; Union Army.

Clark, Wyndham D., viii
Clough, Arthur Hugh, 264
Colonial Army at Concord, 268–269
Comfort: importance of, in America, 11; in trains, *see* Railroads.
Common Council of New York, 281
Concord, Massachusetts, 268–270; appearance, 269; battle, 268–269
Confederate Army: in Border States, 182, 191; cruelties against Union prisoners, 278; determination, 295; Kentucky regiments in, 178; in Nashville, 182; resources, 296; retreat from Manassas, 153–154; volunteers in, 295
Congress, 68–73; access to, 68; committees of, 73; compared with Parliament, 70–71, 73; conduct of visitors in, 69;

Congress—*Continued.*
Houses of, *see* Capitol, U.S.; oratory of members, 70–71; orderliness, 72; public interest in, 72; secrecy in, 73. *See also* Government.

Constitution, American, 286–287; disregard for, 200; limitations on Government (*see* Government, constitutional limitations on; State rights); public opinion toward, in North, 79; restrictions on Abolition, 235; and slavery, 85
Conway, Moncure, 251
Corinth, 208; battle of, 191
Courts, U.S., 58–59, 67
Cumberland, Maryland, 162, 163–164
Cushing, Caleb, 101

Dancing, 266
De Tocqueville, Alexis, ix
Death, of soldiers, 274–275
Declaration of Independence, 283, 294
Democratic party, 55, 57, 78, 85, 99; attitude toward insurgency, 180–181; compared with Republican party, 230–231; opinions regarding Abolition, 82
Dicey, Edward, vii–viii, ix–xv
District of Columbia. *See* Washington, D.C.
Douglas, Stephen, 232
Drinking, xi–xii; in Congress, 67; in New York, 12; in St. Louis, 197; on steamboats, 172–173; on trains, 39. *See also* Saloons.
Dunlap, Lloyd A., viii

East River, 9
Education: of free Negroes, 47–48, 49; importance to Amer-